Swim to Win
Train Like a Champion

Swim to Win
Train Like a Champion

Coach Ed Nessel

STERLING

New York / London
www.sterlingpublishing.com

To my family

STERLING and the distinctive Sterling logo are registered trademarks of Sterling Publishing Co., Inc.

Library of Congress Cataloging-in-Publication Data

Nessel, Ed.
Swim to win : train like a champion / Ed Nessel.
p. cm.
Includes index.
ISBN-13: 978-1-4027-3256-0
ISBN-10: 1-4027-3256-2
1. Swimming—Training. 2. Swimming—Physiological aspects. I. Title.
GV837.7.N47 2007
797.2'1—dc22
2007035335

2 4 6 8 10 9 7 5 3 1

Published by Sterling Publishing Co., Inc.
387 Park Avenue South, New York, NY 10016
Text © 2008 by Ed Nessel
Swimming Illustrations © 2008 Jason Lee
Stretching Illustrations, pages 87–93, copyright © 1992 by Bob and Jean E. Anderson
Fin photo, page 103, copyright © 2008 by Ed Nessel
Medical Illustrations, pages 124–127 © 2004 by S. Karger, A.G.
Distributed in Canada by Sterling Publishing
c/o Canadian Manda Group, 165 Dufferin Street,
Toronto, Ontario, Canada M6K 3H6
Distributed in the United Kingdom by GMC Distribution Services
Castle Place, 166 High Street, Lewes, East Sussex, England BN7 1XU
Distributed in Australia by Capricorn Link (Australia) Pty. Ltd.
P.O. Box 704, Windsor, NSW 2756, Australia

Manufactured in the United States of America
All rights reserved

Sterling ISBN-13: 978-1-4027-3256-0
ISBN-10: 1-4027-3256-2

For information about custom editions, special sales, premium and corporate purchases, please contact Sterling Special Sales Department at 800-805-5489 or specialsales@sterlingpublishing.com.

Acknowledgments

Many people have crossed my path over my long tenure coaching, instructing, motivating, and sharing life's adventures. Most of them have been great people who taught me and let me teach them. If I have had a positive influence on them in any way, I am grateful and pleased that our interaction was worth the time and effort. But the four people who have been closest to me, my immediate family, deserve special recognition. We have shared great things and tragedy, the highs and the very lows of what life has chosen to offer.

My youngest child, Matthew, having to bear from birth the burden of severe cerebral palsy, taught me to cope with imperfection and to adapt to make the best of it in the moment. Since Matt's potential was robbed from birth, his death at age six forced me to rise above deep personal grief and dedicate myself to helping others reach their potential.

My older son, Jason, had the most natural athletic talent I had ever seen. His ability to swim smoothly and fast from the age of eight till his early teens still amazes me. But his shining star dimmed all too soon. Though he nearly broke my heart by giving up swimming just as he was about to blossom, he taught me tolerance and an understanding of how important it is to provide unconditional love. His success early in his military career made me very proud, especially when I heard him say he could trace it way back to his swim training. His death at age 21 in a car crash nearly sank my ship altogether. Again, I had to dig deep down and rise above.

My eldest child, my daughter Lee, proved the adage that hard work with some talent and intellect can produce wonders. She rose to be an All-American swimmer and honors graduate, overcoming physical adversity after being hit by a car while at college. The doctor who told her she would no longer swim and might never walk was unaware of her determination to rise above.

And now my wife of 35 years, Eileen, the one person whom I could always lean on when the world seemed very dark—"Mrs. Coach"—is suffering from a serious form of an aggressive Parkinson's-type disease. Once more it seems life has tapped me on the shoulder and asked me to go for a ride; I only hope I don't fall off this time around. For Eileen to withstand the loss of two children and now suffer the insult of severe disability is a burden that no one should have to endure. Her courage and strength are only reminders once again that the people closest to me inspire me with the ability to rise above.

Many have said I must be "one tough dude." I don't know about that. I do believe I am a survivor, but more than that I think life's vagaries have created a passion in me, an obsession if you will, to help others reach their potential. I've just chosen the venue of the pool.

To the thousands of swimmers of all ages who have trusted me to coach them to improve their movement through water over the years…thank you! You may have not realized it, but I have needed you at least as much as you have needed me.

A Special Thank You

I want to thank Lou Petroziello, head coach of the Jersey Gators, for taking me on as his assistant the last few years I coached in New Jersey. I had had my own team for years but was feeling the effects of the loss of my sons. I was about to give up what I loved the most when Lou heard I would be available and kindly offered his oldest group of swimmers for me to coach. He convinced me that it would be better for me and the sport if I stayed involved in swimming. This says mountains about the man, since most coaches are extremely possessive of their athletes, especially at the senior level.

Lou said he could use someone of my experience, and he liked the way I worked with the swimmers to make them fast. He wanted to watch my style and maybe learn a few things. I would spell him a few days a week so he could begin to "have a life" after so many years as a slave to his program and the sport. I think he was just being kind; maybe he enjoyed watching me put the swimmers through my type of torture—less yardage than he was used to giving but asking the athletes to swim hard for most of the practice. Whatever the reason, we got along great. He learned from me, I learned from him, and best of all, he kept me coaching. Thank you, Lou.

Contents

Introduction

On the surface (pun intended), it seems so easy to move through water. Every four years, after the biggest swim meet in the world has aired on TV, there seems to be an influx of sure-fire Olympic hopefuls joining local swim teams everywhere thinking that what they saw on the home screen looks so easy. But time and experience bring a taste of reality: it's much harder than it looks. Moving through water quickly and over a distance is definitely not for the faint of heart.

I've worked with all sorts of athletes—not just dedicated swimmers—who wanted to improve their swimming ability or simply get stronger from work in the water. The latest non-swimmer group to learn the value of aquatic training was the varsity football team at the Division I school where I coached swimming. After watching several games in which the team hung tough for only the first half, I saw where improvement was needed: their legs. I realized that if these land-based athletes built their leg endurance and power, they would have a much more consistent showing on the gridiron every time out. They would become contenders rather than pretenders. This proved to be a wise choice by the football coaching staff, though it did take some doing on my part to convince them that the water was the absolute best place to build strength, power, and endurance. It allows for gravity-free movement with no extraneous trauma due to pounding against rigid ground.

The players thought what the uninitiated usually think—looks easy, no big deal, let's get to it—until they were put into the deep end of the pool and asked to negotiate a simple 75 feet without being able to touch the bottom. Feeling that they were facing their imminent demise due to severe respiratory distress and complete muscular fatigue, they developed new respect for those who move through water at all, let alone fast. (And the pool training did help their game.)

The water can be a respite from the harried world, a soothing place where swimmer and surrounding liquid dance a harmonious rumba. Or it can be an agonizing torture chamber that sucks the very air from your lungs and drains every ounce of strength and power from your limbs—an unrelenting barrier against which your movement is less effective every moment. The safety of the land is no longer. Your greatest task is keeping the prospect of impending doom from taking over.

As in any demanding sport, I train my experienced, competitive swimmers to work hard so they can make it look easy. They may be "dying" in the water, but I teach them to "share the pain" psychologically and to transfer it emotionally to the rest of the heat. Everyone slows down toward the end of a race; I train my swimmers to slow down less, in the hope that they will finish stronger and either find themselves ahead of their opponents toward the end or swim by the others before they run out of pool. I show them how to relax in the water (not an easy task for the uninitiated) and then how to move through it with gradually increasing effort, all the while being aware of the demands placed on the human body by a surrounding medium a thousand times more dense than air. I prefer to approach the water with the mindset of "making friends" with it, of trying to slip through it rather than trying to plow over it, using the principle of "less is more." To do this, I bring in the various scientific principles, intuitive realizations, and plain common sense that I use in my coaching, training, and presentations all around the country.

As a pharmacist, physiologist, and biochemist for more than three decades, I am well aware of the many topics pertinent to the "science of swimming"—bodies of knowledge that must be studied, understood, and taken seriously if one is to coach athletes to swim fast. As a coach for nearly four decades, in addition to present-day vigorous training and competition in Masters Swimming, I have honed my "coach's eye" to a very fine edge, allowing it to help me see what makes fast swimmers. I also take the title "Coach" very seriously. At the end of most practices I am exhausted or nearly so. I expend much physical and emotional energy while on deck to get my athletes to understand fast movement through water and to believe in themselves.

To coach correctly and thoroughly means to make sure the student/athlete, no matter what his or her age, appropriately understands all the pertinent concepts. Any coach who truly works to enhance the sport must be able to take complicated hydrodynamic principles and make them understandable and believable to the athletes. The coach must combine this with pertinent knowledge of human physiology and a strong empathy for the psychology of competition, all the while constantly exuding the two most important qualities of all, enthusiasm and encouragement: enthusiasm to experiment and learn and try new things; encouragement by showing faith in the athletes and helping them meet the constant challenges of swimming fast. *And this must be brought to the pool every single time.*

Coaches-in-training worthy of their time spent on deck will learn facts and figures, and they will gain experience over time, but they must bring the fever

of enthusiasm with them for others to catch. The swimmers pick up on this more than anything. I want my enthusiasm to be contagious—infectious, if you will—to everyone around me, and I expect my swimmers to catch the fever when they train and learn new concepts about moving through water. How else can I expect them to progress quickly and with the intensity I and they hope for?

I place almost as much emphasis on what happens outside the pool as I do on what takes place in the pool. My philosophy of training aquatic athletes stems from analyzing what it takes to master an event both physically and psychologically and how the body needs to prepare specifically for it. Preparation for competition is a better concept for me than training for competition, because there is so much more to readying a swimmer for a race than perfunctory pool time.

How to Use This Book

In the world of writing, the guiding principle is to "write what you know," and that's what I have set out to do. In the first section of this book, I outline the science of swimming—the physics and physiology that will help the swimmer grasp the principles of efficient movement through water and its attendant conservation of energy in the pool. The second section is dedicated to fully expressing correct form and economical movement for every stroke. Starts, turns, and finishes are equally important in competition, and I explain a few out-of-the-box strategies I've worked on for gaining a real edge against competitors.

The third section of the book lays out a regimen for training the body and the mind for competition. While I'm a firm believer in the value of quality above quantity in training, all swimmers should expect to put in the appropriate amount of time, effort, and distance during this fairly rigorous plan.

In the final section, I present the important concepts coach and athlete need to know in order to keep the swimmer healthy and functioning at full capacity. Real pain signals a serious problem; discomfort doesn't. I explain the difference, the importance of recovery, and how to prevent injury. I also address sports-specific body fuel, hydration, diet, and safe supplements—the sources of energy the aquatic athlete needs to succeed.

Yards or Meters?

Throughout the book you will note that I use yards and meters interchangeably. As there are three primary courses (pool lengths) of competition, each with its own championships, records, and, of course, physiological and psychological demands, I bring them all into the mix. The three venues are: short-course yards, short-course meters, and long-course meters. A yard is 36 inches long; a meter is 39.37 inches, 10% longer. A 25-meter short-course pool is 27.5 yards long. The "metric mile" has been set at 1,500 meters for all sports, which converts to 1,650 yards, the "swimmers' mile." (A true mile is 1,760 yards.)

My take on the different venues is that competing in a long-course (Olympic or 50-meter) pool is more about keeping the stroke long and strong, in an attempt to slip through the water in the most efficient way possible. In a short-course pool, the swimmer needs to work the walls (turns) and power the strokes in crisp, snappy fashion.

Competing in a short-course meters pool yields faster times than competing in a long-course meters pool simply because the swimmer pushes off the wall at faster than swimming speed more often. It is about 10% more demanding to race and train in a short-course meters pool than in a yard pool, but about 15% harder in a long-course meters pool because there are fewer turns. If you've picked up this book, I assume you are serious about moving through water quickly. In the pages that follow, I will give you the tools you need to swim smooth, to swim strong, and, ideally, to swim to win.

PART ONE

The Science of Swimming

CHAPTER 1
Moving Through Water

Moving through water may sound easy; it is not. Just ask anyone experienced enough to have really pushed to go fast in the pool. If you are serious about conditioning for any sport, you know that the moment you reach your comfort zone, it's time to push yourself beyond it. For those of you hoping to swim fast some day, dedicated training can bring out whatever potential your genetics has given you—and maybe a bit more—as you acclimate your body to the rapid transition from "I feel okay" to "*I don't* feel okay" to "*I think I am going to die!*"

It is amazing how quickly fast swimming makes one very uncomfortable in the water. Notice that I said *fast swimming*. Purposeful, efficient movement through water takes concerted effort, understanding of hydrodynamic principles, and a feel for the liquid medium through which you have chosen to move. Slipping through it with as little disturbance as possible is the very essence of swimming fast. The seeming contradiction "less is more" comes into play with every stroke and every decision about how to pace a race.

The Hydrodynamics of Swimming Fast

Fish gotta swim; they are prisoners of their environment. We, on the other hand, are prisoners of our minds: we *choose* to swim. We can also choose to understand the hydrodynamic principles that affect our movement through water. It is established fact that, at sea level, water is a thousand times denser than air with the temperatures at which swimmers usually work; that in itself says much about what swimmers have to contend with, but water's other challenging characteristics—various types of drag related to speed and movement in the horizontal, vertical, and lateral planes—are not so much discussed, probably because most readers are not physicists. Simply put, water, unlike air, changes its persona in response to fast movement through it. This is perhaps the most important aspect of water for the competitive swimmer: as movement becomes more forceful, and speed consequently increases, water's resistance to it increases by the effort *squared!*

To help conceptualize this phenomenon, let's say that you start with a slow, comfortable pace in water, such as a warm-up. Then you approximately double your effort to less than medium speed; still comfortable for the experienced swimmer. You've increased your effort by a factor of two, but the water's resistance to your movement through it has increased by a factor of four (2 squared: $2 \times 2 = 4$). And this assumes smooth, efficient motion throughout. If you fight the water, slap at it and splash around, tangle with water's surface tension, and create counterproductive waves, then the water's resistance explodes by CUBING your increase in effort. In this case, a simple doubling of your effort has caused the water to resist your movement through it

by $2 \times 2 \times 2 = 8$! Not fair, right? The water couldn't care less. but the swimmer better care!

To further illustrate the demands water places on athletes, we simply need to compare swimming times with running times at the elite level for various distances. It takes more time to swim just 50 meters than it takes to run 200 meters—more than a four-to-one ratio. The gap widens as the distances expand. For example, the world 100-meter dash mark is around 9.7 seconds while the world 100-meter freestyle is more than 47 seconds. As I have stated, water increases resistance in response to faster movement through it, which then fatigues the athlete at an ever-increasing rate; yet the air, for all intents and purposes, does not change its resistance as the runner increases speed.

To the uninitiated it almost seems not worth the effort. But those who understand what it means to swim fast and who want to improve constantly must learn to generate propulsive forces that overcome these resistive forces. Appropriate swim training is much more challenging than that for running day-to-day. We can borrow important lessons from another land-based activity, jujitsu, that might help set some certainties in movement through water: *Technique will conquer strength; self-control will defeat arrogance; one need not immediately win, one need only endure, conserving strength until one may improve the position.*

The quickest and most dramatic way to improve movement through water is to ensure that the swimmer understands *proper technique*. A 10% improvement in technique will usually result in a nearly 10% better effort. Since it is human nature to let action faults creep into repetitive movement (even for top athletes), the swimmer must learn and practice the most water-friendly propulsion, both for the specific stroke and for his or her particular style. The second most important element in fast swimming, in my opinion, is the ability to *move water quickly*, which increases as the swimmer becomes first stronger and then more powerful. Finally, *increased condition* (getting in swim shape) plays the third most important part, crucial to holding speed for as much of the race as possible and dealing with the sure-to-come onslaught of increasing discomfort. I call this whole concept Nessel's Assault on Speed.

But think about this: It would take about a 50% improvement in condition to produce the same 10% improvement in effort that better technique affords. To distill all this to its bare essence, we need to realize that the single most important contribution to fast swimming is to know how to move through water efficiently. This brings us to the holy grail of fast swimming: the transfer of power to create *distance per stroke as smoothly as possible*. We will discuss this in depth for each of the competitive strokes. First, let's look more closely at the various forms of resistance water puts in the swimmer's way.

Types of Drag

Resistive Drag

As the human body moves forward through water, streams of water molecules resist its movement and have to be pushed aside to open a momentary "hole" through which the body can propel itself. If the propulsion is greater than the water's resistance, then the swimmer moves forward; if the water's resistance starts to overcome propulsion, the swimmer decelerates (and slows to a stop very quickly if and when propulsion stops altogether). Pushing the water molecules aside is no simple matter, because the resistive drag swimmers encounter is directly proportional to the turbulence they create as they move through the water (see Fig. 1-1).

Two additional concepts, laminar flow and pressure gradients, can help explain the problem of resistive drag. Laminar flow is the way in which water moves in layers along a boundary—in this case, a swimmer's body. Imagine flat sheets of H_2O (water) molecules stacked upon each other. Any body coming into contact with these sheets will cause a disturbance in the layers (see Fig. 1-2). A large, wide swimmer—or one who is not holding a streamlined position—will have to move more water "sheets" with each stroke and will therefore create greater resistive drag than a more streamlined body.

In addition, the movement of water creates pressure gradients depending on where it is being displaced in relation to the body. Water molecules exert greater pressure in front of the swimmer than behind. As the swimmer moves through water, molecules are quickly pushed aside, but as he keeps moving, molecules are relatively slow to fill up the space behind him. This void creates a relative negative pressure, which can actually draw the swimmer backwards. But a swimmer who is trailing behind another swimmer within 5 yards can "drag" off his lane mate (and maybe even off his competitor in the next lane if he hugs the separating lane guide), using the lowered pressure in the other swimmer's wake to reduce his own effort. The trailing swimmer's effort is about 15% less than the leader's in the same lane because he is swimming into a relative vacuum of water molecules, which pulls him along. Take-home point here: it's much tougher to lead the lane in practice than to follow behind.

Form Drag

Mother Nature did not build the average human body for rapid movement through water. Humans were designed to be land-based creatures. It is no

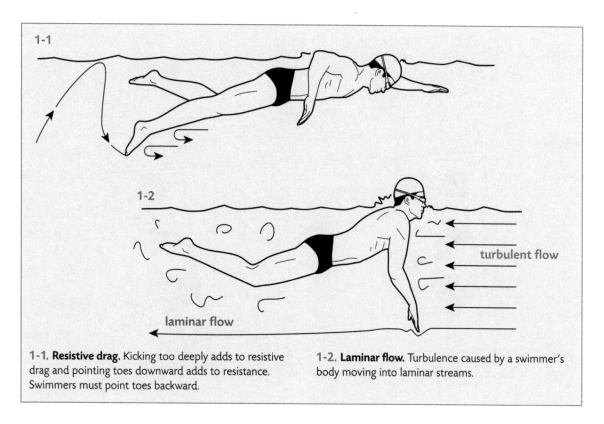

1-1. Resistive drag. Kicking too deeply adds to resistive drag and pointing toes downward adds to resistance. Swimmers must point toes backward.

1-2. Laminar flow. Turbulence caused by a swimmer's body moving into laminar streams.

coincidence that, with a few exceptions, swimmers who rise to the elite level are usually tall and lithe, shaped like torpedos or quick aquatic creatures. The wider and broader a swimmer's shadow, the more water the swimmer must move and the more energy it takes to move it. The drag created by any human form can be lessened by a slimmer, longer, and more streamline-positioned body (see Figs. 1-3 and 1-4).

Swimming Big

Of course, if a talented swimmer is built more like a fire hydrant than a fish, he or she can still perform at a high level by mastering what I call "swimming big." By this I mean streamlining where necessary through every stroke movement and reaching for the best range of motion at all times—things a swimmer must practice over and over at any level of experience.

The America's Cup Boat

Fine tuning and vetting the laws of laminar flow and form drag to a very high degree, designers of the exotic hulls of America's Cup sailboats push the bounds of hull technology every year. Today, the average length of an America's Cup boat is over 80 feet, whereas 40 feet was considered good-sized in the early years of this type of aquatic competition.

- Swimming big requires the swimmer to maximize the streamline off every wall (which takes breath control) and training to do this when in oxygen deprivation.
- Swimming big means extending the body to the maximum reaching position appropriate

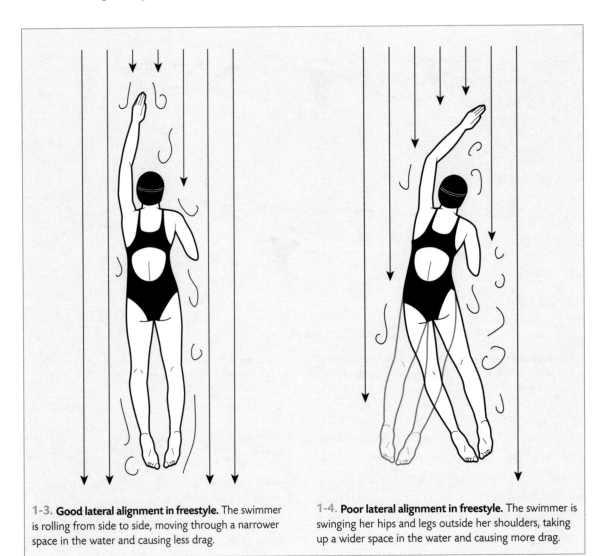

1-3. Good lateral alignment in freestyle. The swimmer is rolling from side to side, moving through a narrower space in the water and causing less drag.

1-4. Poor lateral alignment in freestyle. The swimmer is swinging her hips and legs outside her shoulders, taking up a wider space in the water and causing more drag.

for each stroke, especially when in oxygen debt. Training to have the presence of mind to hold the stroke when in respiratory distress is key to building a champion's attitude. Developing the neuromuscular adaptation to perform this under the combat of racing is key to building a champion.

- Swimming big means not rushing the stroke just to get another quick breath. The tenet of grabbing the most water with each stroke and pulling and/or pushing it away from you at

the finish of each stroke cycle is the essence of producing what I call "easy speed." This is a very important racing concept: taking out a race quickly but in control so as not to fatigue too soon.

- Swimming big brings in the concept that "less is more." Too much effort inappropriately applied during the race will not necessarily make swimmers move faster, but it will most assuredly make them tire faster.

Wave Drag

Modern submarines travel faster submerged than they do at the surface. Why? Wave drag. Swimming any stroke produces bow waves, which, together with surface tension, resist forward movement. These waves increase as forward speed increases. The short-axis strokes (breast and fly) consume a huge amount of energy because their up-and-down movements through the water can create much larger resistive waves than the long-axis strokes (backstroke and freestyle). In fact, as the effort to increase speed in short-axis strokes is doubled, the resistance of the water approaches the cube of the effort—again, meaning water holds the swimmer back eight times as much! Physiological testing shows that the event with the most inherent resistance to movement per unit time is the one that requires the most energy; this is the 200-meter breaststroke. Those competing in butterfly may say they hurt most as a race wears on, but generally their race is faster (that is, finished sooner), so ultimately the breaststrokers suffer most from lactic acid buildup and oxygen and energy consumption as a result of greater wave drag.

Pushing Drag

Pushing drag comes from bad form, as a result of either poor technique or fatigue. It can be the most devastating cause of energy waste in swimming. It comes into play when the leading part of the body that cuts through the water—usually the hands—is placed incorrectly, offering more opposition to the water and creating turbulence that exacerbates all the drag forces discussed above. In addition, the head plays a very important part in correct positioning. If one raises the head too high to look too much forward, water slapping against the face creates a tremendous frontal resistance. The face should be facing the bottom of the pool in breaststroke and in

What Creates Pushing Drag?

- Splashing the water with the hands and arms. The more sound you hear as the swimmer's hands enter the water, the more slap was applied. The more slap, the more drag. Even with fatigue, a competent swimmer will keep hand and arm splashing to an absolute minimum.
- Failing to hold the body parallel to the surface, as long and as streamlined as possible during most or all of each stroke. It is common for the butt to sink or the legs to drop out of streamline as fatigue sets in. Moving in a flat plane and parallel to the surface (even while rolling side-to-side in freestyle and backstroke) is a must all through the race for freestyle and backstroke.
- Holding the head too high. We used to train freestyle sprinters to "get up high in the water and race." But now we know that holding the head up too high creates too much drag at the surface. Better to keep the water coming over the head in freestyle with the eyes looking toward the bottom of the pool.
- Holding the head out of the streamlined position (the streamlined position is in line with the spine). Of course the swimmer needs to breathe, and each stroke has its demands on head placement and movement, but the general rule for good technique dictates that the head needs to be quickly brought back in line with the spine after every breath.

fly when it is inserted into the water, and the head should be kept in line with the spine, eyes looking down and out like the headlights of your car at night when doing freestyle. In backstroke, the head should be placed so it is also in line with the spine. The body always follows the head and moves in the direction of where you are looking. Being aware that the head must be held in a proper position to aid a streamlined movement through water is vital for fast efficient swimming.

Frictional Drag

As a swimmer moves through water, a layer of water molecules clings to the body and is dragged along for the ride. This produces a frictional interaction with the next layer of water molecules surrounding the swimmer. If the friction is allowed to build up, more and more layers of water molecules are disturbed. As frictional drag increases, so does the work the swimmer has to do. End result: greater fatigue earlier in the race, less distance per stroke throughout the race, and greater stroke deterioration toward the end of the race.

The most immediate way to limit frictional drag is to shave down the body. This has proved beneficial to racing results, and not just psychologically. Water clings to the now-hairless skin in just one molecular layer. As the shaved body moves through water, only this one layer of water molecules disturbs oncoming layers. A molecule of water moving against another molecule of water is very slick and presents as allowing greatly reduced frictional movement, and we must realize that even a slight reduction in resistance is magnified throughout the race because of water's density. Depending on the stroke, shaving down can improve time by as much as 2 seconds per 100 meters.

A more technologically sophisticated way to decrease frictional drag is the use of modern full-body racing suits. Original prototypes were taken from downhill ski competitors when it was noticed that dramatic time reductions were produced as aerodynamic friction was reduced. Magnify friction-lowering in a medium 1000 times as dense as air, and you can see why various manufacturers jumped at the premise of producing a hydrodynamic friction-reducer. As with any new product, much marketing hype has preceded the use of full-body racing suits in actual racing, with all sorts of claims and promises made about their benefits for fast swimming. But the several generations of racing suits we have seen so far *have* produced some positive results too strong to overlook. The new gear helps the body stay streamlined throughout the race by limiting the rippling of body tissue (thereby lessening the ensuing muscle fatigue) and creating a near-frictionless boundary around the body. Some suits have added segments of stippling material design that cause water flow to swirl around the body (eddies), seemingly to enhance its movement through the pool. Research is ongoing, and the hype is quickly following to market this expensive racing garb to serious competitors of all ages. The suits are now so good that I don't think record-breaking times would be possible for most swimmers without them. And as long as they are deemed legal, I recommend that swimmers use them to keep the playing field level. Fit and style are usually a matter of individual preference but are very important, so some trial and error may be a necessary task to endure. I also recommend silicone caps over latex, because silicone is a more slippery substance in the water.

CHAPTER 2

Training at the Cellular Level

Back in the early 1960s when I was a young power swimmer, I was trained according to the prevailing thinking: the more yards you swim, the faster you will become. It was not uncommon for my coach to ask for 300 laps per session. (Here, when I say a lap I mean a pool length.) In a short-course pool, this computes to 7,500 yards or meters each time out. Bloodshot eyes, extreme muscular exhaustion, aching joints and nearly asthmatic breathing were all considered badges of honor; we presumed we were true aquatic athletes. Or were we just ignorant of other ways to train fast?

Over my many years of coaching and training I've learned better. Today I believe that much of today's swim training is superfluous at best and counterproductive at worst, which is most of the time. Quality versus quantity is the key for power swimming, and preparing the swimmer for the combat of racing requires more of both swimmer and coach than just doing the mega-yardage on which many programs are based.

As a scientist, I take great care to study what's going on in my swimmers' bodies. As a coach, I strive to learn to take advantage of these mechanisms. This chapter bridges the gap between theory and practice, getting right down to the cellular level to explain the biochemistry and physiology of fast training and to describe the adaptive changes the body can undergo to prepare it for the stresses of competition.

The Biochemistry of Energy Production

We all know that muscles are what make the body move, but many may not know what actually fuels this movement. There are several complicated pathways by which the body produces energy. We'll start by discussing the substances specifically designed to ignite the fuel of activity quickly. Organic chemists and biochemists call them *high-energy adenine nucleotides*. These are composed of three segments: *adenine*, an organic nitrogen-based compound found in protein; *ribose*, a five-carbon sugar produced by the body's breakdown of simple carbohydrates; and *phosphate*, found ubiquitously in all sorts of foods and drink. It is the phosphates that become the carriers of high-energy bonds—the keys to the transference of energy and the essence of what makes the body move (see Figs. 2-1 and 2-2).

Nucleotide Reactions

The high-energy phosphate, denoted by the symbol ~P, comes in three molecular forms: mono- (one),

di- (two), and tri- (three). The highest energy content is found in adenosine triphosphate (ATP), which is the most friable; it gives off one phosphate bond easily and quickly to provide energy for muscular movement, producing a less energy-laden but still viable two-phosphate molecule, adenosine diphosphate (ADP). If more energy is required before molecular rejuvenation can take place—through rest, reoxygenation, or re-phosphating from secondary sources—another phosphate bond is removed, forming the lowest level energy nucleotide, adenosine monophosphate (AMP).

These concepts aren't merely academic. Skeletal and cardiac muscle cells must have a precise ratio of ATP to ADP to AMP to function optimally. When, for example, AMP increases out of proportion at the expense of ATP and ADP due to high-energy-bond depletion from intense and prolonged training, the muscle fiber cells become nonresponsive to AMP and begin to remove AMP compounds altogether, leading to a degradation sequence that is not easily reversed. This poses a real problem for the swimmer or anyone else engaging in intense

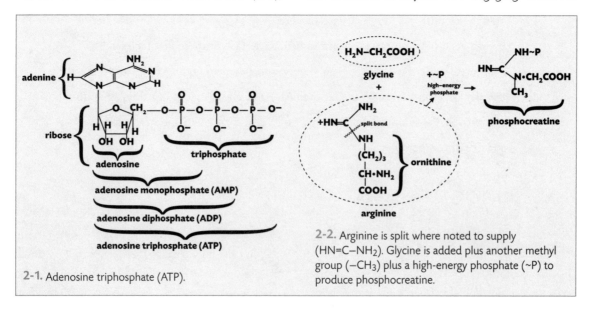

2-1. Adenosine triphosphate (ATP).

2-2. Arginine is split where noted to supply (HN=C–NH$_2$). Glycine is added plus another methyl group (–CH$_3$) plus a high-energy phosphate (~P) to produce phosphocreatine.

physical activity for an extended period of time, since every bit of the body's adenosine nucleotide pool is necessary to regenerate the high-energy molecules that power the cells. If the raw material for the high-energy bonds is missing, the body cannot generate enough energy on demand; performance suffers and recovery can be extensively delayed. Or worse: the heart can be damaged.

In patients with narrowed or partially clogged arteries, heart muscle has been shown to become severely depleted of ATP when it is deprived of oxygen due to reduced blood flow (ischemia). This can produce the marquee symptom of cardiac dysfunction: chest pain (angina) in response to demanding physical activity. Even if the blood supply is returned to normal, it may take up to 72 hours for the muscle tissue of the heart to regenerate the original supply of ATP.

ATP can also become depleted in healthy hearts (though not to the extent of a heart with arterial disease). Since the human body only stores about 85 grams of ATP all around at any one time, and this amount can be totally used up in as little as 10 to 30 seconds under vigorous stress, quick regeneration is crucial—if ATP isn't re-supplied quickly, dangerous depletion can last for at least 24 hours and can even leave its mark after 96 hours. Anything that speeds regeneration will allow for faster recovery and will enable the athlete to train at a higher level (which can translate into faster swims at multi-event competitions).

Of the three components of ATP, the ribose molecule is the limiting factor in regeneration. Without an external source of the 5-carbon ribose, the body must break down various other forms of carbohydrate to first produce the 6-carbon glucose, which is then converted to the necessary 5-carbon ribose sugar molecule. With training, this biochemical enzyme system can adapt over time and ultimately increase your available supply of ATP. However, when instant energy is needed to fuel intense muscular contraction for more than a few seconds, ribose is what provides a supply of ATP quickly for an extended ergogenic (work-enhancing) effect. Ribose also aids in the "salvage pathway" of ATP regeneration. This means that with sufficient ribose, it is unlikely that much AMP will be produced, keeping ADP and ATP levels higher in the various tissues. (For more information on sources of ribose, see Chapter 22.)

During intense exercise, muscle fibers use as much as 200 times the energy that they do at rest. After about 10 seconds of constant, intense movement, the ATP stores in muscles become depleted. If there is no more ATP available, there can be no more muscular contraction. Fortunately for us, nature provides a redundant system. To prevent total muscle failure, the body has a strong and functioning backup energy source: phosphocreatine (PCr). This works with the associated enzyme, creatine kinase, to release its high-energy phosphate ($\sim P$) bond to regenerate ATP as it is being consumed. The PCr-to-ATP reaction does not need oxygen to function, and, in fact, occurs before oxygen actually has time to come into play. But this is an immediate, involuntary response that your body will not support for long, because the natural reserve of creatine in muscle tissues is limited; the body makes only 1 to 2 grams per day.

Lactic Acid

After the body has gone through the quick-responding PCr-ATP energy system, and if the muscles are still needed to fire anaerobically (without oxygen), lactic acid is produced as an *in situ* (in the exact area of formation) waste product. This happens quickly. Though lactic acid can be re-oxidized in the liver to pyruvate and utilized as fuel and energy again if and when sufficient oxygen becomes available as it naturally dissipates from muscle tissue, I see it as an immediate waste product because in its presence, muscle function shuts down quickly and movement becomes very difficult Lactic acid concentration can rise to as much as 25 times the resting level in as little as 1 minute. The problem with lactic acid, or lactate (as it is called when found in ionic or salt form in the blood), is that it lowers the pH of the muscle environment, increasing the acidity in the muscle, which in turn inhibits energy-producing enzymes. The result is lowered performance, muscle spasms, and even complete shutdown.

With the proper warm-down at about 60% effort, much of the built-up lactate can be forced out of the offended muscles and converted by the liver and used as fuel to move the muscles at a mild to moderate level. Recovery massage (within less than an

Sources of Creatine

The best building blocks for the body's own manufactured supply of creatine come from red meat, and red meat provides another beneficial additive—iron for the molecule heme, which is a major component of hemoglobin to help in oxygen transport to the muscles. We know that too much red meat carries its own risks (excess fat and cholesterol and an unhealthy environment in the intestines and colon). But it is also possible to supplement the athlete's diet with pure creatine in careful doses for a slow and safe buildup in the muscle fibers. For more information on safe supplementation with creatine, see Chapter 22.

hour of the vigorous exercise bout) and large quantities of water will also help flush away the squeezed-out lactic acid. Taking a massage longer than an hour after exercise will provide a feeling of recovery and comfort and may even help repair the micro-tears that occur as a result of strenuous movement, but it won't help in lactic acid removal, because most or all of the acid will have dissipated by then.

The most intense moments athletes can subject themselves to, outside of flat-out sprinting, come in lactate-tolerance training. In this difficult but effective form of biochemical conditioning, the swimmer continues at push-pace effort even as lactic acid is mounting. Without sufficient recovery time between swims to release it, lactate mounts quickly, bringing along its discomfort, which shifts into out-and-out pain. If you're training correctly, you will have left your comfort zone far behind. The goal is the creation of lactate buffers, substances the body produces in blood and cells to help neutralize or delay lactate buildup and keep the pH of the muscles from dropping too much, too quickly. The appropriate distance to induce this adaptation is from 150 to 300 yard/meter repeats. Lactate training should not be attempted more than twice weekly for sprinters or once weekly for mid-distance and distance swimmers. (See Chapter 4 for a more in-depth look at how lactic acid works.)

Training the Mitochondria

As we delve more deeply into the study of energy production at the subcellular level, we see more and more clearly that the most efficient training methods attempt to maximize the time spent adapting the body to move quickly through water. We don't need to count the laps; we need to make the laps count.

The "factories" that produce ATP within muscle fibers are the mitochondria, sites of cellular respiration that provide energy to the cell. These are the only structures that produce ATP, and they seem to be the limiting factor in the production of energy on demand. The greater the size and number of mitochondria, the more energy can be produced per unit time, and the more work can be accomplished through muscular contraction. As you train both aerobically (with oxygen) and anaerobically (without oxygen) you increase the number of capillaries in your muscles. The more capillaries you have, the more oxygen your blood will distribute throughout your body. Energy (in the form of ATP) is produced in the mitochondria when fats, glycogen, or lactic acid are metabolized in the presence of this oxygen. Slow-to-moderate exercise over distance consumes fats for energy; fast, intense exercise consumes carbohydrates.

If we increase the number and size of mitochondria, we can produce energy more rapidly. To do this, we have to place stress on them by training at a high heart rate and high rate of oxygen consumption. Translation: relatively short distances (100 meters or less) of fast swimming mixed with longer recovery swims.

The Physiology of Energy Production

Now that we've examined the biochemistry of energy production on a cellular level, we move to the physiology. Every muscle in the body is made up of a mix of three fiber types: white fast-twitch (the largest) surrounded by red fast-twitch and red slow-twitch fibers (the smallest). White fibers have no capillaries and therefore no red blood cells in their tissues, so they work anaerobically. Red fibers, filled with capillaries and blood, work aerobically. Any glycogen used by the white fibers produces lactic acid as immediate

How Mitochondria Increase

Mitochondria increase in number the way most things in nature do: by dividing. The first stage of division (mitosis) takes about 3 days and requires iron for the recombination of proteins. The building and housing of these proteins takes an additional week or so. While this is going on, the mitochondria cannot take part in energy production, so for 10 days the intensely training athlete may have less than optimal oxygen utilization. The effects may include faster heart rates for given intervals, loss of breath, and a sluggish or heavy feeling in the water. Such a sense of setback could also come from overtraining or fighting an illness, but coach and athlete should keep in mind that the natural adaptation of the energy system might well be the cause.

waste. Red fibers, on the other hand, produce carbon dioxide (CO_2).

In a sprint, if lactic acid is allowed to build up, the pH dips, creating an acid-rich environment. The fibers that actually do the contracting cannot work in the presence of acid, so they shut down. Those fibers not yet awash in the lactic acid are forced to work extra hard and can tear, creating a delayed onset of muscle soreness (DOMS)—those aches and pains you feel the day after working out. (For more on DOMS, see Chapter 4.)

Muscular Adaptations

I've had the honor of coaching Cullen Jones, who won the 2006 Pan Pacific Games and was the fastest swimmer in the world that year. There are many factors that make Cullen a champion: desire, physique, adaptability. But a big reason he's an incredible powerhouse is that he is unique. Cullen was born with more fast-twitch fibers than any other swimmer I've seen. But you don't need to have Cullen's swimming genetics. Correct training will allow all three muscle fiber types to adapt to fast swimming in two ways. Under the right circumstances some of the white fibers will actually change to red fast-twitch fibers with their attendant capillary system that washes away the lactic acid. The body will also increase production of lactate-transporting enzymes to help rid the white fibers of the waste product. The overall strength of the changing muscle may decrease somewhat initially, but the newly formed red fast-twitch fibers will have increased power and endurance, so the swimmer will ultimately move through water faster and longer. In addition, research has shown that up to 80% of the lactic acid can be oxidized with bypass through the liver and reused as fuel to make more ATP once it is carried into the blood-bathed red fiber system.

Training Strategies

A strong training method to trigger these adaptations uses intervals of broken 100s (that is, a 100-meter swim done in 25-meter segments) or full 75-meter sprints, swimming at race pace with adequate rest between swims. This produces high muscle-lactate levels, which in turn train the transporting enzymes to increase their efficiency in removing lactic acid. These speed intervals must be followed by moderate swims over longer distances (200 to 400 yards/meters) for recovery. In this way, the capillaries and the cardiovascular system increase in efficiency and further carry away lactate down the road to re-oxygenation.

A newer method is to add on yardage quickly after an initial hard swim. If 100-yard distances are used as primary swims, then after 20 seconds of rest (5 seconds per lap partial rest/recovery), add either 25, 50, or 100 yards at push-pace. Though painful and psychologically taxing, this is one of the best ways I know to add both air and energy to the racing machine we are trying to develop.

Since the white muscle fibers have the least stored glycogen of the three types of fibers, they can become depleted in a little as 8 minutes at race-pace swimming and can take as long as 3 days to re-energize. Both types of red fibers can be refueled with adequate and correct nutrition, including ribose and creatine, in about 14 hours. So adaptation training is a tricky business.

A maximum of 800 to 1,000 yards/meters at race-pace speed is all the muscle fibers can handle in a training session. And, again, unless special nutritional measures are taken to re-energize the fiber cells, the swimmer must wait up to 3 days before another bout of "power swimming" will be beneficial. An average of two sessions per week provides the needed adaptations for enhanced power swimming and yet spares the body the consequences of overtraining and extreme muscular fatigue.

CHAPTER 3

Breathing Patterns for Racing

"You leave me breathless." These words from the 1950s rock-and-roll classic should ring true to every swimmer who honestly trains to go faster. Rapid vigorous movement causes increased depth and rapidity of breathing. This is one of the human body's most visible compensating mechanisms: when we work hard, we breathe hard.

Most animals that move on the Earth require adequate air-exchange utilizing lung tissue. Though we cannot increase actual lung capacity in a full grown human, we can increase the ability to breathe under vigorous exercise by strengthening the skeletal muscles used for chest expansion and contraction (intercostals). The better we can do this, the more easily we can positively exchange air.

Those athletes who have breathing difficulties (e.g., asthmatics) will breathe better. Those who do not suffer from respiratory dysfunction will breathe better. Anyone undergoing vigorous exercise will breathe better.

Since the limiting factor in extended vigorous exercise is the ability to efficiently exchange air, attention to the detail is very important for someone wanting to be able to swim fast.

Oxygen and Carbon Dioxide

There have been a number of studies in which normal athletes at sea level were given pure oxygen to inhale before and after intense exercise. The assumption was that this would forestall oxygen debt and enhance recovery. However, the oxygen content of the athletes' arterial blood was not increased, nor was their recovery time decreased. Since this proves that the body cannot store or accumulate oxygen to any great extent, we might draw the conclusion that the intense breathing response occurring with intense exercise is simply the body's way of bringing back its supply of usable oxygen. But this is only partly correct. I submit that the sometimes nearly paralyzing sense of breathlessness we experience when we work hard is mainly caused not by oxygen debt, but by the buildup of carbon dioxide (CO_2). We aren't simply trying to gulp oxygen when we breathe hard during vigorous exercise; we're trying to get rid of built-up CO_2.

We experience CO_2 buildup every day. When we're sleepy, our breathing slows down, and to compensate, we yawn. This happens more to force exhalation of increased CO_2 rather than to inhale more oxygen. Ever wonder why you get drowsy in a crowded, unventilated car? It's not simply because the oxygen content of the ambient air has decreased measurably; it's mostly because everyone's exhalations have increased the CO_2. This effect would be even more pronounced in highly aerobically conditioned athletes, because they extract more oxygen from the air per unit time and exhale more CO_2 once the oxygen has been consumed. I have also noticed that exposure to cold can bring on the yawning reflex; this is because the increased metabolism necessary to raise body temperature (by shivering) produces excess CO_2 that must be blown off forcefully.

Moving fast for more than just a few seconds creates biochemical demands that must be metabolically dealt with by the body. The forced deep exhalations that follow vigorous movement are one way the body tries to bring back its overall pre-activity condition (homeostasis). Carbon dioxide is one of the end products of aerobic metabolism; it can't be prevented from forming, but its buildup can be delayed. During light to moderate movement, CO_2 is carried away by blood circulating through the muscles. The CO_2 can then be easily exhaled through the lungs. There will be no buildup and no impulse to breathe vigorously. The better the condition of the athlete, the more movement can be handled this way, since the air exchange has been raised to a higher level of efficiency.

However, when CO_2 production becomes so great that lungs can't expel it all, the blood will leave the lungs with some residual CO_2 on its way to be recirculated through the heart and on to the arterial blood supply and the body's tissues and organ systems. Since the physical law of impenetrability states that two things can not occupy the same space at the same time, if there is more CO_2 in the circulating blood, there is less room for oxygen in the blood. A swimmer who has completed a swim in this state may show one of the physical markers of metabolic cyanosis (reduced presence of oxygen)—a face with blue lips. At this point, a sort of rescue mechanism kicks in: CO_2 sensors in the arterial blood supply are stimulated and produce the sensation of "air hunger." I contend that these CO_2 sensors, not the perceived lack of oxygen, trigger the breathing center of the brain to force deep respiration. A buildup of CO_2 tells the brain: "BREATHE NOW!"

Furthermore, the oxygen exchange and replenishment is really not as dramatic as we think during rapid inhalation and exhalation. For example, someone giving CPR takes quick breaths of ambient air, which contains about 21% oxygen on average; forced air from a rescuer into a victim contains about 16% oxygen. This shows that the body removes only about 5% of oxygen from air inhaled quickly. (Of course, the amount of oxygen available in the ambient air where vigorous movement takes place does have an effect on athletic performance. Here, we assume conditions at sea level. See the sidebar for a discussion of respiration at higher altitudes.)

Breath Control for Swimming Fast

What does all this mean for the competitive swimmer who wants to turn breathing into an advantage rather than an obstacle? Depending on the duration, intensity, and type of movement through water, as well as the athlete's condition and skill level, *breathlessness* is the endpoint for which to train.

This is not an easy thing to ask of an athlete. It is one thing to become short of breath during vigorous *land-based* exercise; the body usually responds in its natural way of rapid respiration, in and out, without the athlete giving much thought to controlling this process other than the desire to recover as quickly as possible. But do the same in water and it's another story. No matter how athletic the swimmer, if he or she cannot control the breathing part of the stroke for as long as the race lasts, technique usually breaks down and movement through water becomes at first less efficient and then downright counterproductive. Suffer the perception of being out of air, force the face into the water to effect a better streamlined position while swimming, and finally blow out forcefully under water any residual "stale" air that might remain in the lungs to allow a fresh supply to enter when the face is above water,

Breathing at Higher Altitudes

At sea level, where the relative oxygen content of the ambient air is 21%, the barometric pressure is 760 mmHg, and the atmospheric oxygen pressure is 160 mmHg, the oxygen pressure in the lungs (also called alveolar pressure) averages about 110 mmHg and the arterial blood oxygen pressure rises to 96 mmHg.

Take the altitude up to 3,000 feet and the barometric pressure drops to 687 mmHg, the atmospheric oxygen pressure drops to 142 mmHg, the lung oxygen pressure drops to 94 mmHg, and the arterial blood oxygen pressure drops to 83 mmHg—almost a 14% dip in blood oxygen content from sea level.

Go to a mile high and the parameters drop to 631 mmHg barometric pressure, 132 mmHg atmospheric oxygen pressure, 85 mmHg alveolar oxygen pressure, and 75 mmHg arterial blood oxygen pressure—a 22% drop in blood oxygen content from sea level.

At 8,000 feet, alveolar oxygen pressure drops to 69 mmHg and arterial blood oxygen pressure falls to 63 mmHg—an almost 35% drop in blood content of oxygen from sea level to 8,000 feet.

Lung and blood oxygen contents are reduced by another 10 to 15 mmHg in older athletes. And an athlete who is poorly adapted to training hard at high altitudes will accumulate CO_2 sooner and thus will feel air-deprived sooner and more intensely. The result is often "dragon breathing," an involuntary reflex in which the distressed athlete gasps for air with a facial grimace and neck muscle contractions.

and you have the makings of one intimidating set of motions. Most uninitiated athletes, no matter how talented, simply will not endure this situation for more than a few seconds before giving up the swim and stopping dead in the water or trying to hold onto something for immediate support.

An experienced swimmer comes to realize that in the final analysis, it is breath control that dictates speed throughout the race. Mis-pace the race by taking it out too fast, or make the mistake of holding the breath too much in the beginning, and all too often the back end of the swim becomes more of a struggle than the swimmer bargained for, all because of the *sensation* that oxygen is in very short supply (which we now know is really the resultant of CO_2 in excess supply).

Specific Breathing Patterns

Several studies have looked into the breathing patterns of the various strokes (and even segments of breathing patterns). After analyzing various results, I have come to my conclusions based on the science of swimming and human physiology. I agree with the finding that the inhalation segment of the breathing cycle is noticeably shorter than the exhalation segment for all the strokes. This fact alone has many ramifications. First, for asthmatic swimmers, the usual difficulty in blowing out used air due to constricted bronchioles is made worse if the asthma is not controlled by medication, because the sufferer cannot get new air in quickly enough in the racing cycle to replace the stale air. Second, the *intercostal muscles* between the ribs that expand and contract with breathing need to be made as strong as possible by regular training to facilitate the labored respiration that inevitably occurs with racing. Third, swimmers should learn to breathe in with the mouth, but *blow out with the mouth and*

nose, to expel more stale air more quickly so new air can fill the lungs naturally by negative pressure at the correct moment in each cycle. Fourth, however, they should not try too hard to force all the air out each time, as this can bring on a feeling of breathlessness sooner in the race than planned.

We are looking for rhythmic and smooth movements throughout all the strokes, including the very important breathing segment of each stroke. This comes with practice and racing experience. Learning to pace a race and control the breathing cycle is just as important as knowing how to swim the required stroke, maybe even more so. Many a good swimmer has taken a race out too hard and wished he hadn't; some are able to "feel" the mistake quickly and draw on their reserves of aerobic and anaerobic conditioning to salvage the effort, but for most, the damage for that race is done, and the results will usually be disappointing. I've seen this all too often with enthusiastic and energetic age-groupers in a race. They get caught up in the moment and forget the importance of breath control for the whole race.

The 100-yard/meter freestyle is a good example. This race is usually thought of as short enough to allow breath-holding, as in the 50-yard/meter freestyle. But in fact, doubling the distance (50 to 100) in water at full blast requires almost four times the energy (actual and perceived), since stressful metabolic changes are already under way, and the back half of the race takes place in an already "unfriendly" physiological environment.

I suggest that swimmers hold their breath only in the 50 freestyle, and even here, they will need regular exhalations of CO_2 to ensure a breath-holding strong finish. Though most coaches teach alternate side breathing in all freestyle events, I am against this practice. CO_2 can build up more quickly when breathing every third stroke than every second. Remember, we want to delay CO_2 buildup for as long as possible.

In the 100 freestyle, the swimmer should breathe once every cycle and to the power side going into the last 25 yards/meters, in which appropriate training and the ability to breath-hold during increasing discomfort will allow the quickest, strongest finish possible. Needless to say, this type of breath control needs to be practiced over and over for all freestyle events above the 50 so it becomes automatic during the combat of racing.

I am against "double breathing" in *backstroke* only because of the negative influence on the smoothness of the stroke cycle. Some gravitate to this breathing cycle because the head is out of the water and coordination of head movement with breathing is not absolutely necessary. But the stroke should be trained with the same breath control as freestyle: inhalation on one arm, exhalation on the other arm.

The correct *breaststroke* rhythm dictates one breath per cycle, and here the inhalation is much shorter than the exhalation if one is to maximize the efficiency of the underwater glide. This gives a good chance to blow out enough of the mounting CO_2 rhythmically but not too forcefully.

The *butterfly*, which appears to the swimmer to consume the most energy per unit time of swimming, requires regular inhalation and exhalation. Past established routines for race-breathing have stressed "one-up, one-down": head up for a breath on one stroke, then head kept down in the water on the next stroke. But this costs oxygen and energy in the most taxing stroke. World records have now been set by butterflyers breathing every cycle, as much for controlling the breath and keeping the sense of breathlessness at bay longer into the race as for maintaining the rhythm of the stroke.

Everyone slows down toward the end of a hard race. With proper breath control, my swimmers slow down less than their competition. Even a race car needs an unrestricted clean air system to let it "breathe" for fast, powerful running. Breath control: It keeps you in it to win it!

CHAPTER 4

Even My Eyebrows Hurt

Discomfort, occasionally intense discomfort, is simply part and parcel of the athlete's life. Just about everyone who strives to be the best he or she can be is going to develop sore muscles at one time or another. But the fact is, the cause of this discomfort is still something of a mystery. We know that being dehydrated, and losing essential electrolytes in the process, can make the muscles feel achy and sluggish, both in the pool and everywhere else after practice. We know that unconditioned muscles tire more easily than conditioned ones and feel the effects of vigorous training longer. And, as mentioned in Chapter 2, we know that lactic acid buildup diminishes performance and can contribute to lingering muscle spasms when and if they occur. However, consider this: we can analyze muscle tissue under a microscope and see what condition it is in but we really don't understand the *exact* source of pain, and we don't understand why it takes so long to show up or to go away.

If you overdo any kind of physical effort—working out longer or harder than usual or placing excess stress on specific parts of the body—about 12 to 48 hours later you will probably develop stiff, sore muscles and achy, tender joints. In sports medicine vernacular, this is called delayed onset of muscle soreness—DOMS, for short. Athletes training for competition usually taper down their intense daily routines a few weeks before a race to help their bodies heal and ideally become stronger. With swimming, the taper—usually involving a three-week period—allows us to push during the time swimmers *do* spend in the water and approximate race-pace effort. Under this regimen, a swimmer entering the beginning stages of a taper often experiences generalized discomfort different from what he has felt during his main training sessions. This could arise because of increased pushing through the water as speed adaptations are sought in the body; or it could be part of the psychological aspect of getting the body ready to compete seriously just a few weeks away. You can feel as if everything bothers you—even your eyebrows will hurt! This might be the price we pay for swimming fast, but pain is still a signal that something is not right. So let's look at what we do know about cause and effect and see what can be done to minimize the problem.

The Causes of DOMS

Muscle damage comes free with hard exercise. Whether in the pool, in the gym, or in the field, increases in intensity and duration of intense training or vigorous generalized movement can bring about DOMS. Large forces applied to the relatively small cross-sectional areas of muscles rupture their cell membranes, causing leakage of important electrolytes (mainly calcium) from the cells. With extreme demands on the muscles, these ruptures can cause cell death (necrosis). We don't want to go to this extreme; our goal, instead, is muscle hypertrophy—stressing the muscles enough so the fibers and membranes mend bigger and stronger during the repair process, which can only occur during the rest and recovery period.

If you were able to view intensely-exercised muscle tissue under a microscope, you would see ruptured (torn) individual muscle cells and the breakdown of the membranes between them. Since the broken membranes have now lost their integrity, they allow large tissue substances such as the important energy enzyme creatinine kinase (CK) to pass into the bloodstream. This "footprint," and others like it circulating in the blood, definitely mean muscle cell damage. Finding a marker such as the enzyme lactate dehydrogenase means that the actual cell membranes surrounding muscle tissue

cells have been ruptured. Depending upon the type, duration, and intensity of the training bout, levels of these enzymes in circulation can be from 2 to 10 times higher than normal. (This is useful information for physiologists and a biological bonus for the athlete, since blood testing is a much easier diagnostic process than a painful muscle biopsy to get to the source of an athlete's pain.)

Muscle cell damage not only leaves you stiff and sore, you also lose some strength. Swelling in the muscles, due to broken capillaries, is also not uncommon. Most physiologists believe that the swollen muscles then press against nearby nerves, causing pain, though this has yet to be conclusively proved. The type of exercise you do can affect how you feel afterward: land-based exercises usually cause more muscular breakdown per unit time and thus can bring on more discomfort, but extended intense exercise of any kind can bring on the type of tissue damage described above.

Quite often your muscles are subjected to movements that force them into recovery positions that cause extension rather than the normal contraction. This *elongation* rather than *contraction* seems to be the main culprit in muscle damage. This type of movement, called eccentric, is the main cause of the fiber and membrane tearing that starts the chain of cellular events we've described. Examples of eccentric movement include running downhill and forcing the hands and arms ahead of you as you recover in all the swimming strokes to start the power segment again. An example would be throwing the hands and arms forward in the breaststroke glide. Also in the breaststroke, the backward leg extension as the kick finishes and the heels come together can induce strong eccentric movements that produce pain in the legs several hours after an intense race. This is one reason why stretching is so important: if muscles have not been adequately stretched, they will have a limited range of motion (ROM), so their full extension will become more of an eccentric movement.

When the muscles are forced to contract first and then allowed to return to their original size, we call this *concentric* movement. This is a more normal activity for the muscles; contracting against force is what they are built to do. Here, pre-stretching will help prevent muscle tearing as the muscle tries to move through its accustomed ROM. In the water, contraction occurs during the main propulsive movements of each stroke, while elongation of the muscle fibers occurs during the recovery phases of each stroke. Forced elongation of muscle fibers is needed during fast swimming because we usually hustle through the recovery phase of each stroke in order to get to the propulsive power phase as quickly as possible.

Repair and Recovery

A perplexing aspect of DOMS is that muscles become sorer after fast movement than after more intense work performed at slower speeds. The loss of protein from fast movement is often pointed to as the cause, but I question this. It is true that exercise increases the body's need for protein because of tissue breakdown and repair, but the amount needed is much less than once thought.

Most Americans get about 15% of their total calories from protein, which is twice the recommended dietary allowance for the general sedentary adult population. This recommendation does not hold true for those athletes engaged in high-intensity, strength-demanding endeavors. They will need much more quality protein and/or muscle-friendly amino acids than their sedentary counterparts. In

The Cause of Muscle Soreness

Almost all current theories acknowledge that most of the discomfort felt in the muscles comes from fiber and membrane tears due to *forced elongation, not forced contraction*. This was shown in studies done at East Carolina University and the University of Wyoming in the 1980s. Test subjects were asked to run on a treadmill for 45 minutes on two separate days. Initially, all would run on a level grade. Four days later some subjects would run on a 10% downhill grade. Those running downhill had considerably more soreness than those running level even though more lactic acid accumulated in the level runners. This study questioned the importance of lactic acid in creating muscle soreness.

fact, depending upon muscular demand, body type, and frequency of exercise, as much as one gram of protein per pound of body weight might be needed to build, sustain, and help repair muscles. However, the damage to muscles is not immediately helped to any great extent by simply taking in more protein. If it were, consuming lots of muscle-friendly protein immediately after intense exercise would most likely prevent DOMS altogether. (We will go into nutrition and ergogenics for power swimmers later, in Chapters 20 and 22, but it should be noted here that no one should take supplements, including amino acids, without the supervision of an educated and experienced nutritionist or other professional, such as a biochemist, physiologist, or pharmacologist.)

During vigorous exercise, your body also needs more oxygen to keep up with the demands of burning muscle fuel and to deal with your rising carbon dioxide and lactic acid levels. Some of this extra oxygen can also increase the production of free radicals, which contribute to inflammatory damage. So you would think that antioxidant vitamins would help mitigate muscle soreness. Sadly, this isn't the case. In several studies, vitamins C and E and beta-carotene had no effect on discomfort after intense training. Unfortunately, physiology researchers haven't come up with any real solutions to the problems of DOMS as yet.

Active recovery in the form of "recovery swims" (lengths of easy swimming) within a workout after a demanding set has been shown to help the musculature rebound faster than if there were nothing but rest (passive recovery). In addition, it is wise to have whole recovery *practices* after very demanding training sessions. The coach needs to balance what he or she feels will get the athletes to their highest level of preparedness over a specific amount of time against their physical and emotional need to recover from same. The body can handle just so much day to day, and it takes a knowledgeable coach to understand the *stress/recovery ratio* in training. If this is not kept in balance, the athletes are at real risk of breaking down, and all the great expectations may vanish like the early morning mist hanging over the pool as the sun rises.

Small amounts of light to moderate exercise (active recovery) that mimic the actions taken during the preceding intense activity work best—better than just any movement and certainly better than no movement at all (passive recovery). For example, after a breaststroke race, doing the movements of breaststroke (but easily) would prove more beneficial to the muscles than simply swimming some yards of freestyle. Giving the body an appropriate "prod" to stimulate the natural healing process, but not

enough to cause more damage, has proved to be the fastest way to recovery. About 60% effort is what the body needs to recover most in the shortest time—intense enough to force the lactate out of the muscles, but not intense enough to create more lactate.

There are several products on the market that claim to help the body handle the physical stresses of intense training while enhancing its ability to recover. Pacific Health Labs of New Jersey has come up with one such formulation that actually does what it promises—a patented 4:1 ratio of slow- and fast-absorbed carbohydrate to muscle-friendly whey protein and branched-chain amino acids. This 4:1 ratio, combined with the proper electrolyte mix, allows for the maximum amount of reparative nutrient absorption to aid in muscular recovery, more than would otherwise occur with either carbohydrates or protein alone, and it works better and more consistently than a mixed diet. (See Chapter 22 for more on this and other useful supplements to the athlete's diet.)

Strategies for Relief

If you follow the ground rules but end up sore anyway, what then? The use of non-steroidal anti-inflammatory drugs (NSAIDs) would seem a logical choice to lessen inflammation, but products like Aleve, Motrin, and Celebrex have not been shown to actually heal the damage that strenuous exercise does to the muscles. At times they do provide temporary relief, perhaps through their moderate analgesic effect, but as often as not, the muscular damage from exercise lingers after several doses. There is a balancing act that needs to occur with usage of this type of medication. Short usage (five days on, two days off with one repeated cycle if needed) can bring about reduced inflammation and swelling, allowing the body to help heal itself more quickly. But with protracted ingestion, an actual delay in the total healing cascade has often been seen. Recommended protocol for NSAIDs: five days on (medication taken only with food, never on empty stomach), two days off as a "drug holiday." Repeat for one cycle. If no better, then other medical methods of attack should be sought.

Warming topical creams with ingredients like menthol and eucalyptol can give you a temporary sense of feeling better as well. Anything that brings warmth, or at least the sensation of warmth, to an area in pain usually provides some relief. When pain arrives, muscle spasms usually follow, starting a vicious cycle: pain makes spasms, which make more pain. Warmth with gentle stretching can relieve the spasms, break the cycle, and allow for pain relief.

Even better than creams, direct heat from heating pads or hot showers penetrates deeper to lessen muscle spasms. The opposite approach has some medical logic to it as well: applying cold packs immediately after exercise may reduce swelling by lessening micro-bleeds from muscle micro-tears and may limit potential damage. If there is swelling, redness, and tenderness, the cold may prevent them from getting worse, which in itself can make you feel better.

You may want to try massage; most who do find it makes them feel good, even though it hasn't been proved to speed healing. A series of tests has shown that when athletes worked out hard and followed up within 2 hours with 30 to 45 minutes of massage, their blood creatinine kinase (CK) levels were lower and the white blood cells called neutrophils (which help fight inflammation) had increased. The athletes also reported lower levels of DOMS, compared with a group given a placebo treatment with "medication."

Though this may seem a bit of a "stretch" (pun intended) to some traditionalists, the healing enzymes in tropical fruits have also proved to be beneficial for recovery from intense muscular movement. These enzymes reduce edema (swelling) and inflammation and break up dead and damaged tissue to help heal and repair muscles sooner for the next bout of exercise. (For more on healing enzymes, see Chapter 22.)

Preventing DOMS

If you are serious about athletic training, preventing DOMS is tough. Good training habits help. Preparing for each practice or competition with a slow extended warm-up is vital to protecting the muscles. Cold muscles suddenly asked to work vigorously are much more likely to become damaged than warm muscles, especially as the athlete ages and/or becomes stronger and better developed. In addition, a good warm-up helps the athlete relax and get in the correct frame of mind to tackle a challenging workout or race. After the warm-up but before any serious swimming, some appropriate stretching should be considered, especially in the areas that have barked out previous warnings of muscular discomfort. (We will discuss specific warm-up, stretching, and cool-down routines in Chapter 12.)

Every athlete should aim to build a training program that will maximize positive results but minimize negative effects on the body. It is best to keep the intensity and duration level of appropriate exercises steady for 1 to 3 weeks at a time before ratcheting up all the training demands to get to a higher level all around. Depending upon the condition of the athlete and his or her natural physiologic response to the training effect, the 1- to 3-week

A New Frontier in Pain Research

To add to what sports scientists know about the causes and effects of DOMS, new research is being done on substances produced naturally by the body in response to vigorous exercise that show possible advantages in effort and recovery. These substances, called *heat-shock proteins* (HSPs), reside in the body at low but constant levels and are almost dormant until they are released by physical stress. As the body endures intense muscular stress and raises its temperature *in situ* (at the site), it sends out biochemical signals that activate the HSPs, whose blood levels then rise. It is this event that may play a role in the fitness recovery process by helping to keep muscles strong and lessening the damage they sustain after intense use.

A Japanese study has shown that if the muscles are pre-heated to between 40°C and 42°C (104° to 108°F) up to 24 hours before they are used during an intense workout, their strength and recovery are enhanced even after the temperature returns to normal. The researchers theorize that the subsequent rise in HSPs protects the muscles from damage and speeds recovery after muscular stress.

A study from Germany confirms the rise in HSPs after prolonged workouts in runners, swimmers, and cyclists. This research shows that, in most cases, the activation process takes more than 3 hours to kick in after the physical stress begins. Compared with athletes who rest more, as opposed to those working out for longer periods of time, the longer workout group shows a much higher HSP concentration in the blood; it could be that HSPs help them to maintain their fitness and strength through regular exercise bouts even after intense regular workouts. Still, it's too early to say for sure whether the presence of HSPs actually makes a difference in recovery and performance over a large sampling of athletes engaged in all sorts of activities.

setup can be modified somewhat to allow for individual adaptation. This places more responsibility on the coach, but that is a small price to pay for bringing out the best in talented athletes.

An experienced athlete listens to his or her body and honestly evaluates the adaptive process; there is a big difference between discomfort and pain, and the interpretation of each should be the responsibility of both coach and athlete. Modifications may have to be made to the training regimen to prevent serious tissue damage that could bring on down time, which no athlete wants. No need to rush things and push too hard too soon. If you've given yourself adequate training time to prepare for important competitions and you follow a timetable of expected results from the training program, you should be able to meet appropriate goals.

Why Lactic Acid?

Let's look at the infamous lactic acid in more detail and see just why it casts such a dark shadow. Here's how it works: You swim fast, your muscles go anaerobic (without oxygen), and *lactic acid* forms. You continue to swim with intensity; lactic acid continues to build up, your muscles burn, and you involuntarily slow down. This is due mainly to the rise in the actual acid molecules forming directly in the contracting muscles. Even if we can induce natural antacid buffers like bicarbonate with appropriate training, the acid content will most assuredly rise as intense muscular movement continues through forced-effort swims. Whereas the pH of the muscles normally hovers around 7.1 (near neutral but slightly basic), a drop to below 6.5 can wreak havoc on muscular function. The vital energy-producing enzymes shut down so no adenosine triphosphate (ATP) can be manufactured, and even the muscle fibers themselves refuse to contract in this inhospitable acidic environment.

All this seemed straightforward for so many years, but not anymore. New ideas about lactic-acid formation and utilization have come to the fore. Some new research is showing that athletes should train fast, not only to improve the body's ability to function with oxygen depletion, but to get rid of lactate faster and even use some of it to refuel the musculature by way of re-oxidation by way of the liver.

Lactic acid is produced when carbohydrates are broken down to simple sugars, usually *glucose*, which is the easiest sugar for the body's energy systems to handle. Then glucose (a six-carbon chain molecule) is further metabolized in muscle cells, mostly to *pyruvate* (a three-carbon chain molecule) to produce energy in the mitochondria if there is an adequate supply of oxygen, while a portion is reduced to lactic acid through the action of an enzyme called *lactate dehydrogenase* (LDH) when oxygen is depleted. The more oxygen that is present, the more pyruvate is produced. The less oxygen that is available, the more lactic acid results. Lactic acid can also be produced when the rate of glucose-to-pyruvate conversion is greater than the rate of pyruvate use by the mitochondria.

If this is taking place in an environment where there is very little oxygen (such as the muscular activity of sprinting), then lactic acid really begins to accumulate.

The concentration of *lactate*, as lactic acid is called when it is found in the blood, represents a balance among lactic acid production by the skeletal muscles, its diffusion from the muscles into the blood, and finally its consumption by the muscles, heart, liver, and kidneys as fuel itself. Lactic acid is constantly being produced, even at rest. As long as production equals consumption (a ratio called *clearance*), blood lactate does not rise. As rest progresses to easy activity, and then on to more intense movement, the rates of lactic acid production and clearance in the muscles themselves both increase; the better the condition of the athlete, the longer the production and the clearance can stay in balance. Although the absolute blood concentration of lactate does not increase at this point, the rate of turnover (production and removal) may multiply several times.

As exercise increases, a point is reached where muscle and blood lactate levels begin to climb. As the pace of exercise steps up further into sprinting, the rate of lactate production continues to increase, but now the rate of clearance cannot keep up. Lactic acid is still being produced and cleared, but the two processes are no longer in balance. The point at which this begins to occur is called the *lactate threshold*.

The body has several pathways that can clear lactic acid from the muscles, but the percentage of acid that follows each pathway varies, depending upon whether the body is at rest, exercising, or recovering from activity. Some lactic acid is oxidized to produce energy in the working muscles, while the rest eventually diffuses out of the muscles into the blood. If lactic acid is produced and consumed to the same extent in the same muscle, it never reaches the bloodstream and does not raise blood lactate. With quick, high-intensity muscular movement, however, there is the inevitable delay between the lactic acid concentration immediately being formed in the muscle fibers and the concentration that cascades into the blood as lactate during intense exercise.

If the muscles have a blood supply, lactic acid may be oxidized within the same muscle fibers that produced it or may migrate to other fibers with blood supply (fast-twitch red, for high-energy activity, and slow-twitch red, used for endurance). Remember from our discussion in Chapter 2 that the most quickly reacting muscle fibers (fast-twitch white, used for all-out sprints) have no blood supply at all, and any lactic acid produced here must be diffused out to other areas for oxidizing. This is why, after a race, a swimmer does a recovery swim using the same stroke at about 60% effort—to use the exact muscle fibers doing the exact movements that were just utilized for propulsion so as to help squeeze the lactic acid more efficiently out of them to where it can be handled by the body's oxidizing systems.

The body's reaction to lactic acid is not one of complacency; it works very hard to eliminate this by-product of muscular activity. Eventually, if the muscular activity is pushed high enough and long enough, the concentration of lactic acid will rise sufficiently to cause a migration of the excess into the blood as blood lactate. After diffusing into the bloodstream, lactate is either converted to pyruvate, which then builds to glucose in the liver, or it is oxidized in the skeletal muscle or heart. If there is no immediate need for glucose, the liver produces glycogen (a complex carbohydrate made up of long chains of glucose molecules) as a stored form of energy, which can be reconverted into glucose for the muscles and the brain to use upon demand. Liver glycogen formed this way can be thought of as recycled lactic acid from muscle contractions; this whole sequence is called the *lactate shuttle*.

Training my athletes to swim fast at practice and to hover at or above push-pace through a great portion of the session helps them turn this process to advantage by producing biochemical adaptations that improve both lactic-acid clearance and tolerance to lactic-acid buildup so the muscles can fire more strongly and longer throughout the race.

PART TWO

Strokes, Form, and Pacing

CHAPTER 5

Swimming and Racing Freestyle

I relate this thought to my swim racers often throughout the main competition season: your mind-set has to be such that when you step to the blocks you may lose (it happens to the best of us) but you must push yourself hard enough that if your competitors get to the wall ahead of you they will have to die trying.

In competition, I want my swimmers to just intuitively swim hard, with perfect form. I don't want them to think. During training, I do want them to think. A lot. I want them to think about the counterproductive forces of water, their own bio-mechanics, and how to condition themselves properly. However, concentrating on, and ultimately mastering, correct form and technique are the most important tools in any speed swimmer's arsenal. A 50% improvement in condition will produce about the same result as a 10% improvement in technique. Without correct form, you'll develop bad habits, overwork, and perhaps injure yourself. Even worse, you'll never master race pacing.

The stroke used most often as the anchor for training is *freestyle*. As the fastest competitive stroke, it also requires the least amount of energy per unit time. It is a long-axis stroke whose power comes from a side-to-side roll emanating from the hips, but which includes the whole body.

Since it is the easiest way to move through water when pushing the pace, freestyle is the stroke assigned by most coaches when they are concerned with upping yardage during training. This has some validity in that it does train several enzyme systems, but it is swum in training more than it should be for those who race the other strokes or individual medley. Though it may be the easiest way to move through water, freestyle should not be taken lightly. The technical requirements for powerful, efficient execution are many and must first be understood, then learned correctly, then perfected, and finally, made automatic if one is to swim this stroke fast under the stresses of competition. Along with the technique, the swimmer must have a sense of rhythm and aesthetics. In fact, the best swimmers are usually those who are musicians, artists, or dancers or who have the innate ability to control body movements well.

Freestyle Speed

On a relative scale of energy consumption per 100-meter race, assuming swimmers are at the same level of proficiency in their respective strokes, freestyle is at the bottom. Racing backstroke the same distance would require about 1.8 times the energy and oxygen consumption. Breaststroke comes in next at 2.4 times the energy necessary for freestyle (though in elite competition, the 200-meter breaststroke is the single race that requires the most energy throughout the event). Butterfly tops the list with 2.6 times what freestyle would demand.

It has been hypothesized with stroke/movement analysis that *butterfly* should be the fastest way to move through water for short distances because of the extra push from the kick. But though it is close

(butterfly is about 1.5 seconds slower at the elite level for a 50-meter sprint), freestyle will always be faster through the water. The key to freestyle's speed is the mechanical advantage of rolling the whole body side to side and thus slipping through the water more efficiently. (Fly requires the legs to put forth about 30% of the total energy required to complete the stroke adequately, whereas freestyle only requires 5% for distance swimmers and 10% for sprinters.) As the swimmer forcefully rolls, the leading shoulder drops into the water, in essence creating a deep "V" shape, like the hull of a racing boat cutting through the water. Unlike the other long-axis stroke, the backstroke, in which the swimmer pushes the water while the arms are submerged, in freestyle the swimmer pulls the water. Because of this, freestyle allows for both greater distance-per-stroke and more generated power per unit time. As stated above, there is a mechanical advantage to movement by freestyle over the other strokes.

To understand the importance of mechanical advantage, think of the movement of the body swimming through water as parallel with the functioning of an internal combustion engine powering an automobile. Picture the up-and-down motion of the pistons and how the energy created in that direction is transferred by way of the connecting rods to the rotating crankshaft, which in turn transfers energy to another direction to drive the wheels so the car can move. The body's corresponding elements are the hands (pistons), which grab hold of the water; the arms (connecting rods), which carry this energy to act in another plane; and the torso (crankshaft), which takes this forward-and-back motion from the hands and arms and turns it into rotational motion (rolling of the trunk, the core) so the body can move through water. The body's side-to-side roll is as vital as the crankshaft is to an engine: they both place the energy in the proper direction. The roll must be practiced forever and always, because as fatigue sets in and focus is lost; it is this constant, powerful, smooth side-to-side rolling motion that will "get you home."

Freestyle Arms and Hands

With freestyle, for convenience of instruction and appropriateness of function, I bring out the concept of "bending and extending" the arms, alternating throughout the stroke cycle. Extending the arm forward and grabbing water as far out in front of you as can be done smoothly in time with the roll correctly initiates good distance-per-stroke (DPS). The reaching arm (and hand) now catches the water and pulls it back toward the hips. But for the most power to occur, the elbow must start to bend and wind up pointing out to the side away from the body while still under water. This is called producing a "high elbow." When the pull has been completed, the arm should find itself extended backwards past the hips with hands still pushing the water toward the rear (arm now in a straight position). In order to keep the freestyle cycle going smoothly, the arm and hand must be brought forward for recovery above water in the quickest manner (which if done correctly will protect the swimmer's shoulder); "quickest" requires that the hand must follow the shortest distance between two points, a straight line. The only way to allow the hand to follow a straight-line path so it can be placed again in front of the body is to bend the elbow. Thus, we see the alternating bend-and-extend cycle of the arms and hands over and over as the swimmer moves through water. There cannot be two bends or two straight positions in a row, otherwise the most efficient way to swim freestyle

has been violated. No matter where you start in the freestyle cycle, if you just finished with a bent arm, you *must* have a straight arm following, and vice versa, of course.

Since the hands are the leading parts of the body that enter the water, they have a greater influence on smooth forward motion than many think. There are two distinct hand entrances into the water: one for sprint (power) freestyle and the other for distance (endurance) freestyle. The sprinters place their hands into the water in a neutral position: hand flat, slightly pitched downward with the fingers slightly apart, the fingertips hitting the water all at the same time (see Fig. 5-1). Eliminating splash as the hands enter the water is crucial because splash creates drag at the surface, which, as we've seen, adds to frontal resistance.

Many distance swimmers seem to prefer having the hands enter the water thumbs first, which they feel allows them to start a wider sweep sooner in the stroke cycle for more distance-per-stroke (see Fig. 5-2). But in reality, most of the swimmers who choose either way are not aware of this difference or how their hands actually enter the water until it is brought to their attention. Not being aware of its importance, most swimmers come by hand entrance intuitively and go by how best it feels for them. I believe in letting each swimmer decide what is best and try to make it work. But I also think that these strokes must be as body-friendly as possible, because after thousands of arm motions each day extended over a whole year's training regimen for several years, injury to a swimmer's shoulders could be just a lap or two away at any time. The thumbs-first entry forces the shoulders to rotate medially (inward), which then places too much strain on the shoulder girdle's inner structures. This, combined with the long yardage training that

5-1. Hand entrance for freestyle (sprint). A sprinter places his hand into the water in a neutral position: hand flat and slightly pitched downward, with the fingers spread slightly apart, the tips hitting the water at the same time.

5-2. Hand entrance for freestyle (distance). Many distance swimmers seem to prefer having their hands enter the water thumbs first, which they feel allows them to start a wider sweep sooner in the stroke cycle.

many coaches feel distance people need day after day, could quite possibly lay out the conditions that result in "swimmer's shoulder."

For correct hand entry to occur, this visualization of concept should be understood and practiced: they must be placed into the water where the shoulder pocket will be in the next second as the swimmer moves forward. The shoulder pocket is that indented area just inside the bulging shoulder proper; it is bordered on the top by the collarbone and on the bottom by the thick chest muscle (pectoralis). Concentrating on working the entry into this target area causes the swimmer to want to roll his body to the side and reach out in front. This is good; it makes the swimmer want to reach for all he is worth on each hand entry and get the most distance-per-stroke for each arm. This, too, is good because we all have favorite sides and arms. When fatigue sets in, we favor the strong side at the weak side's expense. Working this entry produces a balanced set of movements where each side is worked equally. Once the hands are correctly placed, the catch becomes the next important element. The pitch of the hand acts like the blade of a propeller; as the hand moves backward through the stroke it

propels the swimmer forward. (Newton's Third Law of Motion teaches us that moving rapidly in one direction requires an equal and opposite movement in the opposite direction.)

Water is not rigid, of course, so you can't actually grab hold of it and pull yourself along as if you were on land working with something solid. Instead, you need to hone what I call a feel for the water. This is a major reason why I don't like my swimmers to train with paddles. No matter how much manufacturers hype these devices, I don't want anything to interfere with that *aquatic feel*.

In freestyle, there are areas of the stroke cycle where the arms and hands must move faster than at other times. Hand and arm acceleration is an absolute for fast swimming, but the grip on the water must not be lost. Simply slipping the arms through the water or bending the wrists (what I call "feathering the water") to move the hands faster actually fatigues the swimmer more quickly. These movements are absolutely less propulsive and less economical through the course of the swim. The ensuing loose grip on the water and reduced distance-per-stroke will always keep the swimmer from reaching his or her full speed potential.

Freestyle Head Alignment

Head position is also extremely important in freestyle. It is an established principle that body movement is strongly influenced by where the head is turned and the eyes look. Years ago, freestyle sprinters were coached to rise as high as possible on top of the water, head up, with the waterline just above the eyebrows, the eyes looking forward, and the back arched. This was emphasized from the very first stroke coming out of the streamline off the dive to start actual swim racing. It was thought that this would give the body a "hydroplaning" position up high over the water. Now we know better. Above-water and underwater video and digital modeling of the body in various positions moving quickly has shown that tilting the head down more so it is further in line with the spine (the eyes are looking down and out while submerged) allows water to flow more easily over the head and reduces frontal resistance (see Fig. 5-3). And in terms of breathing, instead of twisting the neck to catch air (as we used to teach), it is smoother and more efficient to roll the whole body, keeping the head and neck always in line with the spine and taking a "bite" of air as the face breaks the surface (see Fig. 5-4).

Freestyle Breathing

In power swimming, the breathing cycle is all-important; correct breathing technique on every stroke is critical. In freestyle, I almost never advise a swimmer to hold his breath except when competing in the 50. Though the 100 is twice the distance of the 50, it requires about four times the energy, both actual and perceived. Holding the breath the first half of the 100 will prove fatal when trying to bring the race home. In races over 50 meters, the only times you should not be breathing are during the stroke-to-surface breakout from the dive, during the streamline after the first turn, and in the red zone finish, the last 5 meters of the race. This may not seem like much breath-holding, but you need to train for it every day.

Breathing every third arm movement, as many coaches like to emphasize because they feel it will produce a more balanced stroke, will only cause more of an oxygen debt sooner into the race than breathing once every cycle. Holding the breath for every other complete stroke cycle, at speed, can bring on an oxygen debt that will scream to the brain to breathe, and oxygen debt early in the race will lead to labored breathing and a less than opti-

5-3. Head position between breaths. Tilting the head, so the eyes are looking down and out while submerged, allows water to flow over the head and reduces frontal resistance.

5-4. Head position while breathing. Instead of twisting the neck to catch air, it is smoother and more efficient to roll the whole body, keeping the head and neck in line with the spine and taking a "bite" of air as the face breaks the surface.

mal performance as the race moves to the back half coming home.

I recommend breathing to the power side (everyone has a physical and psychological power side) because it allows for the best air exchange (transfer of CO_2 for oxygenated air). The better able the swimmer is to blow off CO_2 throughout much of the race, the stronger he should finish. When the going gets uncomfortable toward the final third of the race, favoring the power side can help the swimmer to marshal any remaining inner energies in order to finish as strong as possible. As I explained in Chapter 3, everyone slows down toward the end of a race. I coach my swimmers to slow down less and, we hope, catch the competition before they run out of pool.

Freestyle Legs

Though the legs provide only about 5% of propulsion in distance freestyle and about 10% in free sprints, they shouldn't be neglected in training or racing. The legs are the single largest mass of muscle used at any one time in a race, and they consume correspondingly large amounts of energy and oxygen. Conditioning the legs ensures that they will not desert you when you need them most: to push you to the wall when you are in the "I think I am going to die" mode.

Even the simple act of pointing your toes as much as you can toward the back of the pool can add to the streamline effect every minute you are moving through water. Letting the toes drift down so they point to the bottom of the pool creates a parachute effect, catching too much water and interfering with the desired streamline. End result: consuming more energy than you need to per unit time, which violates the holy grail of athletics: *economy of effort*. The faster swimmers over the

course of any race usually take fewer strokes than everyone else.

To initiate movement off the dive and every turn, the dolphin kick proves best. This is the most propulsive kick, but it comes at a cost of energy and oxygen. By training daily with this method of streamline propulsion, the body will adapt to the rigors of fast racing by acclimating to the energy costs involved. Skipping over this in practice will usually prove a big mistake in a race. Thinking that in the race it will take care of itself has given many a swimmer a wake-up call they never forget. *How you train is how you race* (see Figs. 5-5 through 5-9).

Freestyle Race Pacing

In a race longer than 50 yards or meters, you can't go all out in the first 50 or you will fatigue too greatly coming home. Here and in the three chapters that follow, I suggest formulas for determining race pacing, with target times for each 50 based on a swimmer's best time over that distance and accounting for increasing fatigue as the race progresses. Note: Formulas are divided into the take-out and bring-back time.

Racing Formula for the 100 Freestyle

The optimal racing formula for the 100 freestyle is the total of the take-out and bring back, and is based on the best 50 freestyle:

take-out = (best 50 freestyle time + 1 sec)

bring-back = (take-out time + 1.5 sec)

Example 1: If the best 50 freestyle is 23 sec: 24.0 sec + 25.5 = 49.5 sec total.

Example 2: If the best 50 freestyle is 25 sec: 26.0 sec + 27.5 = 53.5 sec total.

Example 3: If the best 50 freestyle is 19.3 sec: 20.3 sec + 21.8 = 42.1 sec total.

Freestyle swimming cycle.

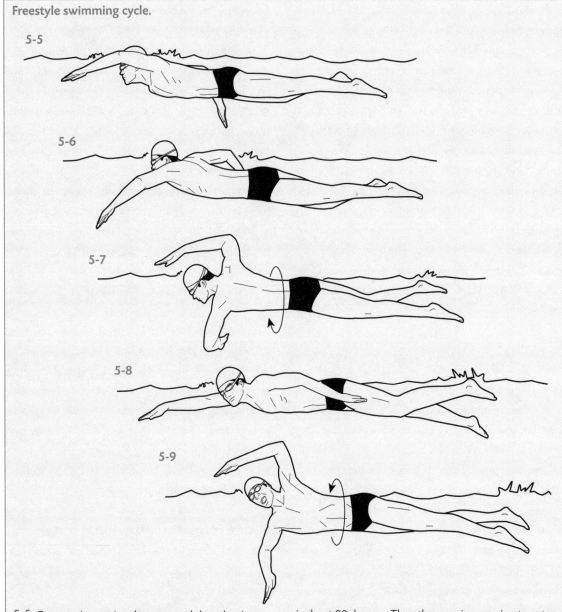

5-5

5-6

5-7

5-8

5-9

5-5. One arm is entering the water and the other is beginning the recovery with a bent elbow. The legs are moving up and down in a steady flutter kick throughout.

5-6. The catch has been made, and the S pattern of the arm pull begins. The elbow is held up high and the body begins to roll.

5-7. The body rolls as the pulling arm passes under the chest and the elbow reaches its maximum bend, which

is about 90 degrees. The other arm is preparing to enter the water, where the shoulder pocket will be in the next second as the swimmer moves forward.

5-8. The swimmer begins to rotate his head to the recovering side, to inhale, as he completes the pull.

5-9. The body achieves maximum roll as the swimmer inhales. The top hand enters the water to begin the next stroke.

All three examples show an aggressive attack to the race for various levels of ability and are the goals that should be sought by the competitor.

Racing Formulas for the 200 Freestyle

With the 200 freestyle, we can see two different formulas at work, depending upon the gender, size, and power of the athletes. A big, strong, determined female can usually swim more powerfully and, thus, aggressively than one of average size.

For female swimmers who are well trained, aggressive, and courageous, but of average size, the formula is about 1 minute plus their best 100 freestyle time.

> **Example 1:** A 53.0 100 freestyler should be able to swim a 1:53 200 freestyle. But a big, powerful female would probably come closer to producing according to the formula below, which applies for male swimmers as well. The 200 freestyle formula with splits by 50s, where Time = best 50 take-out split in the 200:
> (best 50 freestyle + 2 sec) + (Time + 1.8 sec) + (Time + 2 sec) + (Time + 2.4 sec).
> **Example 2:** Where best 50 time is 23.5 sec: 25.5 sec (easy speed) + 27.3 sec + 27.5 sec + 27.9 sec = 1:48.2.

Racing Formulas for the 500 Freestyle

The 500 freestyle obviously requires more endurance at a push-pace level and a strong pacing ability.

There are two main ways to race the 500 freestyle. The first method of attack is to take the race at easy speed, mainly concentrating on controlling the breathing and staying relaxed for as long as possible. Lap 15 brings on the big push. This signals that there are 150 more yards left to race and that the swimmer should begin to pick up the pace and expend more energy. This is done in three 50-yard segments. In the first, the swimmer begins to pull harder with each stroke but becomes more conscious of the need to roll side-to-side. The emphasis is reversed in the second 50: the swimmer rolls side to side with more emphasis and faster while still grabbing hold of the water. The last 50 yards is a sprint to the wall with all the attending needs of speed: extra kick, strong rolling side-to-side, and the three components of the "red-zone finish": giving everything left in the legs, no more breathing, and the lunge to the wall.

The second method is for the advanced 500 freestyler. He or she negotiates the first 50 yards in an "easy speed" time that is swum under control. The second 50 is done with the first take-out time plus 2 seconds; the third 50 has another second added, and the fourth 50 has one more second added. At this point the swimmer has to hold pace of the fourth 50.

> **Example:** If best 50 free is 25.0 sec, then take-out 50 = 27.0 sec
>   take-out 50 yards = 27.0 sec
>   + 2nd 50 = 27 + 2 = 29 sec
>   + 3rd 50 = 27 + 3 = 30 sec
>   + 4th 50 = 27 + 4 = 31 sec
> It is this 4th 50 that must be held in place for the rest of the race.
> With this example: The first 200 free is swum in 1:57 sec. Then the following 300 freestyle is swum in 3:06 (31 sec × 6); total time for the 500: 1:57 + 3:06 = 5:03

Stroke Rate Pacing

There is another way to approach pacing for speed swimming, and that entails *stroke rates*. Stroke rate X distance per stroke = speed. The most important premise here is for the swimmer to hold the goal pace (strokes per minute) no matter what. Strength and power play a great role. We usually reserve this concept for older, more experienced swimmers. Though much easier to accomplish on a bicycle, the premise is the same: get into a strong competitive pace and HOLD IT! However, unless they are specifically well trained to hold pace, even these swimmers will be struggling to hold stroke toward the end, as fatigue sets in.

This sort of training quite often assumes too much. Most swimmers who try this approach lack the ability to hold the pace as fatigue sets in, but it does give us a starting point for the swimmer to understand what on-pace swimming feels like for a specific distance to be covered in a goal time. The all-important side-to-side roll acts like a musician's metronome keeping time. If any portion of the race can be held at this pace, then later we can work to expand this speed to more of the race, so as to "bring home" the swim in strong fashion, having negotiated the early part under easy speed

conditions. Core strength and endurance are most important for this concept to work.

This works much better in short-course racing, in which the walls can help with increased relative speed. All pacing in long course needs to be slowed down to account for the extra 15% effort required to hold speed in a 50-meter pool. Attempting this first with fins is the smart choice, so the swimmer has help holding the necessary speed. Obviously, the longer the race, the fewer strokes the swimmer should take per minute (to prevent premature exhaustion). For the 50 all-out freestyle, the ideal stroke rate is 65 complete cycles (right hand and left hand) per minute. For the 100 freestyle, 60 cycles per minute is the goal. The 200 freestyle would need 50 cycles per minute, and in the 500 freestyle, the swimmer should try for 45 cycles per minute. In a more scientific and intelligent way of attacking a race, the use of variable pacing (easy speed, builds, push-pace, race pace) will afford the competitor the best combination of enzyme/energy production over time.

CHAPTER 6

Swimming and Racing Backstroke

Ask any swimmer who has raced both *freestyle* and *backstroke* which stroke is more taxing, and you will most likely get the answer: swimming on the back. Just the psychological challenge of trying to move as fast as possible without being able to see where you are going presents a distinct hardship for many to overcome. I guess the successful backstrokers have built-in SONAR to help their proprioception (knowing where the body is in a 3-D environment) while swimming fast. Add the science that tells us it requires more oxygen and energy to push water while moving on the back than to pull water while on the belly and you have a stroke that, though it resembles freestyle in the overall picture of its movement, is ultimately much harder to swim fast.

Leg stress is greater in backstroke than it is in freestyle. Many of my swimmers relate that in a hard race, their legs hurt more when swimming backstroke than with freestyle. The physicality of kicking hard on your back is more intense than when on your belly, although the kicking motions may appear similar or even mirror-imaged when compared. Vigorous leg movements while on the back place more demands on several supportive muscle groups than is needed with freestyle. The lower back, the upper and lower abdominals, the front (quadriceps) and back (hamstrings) muscle groups of the legs are all more greatly challenged while racing backstroke.

I liken training and racing back vs. free to the on-deck batter in baseball. The on-deck batter swings a weighted bat before he comes to the plate to make the one he takes to the plate feel lighter. Take home point: make your freestylers train and race backstroke to better their freestyle.

Backstroke Alignment

As with freestyle, the body roll is the crucial factor in generating the power and sleekness of movement. Though the timing of the roll side to side must be coordinated with the arm movements in both long-axis strokes, this timing is even more important with backstroke than with freestyle since it is harder to move water by pushing it than by pulling it. The muscles of the trunk are needed to help the shoulder and arm muscles push the water backward.

The two markers that a coach should look for to confirm correct backstroke body roll are: (1) the tip of the shoulder breaking out of the water first, followed by a rifle-barrel straight arm, and (2) when the arm is fully extended backwards after pushing the water away from the body, the palm of the hand should be facing the upturned hip bone, which has rolled upward facing the water's surface. I call this the hip-to-hand position. The faster the desired speed, the faster the body must roll. This concept *must* be kept strongly in mind during training and racing to prevent arms from flailing and slapping the water with every stroke when it is time to swim fast. The hand at the end of the "rifle barrel" should come out of the water thumb-first to keep resistance to a minimum. As the swimmer fatigues, most often the first sign of mechanical breakdown is that the shoulder and arm come out at the same time. This signifies that the crisp, snappy, forceful side-to-side full length body roll has deteriorated to a slight side-to-side rocking of the shoulder.

Backstroke is also the only stroke in which the head must never move except at the start (when it is looking backward) and near the turns and the finish. (For more on starts, turns, and finishes, see Chapter 10.) It calls for a two-point head placement while swimming down the lane: place your head back in the water lying flat, and then drop your chin slightly toward your chest. Alignment is correct when the ears are half-submerged under water. If your ears are totally under water, your head is too far back (too low in the water), and you will lose points of reference by not being able to see where you are in relation to the center of the lane. You will also lose sight of competitors on either side. (Peripheral vision should be at work here, not head-turning.) If your ears are totally out of the water, your head is being held too high, and your legs will begin to sink. This tires the upper back and neck muscles much sooner than need be in a race and also takes the body out of the ideal streamlined flat position on the water, which then increases drag.

Some coaches incorrectly suggest that as the backstroker fatigues and his breathing becomes labored, he should tip his head back further in order to open up the trachea and help stave off oxygen debt. But in fact, this doesn't help with labored breathing; keeping the head in the above-described correct position is the best way to finish the race as quickly and smoothly as possible (see Fig. 6-1).

Backstroke Breathing

Since the face is virtually always out of the water in backstroke, inhalation can be there for the taking no matter where the swimmer is in the stroke cycle. But correct form and technique dictate that breathing in and out should be coordinated as in freestyle: inhalation on one arm's recovery, exhalation on the other. I am against double breathing—inhaling on each arm's recovery. Double breathing allows for more up-and-down movement (a bouncing effect at the surface) that increases drag and wastes energy; it breaks up the smoothness of the stroke and causes the swimmer to blow off CO_2 too rapidly, which

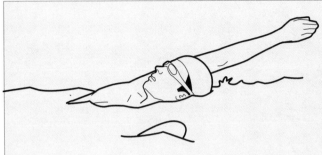

6-1. Close-up of head position in backstroke (side view). A backstroker's head is in the right position when the water line covers half the ear. If the ears are totally under water, the head is too far back, and the swimmer won't be able to see where he or she is in relation to the center of the lane. If the ears are totally out of the water, the head is too high, and the legs will begin to sink.

may bring on the sensation of lightheadedness. As I emphasized above, it is imperative that backstrokers strive to be extra smooth in the water.

Bouncing can arise for another reason: a defect in technique. During the catch phase in the stroke, the hands enter the water behind the head (if you were visualizing a clock facing you, the hands would enter at the 11 o'clock and 1 o'clock positions behind each shoulder). If they are pitched downward toward the bottom of the pool too soon and too sharply, the body will rise up with equal force, creating that up-and-down movement we never want to see an athlete do while swimming on the back.

Backstroke Arms

Three of the four arm positions in the backstroke cycle—the finish, the recovery, and the entry—are absolutely bone-straight, with only the hand positions changing. Only in the power phase does the arm bend, approaching a 90-degree angle, as if the swimmer were shot-putting or arm wrestling for maximum power at that instant. The key here is to keep the elbow tucked in close. Many backstrokers allow their elbows to drift away from the body, which reduces the force with which they can move water. Just keep thinking of the arm position you would choose to use if you were arm wrestling a powerful opponent.

To begin one complete cycle of backstroke, the shoulder tip lifts out of the water at the beginning of the body-roll sequence, with the rest of the arm following quickly and as straight as possible. The hand exits the water in knife-like fashion with the thumb breaking the surface first. The hand then rotates on top of the straight arm as it reaches behind the head so that the pinky enters the water first in either the 1 o'clock (right hand) or 11 o'clock (left hand) positions. This corresponds to where the shoulder pocket will be in the next second as the swimmer propels forward in freestyle. The opposite hand enters the water at either 11 o'clock or 1 o'clock (see Figs. 6-2 through 6-6 for whole sequence).

We don't want the hands to enter the water behind the head in the 12 o'clock position. We call this "crossing over midline," and it is a major error in technique—a common one that many coaches do not take the time to correct. If it is not addressed as soon as it is spotted, the swimmer will continue to practice and reinforce the error, making it very difficult to change later on when he wants to swim fast.

Flawed technique in backstroke will cause an unbalanced roll that will pull the swimmer to one side or the other, making him bounce off the lane guide like a pinball. This mistake in the swim can add 1 to 2 feet in venues such as most long-course pools, where a lane may be as wide as 9 feet. This error is doubled if the swimmer hits the lane guide

Backstroke swimming cycle.

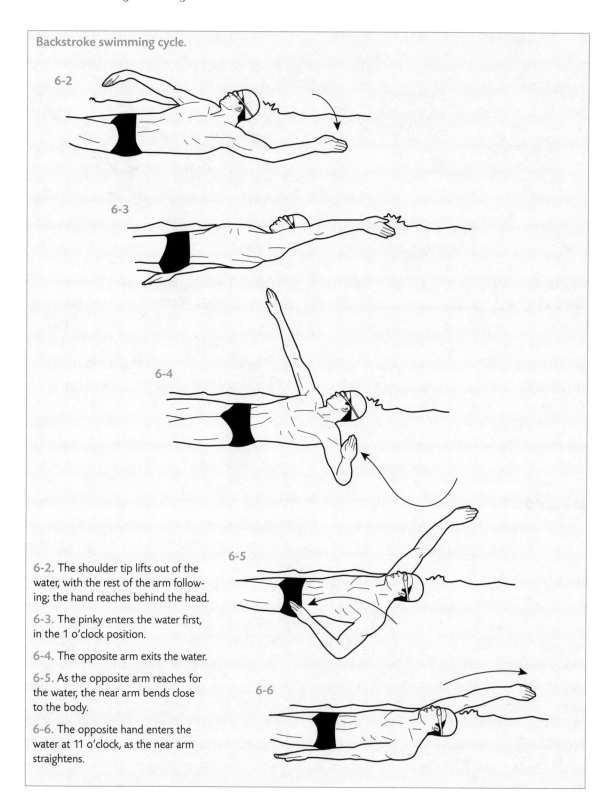

6-2

6-3

6-4

6-5

6-6

6-2. The shoulder tip lifts out of the water, with the rest of the arm following; the hand reaches behind the head.

6-3. The pinky enters the water first, in the 1 o'clock position.

6-4. The opposite arm exits the water.

6-5. As the opposite arm reaches for the water, the near arm bends close to the body.

6-6. The opposite hand enters the water at 11 o'clock, as the near arm straightens.

and then by reflex bounces off it to move back toward the middle. The smart move here is: If you hit the lane guide, stay close to it and use it to keep the path straight the rest of the way down the pool. Don't double the mistake.

Backstroke Legs

If distance freestyle usually requires only about 5% of its power from the legs, and sprint freestyle requires about 10%, it is safe to say that backstroke demands at least twice that of the sprinters, about 20%. Since there is no long-distance backstroke, the kick demands a lot of energy to produce speed over the three main distances: 50, 100, and 200. The kick is like that of freestyle, but, of course, upside down. There is more bending at the knee than in freestyle, and the feet kick just below the surface, making the water look as if it is boiling. When the body rolls side to side, the legs go right along with it, the whole body rolling as one. Here, the ankles must be flexible enough to allow the feet to point away from the swimmer and toward the back of the pool.

Backstroke Race Pacing

Racing Formula for the 100 Backstroke

For speed in the 100 backstroke, the take-out 50 should be about 1 second slower than the best 50 time; so if the best 50 is 30.2 seconds, then the lead-off 50 should be about 31.2 seconds; add 1.4 to 1.5 seconds to the take-out time for the back half of the race, and you get:

take-out = (best 50 backstroke time + 1 sec)
bring-back = (take-out time + 1.4 sec).
Example 1: With a best 50 at 30.2 sec we get:
31.2 sec + 32.6 sec = 1:03.80 min
Example 2: With a take-out 50 of 25.0 sec we get:
25.0 sec + 26.4 sec = 51.40 sec

Racing Formula for the 200 Backstroke

The first 100 should be between 3 and 4 seconds slower than the best 100 time, which again brings in the concept of easy speed. If the best 100 backstroke is 51.50, then the first 100 backstroke split should be about 55.0 seconds; add 3.6 seconds to the take-out for the back half of the race, and you get:

Example: With a take-out 50 of 55 sec, we get:
55.0 sec + 58.6 sec = 1:53.60 min

With Masters swimmers, the fade factor for the second 100 allows for a 5- to 8-second add-on:

Example: If we have a 1:05 100 backstroker, then a strong 200 swim would be: 1:09 min take-out + 1:14 min bring-back = 2:23 min

Ideal target stroke rates are as follows (where one right hand and one left hand = 1 cycle):
- For the 50 backstroke, 55 cycles per minute.
- For the 100 backstroke, 52 cycles per minute.
- For the 200 backstroke: 45 cycles per minute.

Notice that all three stroke rates are slower than for freestyle in the same distances. This illustrates the fact that it is harder to push water than pull it.

CHAPTER 7

Swimming and Racing Breaststroke

Of all the racing strokes, the breaststroke is the only one in which the competitor will live or die by his or her legs. In the other three strokes, a minor but important percentage of forward motion comes from the kick. In breaststroke, the legs can generate anywhere from *50% to 70% of the forward movement.*

I am a breaststroker, or at least I like to think of myself as such. I learned early on that the knees take a huge beating, enduring enormous pressure and tension kick after kick. It is important for the swimmer to develop the muscles around the knee, at the same time taking great care to protect the delicate tissues that make up the inside of the knee joint. So, for the breaststroker, no running, no doing stairs, no kneeling on hard surfaces while doing chores or hobbies. No excessively stressful exercises in the weight room that could place the knees and their surrounding support tissue in harm's way—that includes deep-knee bends, tight-positioned leg presses, and any severe or uncomfortable twisting or rotational motions of the lower body. It is important to develop the musculature around the knee, but with an eye to protecting the delicate tissue there. Bike riding is a good choice for cross-training and leg conditioning because the physical mechanical advantage of the bike and the rubber tires spare the lower-body joints the burden of absorbing prolonged pounding against gravity. (For more on preventing knee and other injuries, see Chapter 18.)

The breaststroke style of swimming resembles the "life-saving" movement through water that most of us are used to seeing. To push the pace and race the stroke costs a lot of oxygen and energy, more so than in any other style of swimming through an event.

Breaststroke Form

The goal of the efficient breaststroke is to maximize the beneficial movements from the kick by getting to streamline as quickly as possible. Getting the body to become as streamlined as possible before each kick allows the swimmer to achieve the maximum effect of the kick and the greatest distance-per-complete-stroke. If the kick comes too soon in the cycle, most of the thrust is wasted in trying to force the body through too much water before it is streamlined—a waste of energy and a definite stroke defect. I often tell my breaststrokers to "hurry up and wait"—hurry to get to streamline but wait to kick until they get there. The goal of every movement should be to achieve the least amount of drag and wave interference. This conserves both oxygen and energy. Breaststroke is quite demanding—all the strokes are, if the swimmer wants to be a champion.

Every part of the breaststroke, including the recovery, is at or below the surface, so the water's resistance is relentless. In fact, the single most taxing race physiologically—this will come as a surprise to the uninitiated, but not to the competitor—is the 200-meter long-course breaststroke, which produces the greatest level of lactate in the muscles and blood and requires more oxygen consumption than any other race. That includes the daunting 200 fly and the 400 individual medley!

Breaststroke is a classic example of less being more. Using too much muscle and not enough finesse, or fighting the timing of the stroke segments, causes even more energy drain. There is a "magic zone" in the stroke where increased muscle contraction will naturally create more speed, but if technique is abandoned in favor of strict muscle force, overall speed will diminish. The goal is to slip through the water rather than plow through it.

Breaststroke Kick and Glide

There are two key concepts that influence fast breaststroke more than any others. As mentioned above, one is how smoothly and efficiently the swimmer can perform the glide and streamline. The second is also unique to this stroke: *breaststroke is the only competitive stroke where you can only go as fast as your kick.*

During the glide, when everything has been set up correctly, the swimmer should set his body to maximum streamline and do nothing but hold that streamline for an appropriate length of time, depending on the event. The shorter the event, the quicker the stroke cycle must be, producing less glide per stroke in short-course sprint breaststroke (50 and 100) and more glide in the 100 and 200 long-course events.

The best way to make the kick work most efficiently is to start with "high heels"—the heels of both feet are pulled up as close as possible to the butt to start the kick cycle. From behind, the swimmer should look like he is making the letter W with his legs. As the kick goes further to completion, the legs are then thrust back quickly and crisply and squeezed toward each other with a rounded, smooth motion, the soles of the feet coming together as the legs extend straight back. It is the soles coming together that I call "the breaststroker's

It's the Kick

I am convinced that the kick makes a champion breaststroker. The 2004 Olympic breaststroke champion is rather short for a world-class swimmer (about 5'9"), but his kick is amazing.

secret." If this can be implemented with each kick, this motion comes close to emulating the angled blades of a propeller, and it provides a few more inches of forward movement per kick. (Stretching the ankles by sitting back on the feet and the use of fins in daily practice are but two ways to increase ankle flexibility to allow for this sole-to-sole action.) You do *not* want to kick too wide, because of increasing drag and resistance. And, remembering one of the tenets of fast breaststroke (you can only go as fast as your kick), if the kick is too wide, it will be too slow. If the range-of-motion of the kick is kept large by bringing the heels up to the butt while keeping the knees no more than 8 to 10 inches apart, and if the width of the kick fits between the shoulders, we get all the ingredients we need to produce a snappy crisp kick and to move water quickly.

Foot positioning must not be left to chance. The ankles must point away from the swimmer during the outsweep. If the feet face down towards the bottom of the pool, they will grab too much water, creating a parachute effect. The ankles should also be powerful and flexible enough to whip the feet inward and outward quickly. It has amazed me all my coaching life when I see some swimmers simply unable to make this physical concept work; it lends credence to the thought that breaststrokers are born, not made. Up to a point, this is true. Though I can coach a good athlete to finally get the "ankles-out, ankles-in" movements, those who come by it naturally usually make the best competitors in this stroke. More so than in any other stroke, a natural propensity for the inherent movements of the kick will allow those competing in breaststroke to be successful at it, since this whip-kick action from the ankles, feet, and lower legs generates the actual push-back movement against the water that brings about the most thrust forward.

Breaststroke Arms

Though the legs are the focus of the breaststroke, the upper body cannot be ignored. The hands, arms, shoulders, and head must be moved in concert as though always swimming downhill. We want to get under the surface during the glide as quickly as possible, head facing the bottom of the pool (face parallel to the bottom), and with the least amount of resistance. To get more distance per stroke and reduce resistive drag, the competent breaststroker uses the wave of water going over the head (as he dives down) as it moves toward the butt, which rises as part of the actual stroke's undulating movement as it comes to the surface. This wave motion actually helps push you forward like a surfer riding a wave to shore. The swimmer cannot see this wave since it is forming behind him, but he can feel it; when the timing is correct, he gets sort of a free ride forward. Those watching him swim can certainly see this wave form. The only caution here is not to allow the legs to press down together in dolphin-like kicking motion within each stroke cycle. This is an immediate disqualification, since breaststroke is the only stroke in which dolphin or butterfly kick is not allowed during the actual swimming of the stroke in a race. The only places it can be instituted are the insertion of one downward press of the legs in dolphin fashion off the dive and in leaving each wall after a turn.

I like to have my swimmers visualize drawing a heart with their hands and arms and then immediately putting an arrow through the center of the "heart" by thrusting the hands and arms forward quickly and forcefully to enter the streamlined glide phase (see Fig. 7-1). I must also point out that although at the surface I ask the swimmer to perform a serpentine or wave-like movement to dive

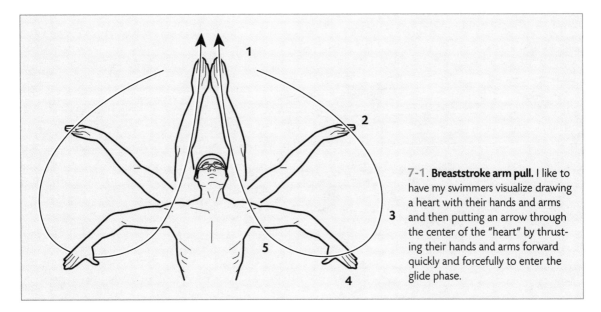

7-1. **Breaststroke arm pull.** I like to have my swimmers visualize drawing a heart with their hands and arms and then putting an arrow through the center of the "heart" by thrusting their hands and arms forward quickly and forcefully to enter the glide phase.

down, once under the water the body must stay flat and streamlined. It would be a waste of time and energy to try to come to the surface from too deep down. The optimum depth of the dive is about 18 inches under the surface—deep enough to eliminate the resistive surface tension but shallow enough to get to the surface quickly for the next stroke cycle.

The position of the fingers is very important since they are the leading edge of the body cutting into the water. The more streamlined and hydro-dynamic they are at all times, the easier it is to move through water. They should be held together and angled slightly downward to help guide the water to stream over the head. We don't want the head bob-bing in such a way as to create extraneous up-and-down movement and thus more resistance, and we don't want the head looking forward so the water can smack the swimmer in the face. Since the body follows the head in movement, we want the head to cut into the water and dive face down as quickly as possible so the swimmer can get under the surface for as long as appropriate in a streamlined fashion.

I like to teach swimmers to try to get their shoulder tips to touch the bottom of each ear lobe. We want to shrink the distance from the ear to the shoulder as much as possible every time we come out of the water to breathe, creating a rounded, hunched-forward position that helps reduce frontal resistance. Correct breaststroke rhythm dictates one breath per cycle. The inhalation is much shorter than the exhalation, to maximize the efficiency of the glide by staying in this position longer (see Figs. 7-2 through 7-6).

Breaststroke Race Pacing

Racing Formula in the 100 Breaststroke
The first 50 (take-out 50) breaststroke is about 1.5 seconds slower than the best 50 swim. If the best 50 swim is 30.5 seconds, then the take-out 50 should be around 32.0 seconds; add 3.3 seconds to the take-out time for the back half 50, and the composite 100 breaststroke time is: (first 50 breaststroke split) + (50 breaststroke + 3.3 sec).

Breaststroke swimming cycle.

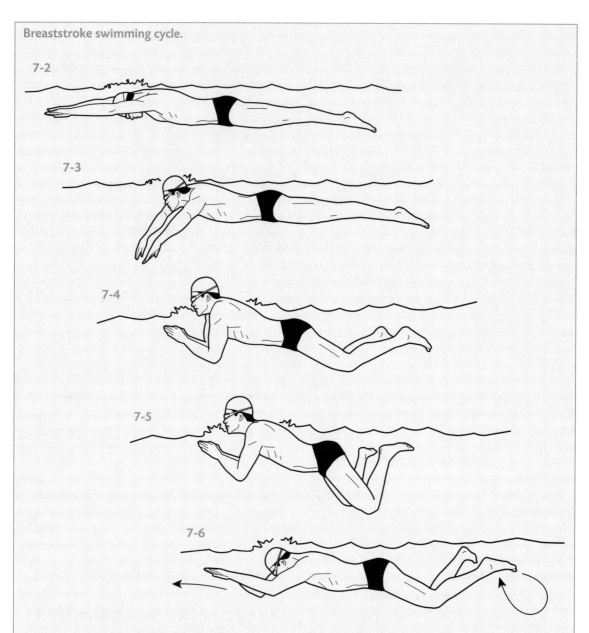

7-2. The stroke begins with the arms and legs fully extended, the feet together, and the body fully streamlined about 18" under the water surface.

7-3. The arms begin to sweep out while the legs stay extended.

7-4. As the hands finish the sweep, the chin is lifted up to breathe and the swimmer hunches forward. The feet are brought up to the buttocks.

7-5. The hands and arms are thrust forward quickly and forcefully, followed by the legs coming up to get set to squeeze water.

7-6. The feet are whipped down, back, and around in a circle while the chin is lowered into the water for the exhale, to make the most of the streamline position of the stroke.

Example 1: If best 50 is 30.5 seconds:
then take-out 50 + bring-home 50 will equal
32.0 sec + 35.3 sec = 1:07.30 min.
Example 2 (to break a minute): 28.0 sec +
31.3 sec = 59.30 sec.
Example 3 (championship time): 25.5 sec +
28.3 sec = 53.80 sec.

Racing Formula in the 200 Breaststroke

The 200 breaststroke is the premier event for physiological challenge if approached with aggression and courage. The oxygen and energy consumptions per unit time and for the whole race are larger than for any other swimming event. Here, also, the formula for a swimmer who attacks the event is to take out the first 100 about 3 seconds slower than his or her best 100 breaststroke swim. It is important to make sure that the lead 100 is done with easy speed generated by working the efficiency of the glide; distance-per-stroke is the key to easy speed in the breaststroke more than with any other event. The second 100 has the first 100 time plus the "fade factor" of 4 to 5 seconds.

Example: Best 100 breaststroke is 56.8 sec:
take-out 100 swim = around 1 min; the bring-home 100 is take-out time + 4 to 5 sec
=60 sec + (64 or 65 sec) = 2:04 to 2:05 total

As athletes approach age 45 and older, the fade factor in the back half of the race is usually more dramatic (5 to 8 seconds slower). Some extraordinary Masters athletes, though, are belying their age with sophisticated training, ideal nutrition, great genetics, high motivation, and space-age racing apparel. Such athletes can do even better than the above formulas.

A good swim for those over age 50 in the 200 breaststroke would be: if the swimmer is a 1:10 min 100 breaststroker, then he takes it out in about 1:13 and brings the second 100 home in 1:13 + 8 seconds (total = 2:34 min).

A 1:07 min 100 breaststroker would have a strong 200 swim if he produced a 1:10 + 1:18 = 2.28 min.

Even more than with the other racing strokes, an important part of the breaststroke cycle needs to be adapted as the racing distances change. The length of glide is reduced for the "short stuff" and increased as the distances expand. The 50 breaststroker has a power swimming rate of 66 complete strokes per minute (0.9 seconds per cycle); the 100 breaststroke swimmer needs to approach 1.1 to 1.2 seconds per complete cycle (50 to 55 complete strokes per minute), and the 200 breaststroker needs to hold 1.4 to 1.6 seconds per cycle, or 40 to 43 strokes per minute.

CHAPTER 8

Swimming and Racing Butterfly

Butterfly is the marquee event that the world has come to associate with elite swimming. It may not be the fastest stroke, but it is eye candy as far as swimming goes. Growing up in the late 1950s and early 1960s, if you were branded a swimmer you had to know how to do fly and look good doing it. I found out early that butterfly really wasn't all about strength and power, it was more about rhythm and timing: in essence, when to do what. With all the strokes, you need to know when to do what; but with fly, timing is everything. What you do in the water can be butterfly or "butter-struggle." It can be butterfly or "wounded moth." It can be barely adequate fly or it can be a thing of beauty. And just like anything else done expertly, when butterfly is made to look both esthetically pleasing and easy to perform, the uninitiated assume that it is no big thing to race—but we know better!

In butterfly, it is not so much pure strength as it is rhythm and timing that gets one across the pool smoothly and efficiently. To perfect the technique and internalize the timing, it takes practice—and everything starts with the kick.

Here, again, it's the legs that will get you to the wall. The legs play an important part moving through the water in fly. If done correctly, the kick provides up to 30% of the forward motion, a sizable portion that must be trained so the legs won't give out as the race progresses.

Butterfly Kick

Unlike the snappy, crisp dolphin kick that is used in streamline off the dive and the walls (all with the same amplitude, or height and depth of motion, and force) the butterfly kick has two distinct motions as dictated by the stroke: a small assistive kick and a larger propulsive kick. The small kick happens when the hands are in front and the head is facing the bottom of the pool. This first kick gives the stroke some leg thrust but also, and most important, it helps maintain the rhythm. The second, deeper and more forceful kick happens when the hands and arms are behind the swimmer. It forces the body forward so the hands can come out of the water more easily for recovery. This is the most demanding part of the stroke and the trick to maintaining pace when fatigue sets in. Trying to "muscle" the hands and arms out of the water to recover properly for the next stroke consumes enormous energy very quickly. This is what breaks a flyer down toward the end of a race (or much sooner if proper pacing and stroke technique are not held). Getting the kick timed right so the tiring arms can be helped out of the water is the secret to extending the fly in a more sustainable fashion.

Flexible ankles add a great deal to the force of the kick. The increased range of motion and the snap of the ankles downward produce explosiveness in every kick motion that propels the swimmer forward. Just try to swim some fly without using your legs, or with no snap of the ankles, and you'll see how important the tail end of the body is for helping the front end move through water.

Butterfly Muscles

Four main muscle groups are critical in the fly. The most important are the core muscles around the

Using Fins

Butterfly can consume so much energy that it is hard to get enough practice yardage in to acclimate the body to perform well under racing conditions. The use of fins usually mitigates this problem, as can one-arm and alternate-arm fly drills. If done correctly and kept smooth with very little splash, the one-arm fly can make an enormous difference in the actual and perceived energy cost of the various training swims. (For more on training drills and fins, see Chapter 14.)

hips. These include the abdominals, the obliques, the lower back, and the hip flexors. The next most important are the muscles of the upper back: the trapezius, the deeper rhomboids, and the *latissimus dorsi*. The specific musculature of the shoulders (the anterior, medial, and posterior segments of the deltoids) is mainly responsible for up-and-over movement (getting the hands and arms from back to front to initiate another cycle of swimming). The muscles of the forearms and upper arms pull the water backward, propelling the swimmer forward. And finally, the muscles of the legs—the quadriceps, the hamstrings, and the calf muscles—all work in concert to provide at least 30% of the forward momentum through the water. Next to the breaststroke, the fly requires the most from the legs.

Butterfly Arms

The fly as I teach and coach it looks somewhat different from what most are used to seeing in the pool. I emphasize a higher elbow as the arms move forward in recovery, resembling sort of a bat wing, with each arm positioned similar to freestyle form

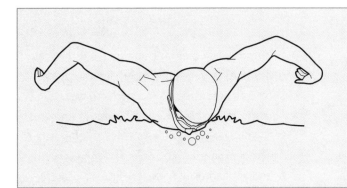

8-1. **Butterfly arm position.** In fly, I emphasize higher elbows, like chicken wings, with each arm positioned similar to freestyle form. Ideally, this makes the motion of the arms as much like a two-handed freestyle as possible. The only difference is the entry into the water. In freestyle, the hands enter in neutral position, all the fingers at the same time. In fly, the thumbs must enter first.

though not as articulated (see Fig. 8-1). What I am looking for the athlete to do is slip into a two-handed simultaneous near-freestyle recovery. The only difference is the entry into the water. In freestyle, the hands enter in "neutral position," the fingers being horizontal and touching the water all at the same time. In fly, the thumbs must enter first. This cuts the splash (and therefore the drag) drastically and prevents wasted energy from interfering with the forward motion.

The idea behind this style is to emphasize a physical absolute: the shortest distance between two points is a straight line. If the elbows are somewhat bent in recovery, the hands travel in a straight line and get to the starting position quicker. This allows for a faster turnover in stroke cycle. It also spares the upper back muscles since the arms and hands do

not need to be lifted a greater distance above the water line.

At first, this will usually seem awkward to swimmers used to the traditional roundhouse swing of the hands and arms. The swimmer may feel that he is not getting enough extension as when he whipped the arms forward or that the hands and arms just feel wrong. But eventually, with personalized refinement to fit the stroke to the body type, the bat-wing technique becomes doable and will allow for even faster recovery of the hands from back to front. The delay in making this an automatic neuromuscular movement is normal for anyone having to be retaught muscle memory, especially after thousands into millions of yards swum a different way. To develop a new "feel" is to produce a new look in the water—much harder than learning it my way from the start.

Butterfly Breathing

Everybody is an Olympian for the first lap; then things can get ugly. Coming up for air requires the swimmer to pull out of the most streamlined, head-down position, which slows him down. But, if you remember, the butterfly also consumes the most energy per unit time, which means the swimmer needs more oxygen per unit time.

Bat-Wing Butterfly

Swimmers who practice my bat-wing fly seem to learn naturally when to put their hands in the water to get the most extension. I encourage this individuality in developing the strokes I teach. As long as my swimmers stay true to the concept of what I am trying to coach, slight variations in execution are absolutely OK.

Breathing in butterfly can follow the ideal pattern, the superhuman pattern, or the reality pattern. Superhuman flyers take two or three down strokes (without breath) for every up stroke (with breath). This is very demanding, and I think too costly for most swimmers in terms of oxygen debt. Instead, I suggest the flyer should breathe at least every other stroke (one-up/one-down). If you train diligently, you should be able to hold this pattern for at least the 100 fly. But if your pace is a little too fast, one-up/one-down may cause an oxygen debt/CO_2 buildup sooner than desired, and you may need to switch to breathing every stroke to save the race. You might think this is poor form and a waste of energy, but Michael Phelps breathes every stroke and sets world records doing it. I have nothing against breathing every stroke as long as the swimmer can maintain speed and confidence for the length of the race (see Figs. 8-2 through 8-6).

Butterfly Race Pacing

Racing Formula for the 100 Butterfly

My formula for a strong, courageous, fast 100 butterfly is to have the take-out time be 1 second slower than the fastest 50 time; add 3 seconds to the take-out time for the bring-back time:

> take-out time = (fastest 50 time + 1 sec)
> bring-back time = (take-out time + 3 sec).
> **Example 1:** If 29 sec = fastest 50 time:
> 30 sec + 33 sec = total 1:03 min
> **Example 2:** If 22 sec = fastest 50 time:
> 23 sec + 26 sec = total 49 sec

If the walls are utilized correctly and streamlines are optimized, the last example can be even faster by about 1.5 seconds.

For Masters swimmers the bring-back 50 is usually 4 to 5 seconds slower than the take-out 50.

Racing Formula for the 200 Butterfly

The 200 butterfly has pacing and courage written all over it. It could be executed in one of two ways, both of which give swimmers a chance to show their motivation. Those who feel they can take it out and hang on should try for the first 100 swim 3 seconds slower than their top 100 swim. Then, relying on and remembering to work the kick (also depending upon how they utilize the walls for short course), they can bring it back with as little as a 3-second fade. More realistically, average age-group and Masters swimmers will experience anywhere from 5 to 10 seconds of fade.

Another tactic is to make the take-out 100 swim 4 to 5 seconds slower than the best 100 but keep the rest of the swim strong (within 4 seconds of the take-out 100, accounting for the dive in the beginning); this is considered a negative split for the second 100, since the swimmer has no dive to help propel him in the second half of the race. The purpose is to "buy back the clock" from an easier first half. Some like to race the two-fly this way, keeping the great discomfort of increasing oxygen debt at bay until much later into the race.

Having this sense of still feeling OK boosts confidence to where and when desire and pride take over to bring the race home. Of course, I have the statement from many of my swimmers after they have recovered from their event: "I know I could have gone faster." I usually respond in one of two ways:

1. If it is a new event for them or if they have only raced it a few times, I offer the fact that they will eventually attack the race and give it a more courageous try next time out, or

2. I say, "Then why didn't you swim faster?"

Butterfly swimming cycle.

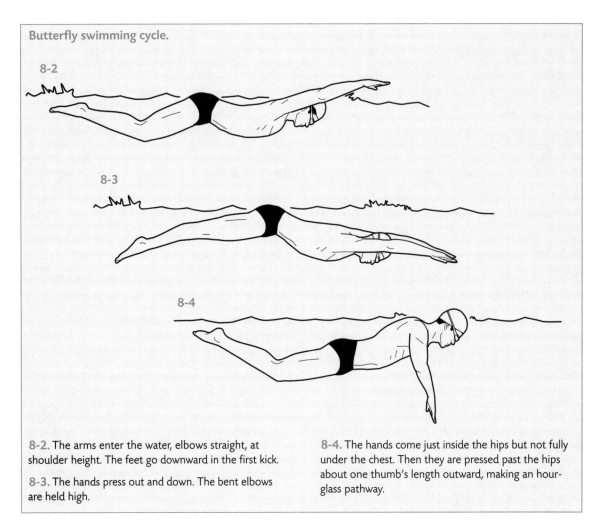

8-2

8-3

8-4

8-2. The arms enter the water, elbows straight, at shoulder height. The feet go downward in the first kick.

8-3. The hands press out and down. The bent elbows are held high.

8-4. The hands come just inside the hips but not fully under the chest. Then they are pressed past the hips about one thumb's length outward, making an hourglass pathway.

I want to solidify the tenet that for that particular moment, it was the best they could do. I can ask nothing more than that.

Example 1: For the 200 fly:

If the best 100 fly = 49 sec then we want to see:

52.0 sec + 55.0 sec = 1:47 min

Example 2: If the best 100 fly = 49 sec then we want to see:

53.5 sec + 54.0 sec = 1:47.5 min

Example 3: If the best 100 fly = 55 sec then we want to see:

58.5 sec + 1:05 min = 2:03.5 min

Ideal stroke rates for butterfly have more to do with courage and experience than with strength and desire. The faster the kicking, the faster the swimming in fly. A 50 flyer should be able to hold stroke at about 60 cycles per minute (1 second per cycle). The 100 and 200 butterfly should be attempted at close to the same rates as the breaststroke:

- 100 fly = 1.1 to 1.2 seconds per cycle (50 to 55 strokes per minute).
- 200 fly = 1.3 to 1.5 seconds per cycle (40 to 50 strokes per minute).

Butterfly swimming cycle *continued*.

8-5

8-6

8-5. While the arms are finishing the pull, a breath is taken and the second kick is made.

8-6. The arms are bent for recovery with the hands aiming forward, thumbs closest to the water. The head is lowered into the water before the hands enter, thumbs first.

CHAPTER 9

Swimming and Racing the Individual Medley

The individual medley (IM), to me, is the decathlon or modern pentathlon of swimming. To succeed in an IM, competitors have to do everything well. But I have seen a pattern over the years where the fastest IMers are strong in the breaststroke. Why? The breaststroke is the slowest stroke and requires the most energy in an IM. Butterfly is first, so the rested swimmer takes this first stroke of the event where he can play off his dive and extended streamline (to the 15 meter mark) to save actual swimming. But by the breaststroke portion of the race, those who are more contender than pretender have already entered the discomfort zone. If behind, strong breaststrokers will be able to catch up to those lacking this talent without expending all their reserve energy. They'll have some "gas in the tank" for the freestyle leg, or if they have worked hard enough to be toward the front of the heat, they can pull away at this point and make the others try and chase them down.

The IM rules are simple: each stroke must be *swum and finished* legally and in this order: butterfly, backstroke, breaststroke, and freestyle (any stroke but the first three). Once the wall is legally touched, swimmers can turn in any fashion they choose. I coach two modified turns in the IM. They take lots of practice to get down well enough for them to help in a race, and they take courage because there is an oxygen cost that must be trained for daily and paid for dearly in the race. However, I feel that they do give the swimmer a distinct advantage.

Transition Turns

After the fly is completed and the required two-hand touch executed, the push-off into backstroke should be done on the body's side, to lower resistance through the water by cutting through it on the body's edge. The swimmer should never push off on the back—too much squared-body resistance. It doesn't look good, and it isn't good racing form. The kick is what I call "waffle," which is strong snappy dolphin kicking on the side. The eyes must be riveted on the lane guide to ensure proper body placement in the water so as not to be rotated over 90 degrees, with the upper shoulder pointing straight up to the water's surface. Here at least four kicks are needed to get the propulsion necessary to edge ahead of those not utilizing this type of turn. After the dolphin kicking, the swimmer rolls over onto his back and begins backstroke kicking as he takes one stroke, pushing the water backward, and rises to the surface and begins backstroke. He must also remember to force his leading shoulder tip to break the surface first so as to ensure that no "bucket of water" is resting on his chest. It would be a big mistake to carry almost one gallon (8.5 pounds) of water (over the chest) up to the surface because of poor form or ignorance.

The other turn is more exotic and is something I only recommend as a way to get more distance off the wall at the last transition turn in the IM. Most swimmers will not like this, and for those who do not train to do this, it is nearly impossible to pull off at this point in the IM. For the last transition turn in the IM, as the breaststroke finishes and the two-handed touch is made, we begin the turn and streamline into freestyle. This is accomplished by holding the streamline as tight as possible and forcing at least three hard, snappy dolphin kicks while on the belly.

The Order of an IM

Butterfly, backstroke, breaststroke, freestyle: this was not always the order of an IM. When all four strokes were incorporated in the late 1950s, the event was swum in the same order as the medley relay, with fly coming third…murder! (Another popular event was originally set up to tax its competitors excessively. The Triathlon administrators had swimming scheduled last. This proved dangerous in enough cases to force the change in order we see today.) Luckily, some logic (and a few kind thoughts) from the administrators of national and international swim competitions made the present order of strokes in the IM de rigueur. Times dropped markedly because the swimmers could use the start off the blocks to help the fly, and they were able to get the fly out of the way while still energized in the race. I wonder how many would choose the event if the order were reversed? Imagine having to swim fly at the end of the event when you are supposed to take out the race strong. I would bet a dozen Krispy Kreme donuts that, if the original order were still in effect, most swimmers would hold back until they came to the fly and then pray real hard to hang on.

Then a strong *two-handed* pull-down with the arms comes next. This is perfectly legal. The main concern at this point is *not* to do a breaststroke kick. We are finished with that stroke and any semblance of it during the freestyle leg is cause for a disqualification (DQ). The only kick I want to see is the dolphin kick right through the pull-down and into the breakout at the surface into freestyle. This turn increases underwater distance by at least 1 1/2 body lengths over the standard turn from breast to free. But it has to be mastered and the swimmer must believe in the concept for it to be workable and productive.

Individual Medley Race Pacing

We try to approach a certain ideal formula for speed through the IM, broken down by stroke. The best way is to take the swim out comfortably in training and try and institute the various segments of the formula to gain a feel for relative speed throughout. We do this with fins at first so the swims are more under control, and we have the option of "playing" with the formula. It is usually at this time that I emphasize the need for best possible streamlines off the walls to help in the effort to try and hold the time segments of the formula for racing each stroke.

Racing Formula for 200 IM
Each total time given below is the sum of the times listed for each of the 4 strokes:

butterfly, backstroke, breaststroke, and freestyle
Total IM time = fly time + (fly time x 1.15) + (fly time x 1.33) + (fly time x 1.09)
Example 1: 25.0 sec butterfly + 28.75 sec backstroke + 33.25 sec breaststroke + 27.25 sec freestyle. Total time = 1:54.25 min
Example 2: 28.0 sec butterfly + 32.20 sec backstroke + 37.24 sec breaststroke + 30.52 sec freestyle. Total time = 2:07.96 min

The above efforts assume an ideal situation, in which the swimmer has no real deficiencies and can hold this "perfect effort swim." Closer to reality is a situation in which we see how fast the swimmer can take it out in the fly and then hold as close as possible to the other relative speeds. Or, in courageous swimmers, it is not just how fast can they hold each segment but really how fast can they finish the race…how fast can they go freestyle when everything hurts, and it feels like there is not enough oxygen on the planet. The bottom line here is total time to the finish wall, not just segmental swims for each stroke, though getting fast in this event should take into account segmental swims in training.

It seems almost intuitive that the swimmer pays the price in the backstroke for the effort in the fly, since he feels he needs to recover somewhat for what lies ahead. Actually, there is a mini-recovery period throughout the race. In short-course individual medley swimming, it can be considered acceptable to take three or four strokes in the easy speed mode in the succeeding segment to enhance at least psychologically a sense of recovery before the swimmer picks up the pace and effort again. Some strokes physically take more out of the swimmer than others; some are more mentally challenging. The secret to a strong IM is really no secret: competing in the event many times and experimenting with the above formula to see whether you fit into it. If it takes a greater effort in one segment as opposed to another to get a fast cumulative time, then we work from there. We work that segment to its fullest while trying to strengthen the other areas as much as time and talent will allow.

As with all events in competitive swimming, attitude plays a very important part in this type of training. Many swimmers with the sprinters' mentality like this event, because it certainly is not boring. Training for the IM and racing the IM brings into play, in a single event, all that swimming has to offer.

CHAPTER 10

Starts, Turns, and Finishes

For those who know fast swimming, starts, turns, and finishes are the finesse portions of any race, expected of any competent swimmer. But to everyone else, they are the I'm-not-exactly-sure-what-I-saw-but-it-looked-like-it-belonged portions. They are important no matter what the course and event. For short-course races in particular, it is definitely about the walls. Next to a good dive, every push off the walls should be the second fastest segment of the race—always faster than actual swimming speed. High-quality races so often come down to the finish—the red zone, as I call it. Inside the flags, a distance of only 5 yards or meters, medal places can change dramatically.

While starts, turns, and finishes only comprise a small portion of the race distances, their impact can produce dramatic results. Much attention should be delegated to their mastery. Every practice session should have a designated segment for their practice. They need to be done automatically under the most taxing circumstances. Relying on the swimmer to do these during intense training can be foolhardy. Definite time segments need to be allotted in each practice so the swimmer can focus, visualize, and develop neuromuscular adaptation to elements that are much more difficult to perform at a high level than would normally seem the case.

Starts

A few important rules and concepts regarding starts must be understood, incorporated into regular practice, and perfected if a great swim is to begin when the gun goes off.

But before I coach my swimmers in the finer points of getting off the blocks, I instruct them to utilize the start and the starting blocks to help them in another important aspect of swim racing. I have my people rub their hands up and down several times on the blocks to cause them to tingle. This does two things: (1) it allows the first few strokes to feel enhanced due to the "lufa effect" we just created in the hands, and (2) while they are doing this maneuver, they have to consciously deep breathe in and out a few times to help control their air-exchange. This also helps to ground my swimmers and aid in their focus just before they step up onto the blocks.

Swimmers have to come down to a set position quickly when commanded by the starter. A slow move to get set can bring a warning. A second warning can bring a disqualification (DQ), though that rarely happens. Sometimes the slow-to-get-ready swimmers are asked if they can hear the start command; if the answer is yes, they had better be ready for the second try.

Once swimmers are down in the ready position, absolutely no movement is allowed. If starters see movement before the gun goes off, they will usually issue a "stand-up" command. At this point if someone falls into the water, it will usually not be a DQ, since the swimmers have been "released" from the hold position of the start. The offending swimmer(s) will be admonished once and then given a second chance to race. But if movement is noticed by the starter and take-off judge or referee too late to halt the start, the race goes on and finishes; the offender will be notified afterward of the bad news. This is so as not to penalize the whole heat for someone's bad start by making everyone get up and start the race a second time.

With breaststroke being the exception, after the dive, all swimmers' heads must break the surface of the water by the 15-meter mark. Each lane line has a contrasting colored disk at the 15-meter mark for ease in gauging this distance. This rule was instituted after the 1988 Olympics, when backstroker David Berkoff swam almost 50 meters under water in his leadoff lap. The officials wanted to keep hydroplaning beneath the surface from replacing swimming at the surface when the former has proved faster than the latter. As mentioned, breaststrokers do not have to adhere to this rule, since at the senior level of swimming most are big and strong enough that their underwater sequence of movement after the start will bring them past the marker.

Leaving the Block

There are three types of starts off the block: the traditional grab start, the more recently instituted track start, and a few forms of the relay start.

Grab Start Sequence

I prefer to coach the grab start. Here, both feet are at the front of the block; the hands can be placed either outside the feet or between them. I prefer the power hand grabbing the front edge of the block, the other hand on top of the first, and both placed between the feet, which are spread to about shoulder width. Heads are down until the sound of the starting device is heard. What follows in quick sequence is:

1. Hands are thrust forward, one hand directly on top of the other, power hand (on the side on which you usually breathe) on the bottom (see Fig. 10-1). The power hand is purposely placed

under the weaker hand because, if we are racing freestyle, the first stroke will be taken as the power hand peels off from the bottom. If it were on top, the bottom hand would be in the way, and it would have to be moved slightly to the side to initiate the first pull; this would cause the hips to roll slightly to the opposite side to compensate, movements which would throw the body slightly out of line to weaken the streamline. Of course this doesn't come into play for the two-handed strokes, fly and breast, but it is best that a particular movement be practiced and permanently incorporated into muscle memory so as not to bring about possible confusion when racing different strokes begins. For backstroke, of course, everything is already upside down; the power hand would be on top.

2. The head is then lifted and forced to look across the pool while the body is in mid-air. The arms and hands are thrust forward but slightly below the head, closer to the water. Since the body follows the direction in which the head is pointed during the dive, looking across the pool will cause the body to extend fully and move explosively away from the block as if shot from a cannon (see Fig. 10-2).

3. The hands and arms, which are already angled toward the water, now present themselves in the proper position for the head to be quickly placed between them. I teach "skin to skin"; by this I mean the skin of each hand is touching and the skin of the ears is touching the skin of the biceps, which are squeezed against each side of the head. This locks the head into place in the most streamlined position, anticipating the next instant when the body enters the water. As a secondary benefit, this position of biceps squeezing against the ears helps press

the goggles to the head and prevents them from coming down and filling with water.

4. The swimmer then tries to dive into an imaginary hole in the water, entering the water with as little splash as possible (splash = drag = bad); see Fig. 10-3.

5. The streamline sequence of movements brings the swimmer to the surface quickly, powerfully, and as far down the pool as allowed by the 15-meter mark (except for breaststroke).

Track Start Tradeoff

More and more swimmers are using the track start, which seems to be all that coaches are showing their age-groupers nowadays. Just as in running track on land, swimmers using this start have one foot in front (over the leading edge of the block) and one foot pushed back (toward the rear of the block). The hands are placed on the front edge with the body's center of gravity shifted slightly to the rear for stability on the block, which should be tilted about 10 degrees downward according to USA and FINA rules of competition. At the "go" signal, the swimmer pulls the body forward with the hands and pushes off with one foot, the hands initially trailing the body off the blocks.

At all but the highest level of competence, the track start is not really faster into the water—and even with elite swimmers, the difference is measured only in a few hundredths of a second. But there is a tradeoff, an important one. The track starter usually enters the water at fewer miles per hour because only one foot pushes off. Former British Olympian Mark Foster has entered the water using the grab start at up to 13 miles per hour, about three miles per hour faster than most of his competitors, who use track starts. This is a very important concept to emphasize. It is not who enters the water the quickest that matters most. It is who gets

Grab start sequence.

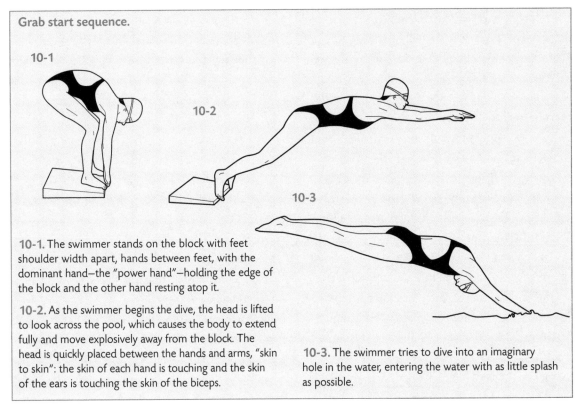

10-1

10-2

10-3

10-1. The swimmer stands on the block with feet shoulder width apart, hands between feet, with the dominant hand—the "power hand"—holding the edge of the block and the other hand resting atop it.

10-2. As the swimmer begins the dive, the head is lifted to look across the pool, which causes the body to extend fully and move explosively away from the block. The head is quickly placed between the hands and arms, "skin to skin": the skin of each hand is touching and the skin of the ears is touching the skin of the biceps.

10-3. The swimmer tries to dive into an imaginary hole in the water, entering the water with as little splash as possible.

farther away from the blocks quickest. I measure the time it takes swimmers to get to the 15-meter mark. It seems that just about everyone who has practiced both starts and compares the two finds that the two-legged push-off with tight streamlining gets them to the marker more quickly. In fact, recent world class competitions have shown the whole Australian Woman's Team reverting back to the grab start. The marquee swimmer is the woman's World Record Holder in the 100 meter freestyle, Libby Lenton. The men's world records set years ago and still standing leading into the 2008 Olympics in the 50 and 100 freestyle were set by swimmers who used grab starts.

The Streamline

In every stroke, the underwater streamline has the same importance. It allows you to get as far down the pool and to the surface as efficiently and as quickly as allowed by the rules of the stroke. The fingers, as the leading edges of the body through the water, need to point to the surface in a smooth, elongated curve upward to allow for the quickest route to the air. This curved route, called a "parabolic trajectory," has been shown to be the fastest way to get the furthest out; it is more efficient than if the swimmer tried to go straight up after the dive.

Once the swimmer is in the water, each stroke has its required sequence of movements that we hope will get the swimmer as far down the pool (below the surface tension) as is needed, in the appropriate amount of time. Too short a time, if the swimmer rushes things, and the swimmer is cheated out of optimum momentum and distance in the race. Too long under water and the swimmer begins to slow down excessively as he watches his competition go by. For freestyle, which requires the least amount of time under water, four things have to be done quickly and in the correct order. The optimum time to come back up to the surface is 4 seconds, and I mean 4 seconds from the time the swimmer's hands enter the water, not from when he or she leaves the blocks. The motions that I coach are: (1) three or four dolphin kicks, (2) four to six freestyle kicks, (3) power hand (bottom hand) pulls the first stroke to the surface, and (4) no breath taken on the first stroke once at the surface. Of course, the head *must* be held facing the bottom of the pool all this time except that as the first stroke to the surface is completed, the head lifts up into proper alignment with the spine.

Let's say that a swimmer holds a good streamline, kicks hard, and correctly utilizes all the proper movements, and strokes to the surface at just the right time, but he has hit the water at eight miles per hour with a one-legged track-start push-off. After four seconds under water, that swimmer cannot have traveled as far as if he had hit the water at 11 miles per hour with the same competence, using a two-legged push-off with the grab start.

The butterfly start has several other components besides the dive that need to be addressed for optimum distance traveled over time. After the entry into the water, anywhere from eight to ten snappy, powerful dolphin kicks are needed to propel the swimmer under water close to the 15-meter mark. This should take less than 6 seconds. In fact, when training for fly starts, the swimmer should focus on time under water, not distance traveled. Remember, the dolphin kick is different from the butterfly kick only in the fact that with the dolphin leg movement, each kick has the same amplitude up and down, no deeper than the thickness of the chest. The butterfly kick has two different amplitudes: shallow kick when the hands are in front, deeper kick when the hands are in back. In essence, the swimmer "kicks his hands out of the water" after each power segment of the stroke.

The Breaststroke Entry

Breaststrokers follow a special entry procedure, and they need to stay under water the longest—7 seconds—to ensure that no part of the allowed sequence of movements is compromised, which would cheat the swimmer out of valuable distance during the race. After the entry into the water, which is slightly deeper than for freestyle or butterfly, the breaststroker simply does nothing but hold the tightest streamline possible, head facing the bottom of the pool. He has to resist wanting to take that first pull-down too soon. A 3-second pause holding the tight streamline position after entry allows the maximum distance at the highest velocity before the swimmer slows down to regular swimming speed. The rules allow another assistive movement: a two-handed pull-down in which the hands are accelerated past the hips in a sort of hourglass movement, followed immediately by a snappy quick downward dolphin kick. The shoulders are rounded to prevent excessive water from grabbing them and producing excessive resistance (drag). This position is held for another 3 seconds, head still facing the bottom of the pool, while the body receives a second acceleration boost.

Now comes the part that is truly helped by experience: preventing the "dead spot." The swimmer should *not* wait until he slows down again to swimming speed or less, but should now take the allowed breaststroke kick and use it as the beginning of a powerful stroke to the surface. This first stroke sets the tone of the race, so it should be as powerful as the moment will allow. This should happen all in one smooth move that takes one quick second to perform, bringing the total time under water to 7 seconds.

A swimmer who slows noticeably after the pull-down and almost comes to a stop needs to practice the quick, smooth kick and stroke to the surface over and over to perfect a continuous cascade of movements that propels him out towards the 15-meter mark. With strength, power, technique, and timing all practiced and recorded in muscle memory, this should never become a weak spot for the competent breaststroker.

The Relay Start

The relay start involves two swimmers, each with an equally important part to play. The swimmer coming into the wall and the take-off swimmer must share responsibility for the legal exchange without leaving too soon ("jumping the gun"). The take-off swimmer needs to anticipate accurately the incoming swimmer's speed and style of finish for the particular stroke being swum. To do this, the take-off swimmer should frame the swimmer coming into the wall with the hands, thumbs touching each other and the other fingers pointing to the ceiling. When the incoming swimmer's head is over the turning T on the bottom of the pool near the wall, the take-off swimmer must begin to create momentum off the blocks.

To accomplish this, I teach what I feel is the best off the blocks; I call it the "wing-back" maneuver, which, when practiced and performed perfectly, is the fastest legal relay exchange. Once the swimmer on the blocks sees the incoming swimmer's head crossing the turning-T, from his position of framing the incoming swimmer, the hands and arms are immediately thrust up and over toward the back in a rounded or circular motion and continued onto the front toward the water's edge. Once the hands and arms are in front over the water, the head follows, looking across the pool, and the swimmer explodes off the blocks. All this motion is per-formed for two very important reasons: (1) to act as a delaying maneuver to keep from "jumping" the start and disqualifying the relay, and (2) to create as much momentum as possible to help in the leap forward, which should carry him up and over his incoming teammate. I emphasize this last maneu-ver by having my outgoing swimmer make sure he is looking down over the incoming swimmer just as he is about to leave the block (Fig. 10-4).

Think of watching a fast-pitch softball pitcher wind up and fling the ball: this is what I am seek-ing, only with both arms and hands at the same time. If the movement is timed correctly, the feet leave the blocks just as the incomer touches the wall (see Fig. 10-5). I call this "cutting a close start." Any other movement of the arms will not create this important momentum boost. This is the fastest type of exchange that usually prevents a DQ for leaving the blocks too soon, but it takes practice, ideally with swimmers who will be on the same relay in competition.

There is a modified version of the relay start that has the relay takeoff swimmer start from the back of the block and take one or two steps forward, timed to correctly leave as the incoming swimmer touches the wall. I find fault with this because even with practice and at the highest level, I see too many ten-tative movements not making the most of momen-tum building as I have described above. What was old is still the best in my opinion. But like anything else, it must be practiced (OFTEN)!

The Backstroke Start

All of the maneuvers off the blocks are called front starts. The backstroke has its own specific rules that require the swimmer to be already in the water. This is the most difficult of the starts, mainly because the swimmer is turned backward and upside down from

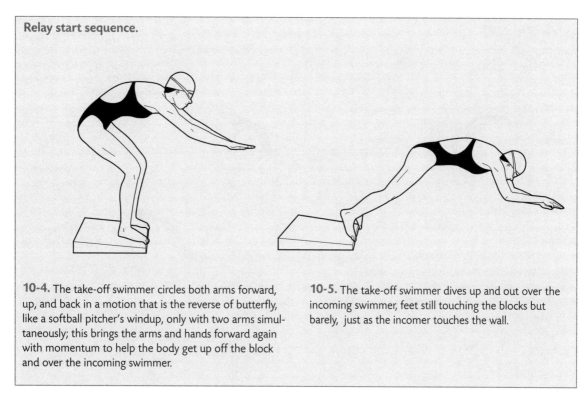

Relay start sequence.

10-4. The take-off swimmer circles both arms forward, up, and back in a motion that is the reverse of butterfly, like a softball pitcher's windup, only with two arms simultaneously; this brings the arms and hands forward again with momentum to help the body get up off the block and over the incoming swimmer.

10-5. The take-off swimmer dives up and out over the incoming swimmer, feet still touching the blocks but barely, just as the incomer touches the wall.

the front-start positions that come more naturally, and also because the swimmer does not have the height mechanical advantage of leverage off the blocks. However, there are certain movements that can make the most of the backstroke start. For a worthy effort to start the race quickly and strongly, a few concepts must be understood and practiced until comfortable, and then mastered to the most of one's potential.

Remembering the important rule that the body follows the head, as the swimmer sets up to leave the wall on command, he must thrust the hands and arms out to the sides and then bring them back behind the head, one on top of the other. The head *must* be looking back toward the far end of the pool. This, we hope, will create the body line we are looking for: an arching motion up over the water where the hands, arms, head, body, legs, and feet will enter in sequence the imaginary "hole" in the water that

we want to dive through with the least amount of splash and drag (see Figs. 10-6 through 10-8).

Under the water, things can get confused. The fingers must point up toward the surface. Since you are now upside down relative to the front start, your fingers will be bending slightly upward, making a cuplike figure with the hands instead of arching backward; it may feel awkward, as if you are pointing *down*, with your hands not in the right position to get to the surface. This is where practicing the body line and all ancillary movements becomes important. You cannot rely on "feel" and thinking you understand; it has to be made automatic. In the heat of competition, the start has to be immediately correct; otherwise you will be left behind. Six to eight dolphin kicks going into six to eight backstroke kicks with a stroke to the surface should ideally bring the backstroker close to the 15-meter mark, and this should take about the same time as in the fly (up to 6 seconds).

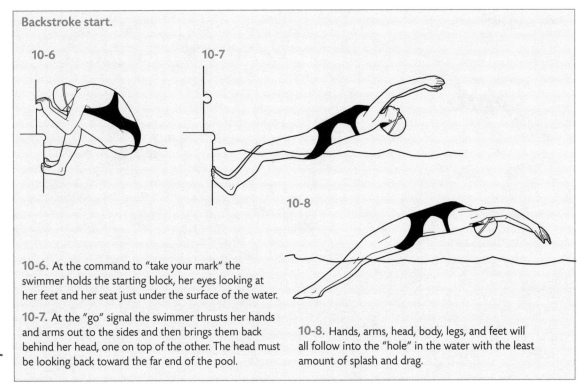

Backstroke start.

10-6

10-7

10-8

10-6. At the command to "take your mark" the swimmer holds the starting block, her eyes looking at her feet and her seat just under the surface of the water.

10-7. At the "go" signal the swimmer thrusts her hands and arms out to the sides and then brings them back behind her head, one on top of the other. The head must be looking back toward the far end of the pool.

10-8. Hands, arms, head, body, legs, and feet will all follow into the "hole" in the water with the least amount of splash and drag.

Turns

As mentioned previously, if the race is short course, turns play a very important role in the outcome. This is not to discount the walls in a long-course event; it is just that a short course brings the swimmers to the walls so much more quickly and more often.

The Freestyle Turn

I have been working on two modified freestyle turns. The difference between mine and the standard issue is that after the quick flip, my swimmer (in Style 1) stays on his back for at least 3 to 5 dolphin kicks, submerged about 18 inches below the surface. Then he begins kicking the backstroke kick and angles upward smoothly to the surface, still on his back, eyes open to see where the skin of the water is. As he is about to break the surface, the power hand, which has been resting on top of the weaker hand in a streamlined position behind the head, is brought down alongside the body to push water backward and create more forward momentum as if he were swimming backstroke. At the surface, the swimmer takes a quick breath while still on his back. Then a snappy roll-over onto the chest allows for an easy transition into swimming freestyle. The advantage here is that this modified turn will get a swimmer farther out from each wall more quickly under water and with less surface tension resistance. But, as with most things in life, there is a price to pay. This turn costs more air to perform correctly, so the body must be trained and allowed to adapt. The second style of modified freestyle turn also brings in the fact that the swimmer leaves the wall on his back, but he immediately starts to dolphin kick—once or twice on his back, twice on his power side (waffle kick), and two or three more dolphins on his belly before freestyle kicking and taking a stroke to the surface to continue racing. This also gets the swimmer out more than a body length further in about the same time but—you guessed it—at a cost of air.

Most coaches and swimmers feel that it is not worth the effort, that the traditional freestyle flip turn (fast flip-over followed quickly by the push-off and corkscrew onto the chest) is the fastest way off the wall when done aggressively. Several years ago the innovative swim coach at the University of Tennessee worked on what became known at the time as the Tennessee Turn, which proved to be the quickest off the wall, once mastered. He wanted his swimmers to flip and stay on their backs while quickly coming off the wall to save time and then move onto the breast while still under water. However, this procedure didn't allow for the full hydrodynamic lift that pushing off on the back creates. It also didn't emphasize the dolphin kicks (which are the most propulsive) while still on the back and leading onto the side and then the chest. The extra dolphin kicks and the extra time under water after each wall create an oxygen debt, as mentioned, that swimmers must train to meet, but the rewards can be scary-fast. At the very least, the extra underwater streamlining brings the body out one full body length past the traditional turn. More often, with experience and training, the difference is over two body lengths per turn. One of my swimmers dropped 13 seconds in the 500 freestyle just by using the new turn, and another dropped 7 seconds even though he could only hold the new turn for 10 out of the 19 walls. Another dropped 7 seconds in the 400-meter long-course freestyle from his best time up to that point.

The Backstroke Turn

My freestyle turn mimics what the backstroke turn requires right up to the last moment when the sur-face is reached, the breath is taken, and the swimmer rolls over. In the backstroke, the turn is a major point of possible DQ. Written rules and their interpretation in the pool can be at odds on occasion. The main thing to learn and remember is that once the shoulder is rolled up and over 90 degrees (past vertical toward the breast), the swimmer is committed to the turn, and now all the movements to get to the wall and turn must be done in one continuous smooth motion as interpreted by the observing official. A trick here is to remember the 90-degree part of the rule. A swimmer can stay on the side all the way down the lane as long as he does not go past 90 degrees (the shoulder pointing straight up toward the ceiling). If a swimmer begins too far away from the wall to make a continuous smooth turn, DQ can still be avoided if the swimmer stays on the side, at 90 degrees or less, until he or she gets closer to the wall to commit to the turn. The swimmer is also allowed to keep kicking in this position to help get closer to the wall until he or she rolls past 90 degrees and commits to the turn.

The rule of thumb, as I teach it, is that if the competitor rolls over onto the stomach while committing to the turn, in one smooth motion, he can take one freestyle stroke and he has about one body's length to make it to the wall on the stomach before the flip turn. Longer than this, and there shows an obvious delay; the turn is no longer "one smooth motion." Also, one dolphin kick is allowed as the head tucks under the body during the flip. More than this on the belly and the stroke becomes freestyle, not backstroke. (These rules are for USA Swimming, which is the main governing body for swimming in America and is in line with international rules. But the NCAA allows continuous kicking into the wall—an obvious advantage if the swimmer has miscalculated the distance to the wall.)

After the turn, the streamline is composed of three main elements: strong dolphin kicking, then backstroke kicking, followed by a strong stroke to the surface. The breakout has been done correctly if the body comes to the surface somewhat on its side, with the lead shoulder tip breaking the water first. This prevents up to a gallon of water (8.5 pounds) from being carried to the surface by the torso and being lifted up through the skin of the water by the swimmer; not the best choice to make at every wall as fatigue sets in.

Butterfly and Breaststroke Turns

The two short-axis strokes (butterfly and breaststroke) have very similar turn mechanisms at the wall; the only obvious differences are the strokes into the wall and the type of streamlines going out (see Fig. 10-9). After the compulsory two-hand simultaneous touch, three things have to happen almost at the same time…no time to think at this point, only reflex movements that will show who has learned, practiced, and adapted to the fastest, most efficient legal moves off the wall.

After the two-handed touch, if the swimmer is a "righty," he turns from right to left; the left hand immediately pulls back from the wall and, with the elbow leading, moves under water, pointing in the opposite direction away from the wall. The right hand has two important tasks: (1) to help guide the swimmer into a straight push-off and (2) to do so with as little splash and as quickly as possible. The right hand must be placed behind the ear when the swimmer is preparing to leave the wall, a move I call "answering the phone." This positioning causes the elbow to bend, which is good, as it allows for faster movement and helps prevent splashing upon re-entry (see Fig. 10-10). The right hand also adds a little extra push to help get the body off the wall

with more force. For "lefty" swimmers, of course, everything is reversed.

While the hand and arm action is going on, the feet need to come up to the wall to allow the swimmer to push back off in the opposite direction. They come up to the wall with the knees facing to the left for "righty" swimmers and to the right for "lefty" swimmers. I also teach that I want one foot touching on top of the other as they come up to the wall, then separate and placed side-by-side one above the other on the wall. The feet must also be placed parallel to the bottom of the pool or the surface of the water. If they are placed so the toes are facing either up or down, the ensuing push-off will not have the correct trajectory. Either the swimmer will head down too deep or come to the surface too soon. Assuming a correct push-off from the wall, this is where the power of the legs comes into play—a weak, perfunctory kick is a waste of time and effort. An explosive two-legged push-off is what gets the swimmer to move out faster than normal swimming speed and usually can make the difference in a closely contested effort.

The most important movement to cause the body to switch directions is that of the head. Remember, the body follows the head, so the head has to be flung in the opposite direction the same time as the feet are coming up to the wall and the arm is going past the ear. The correct position for the head (if the turn is from right to left) is when the swimmer is looking up at about 11 o'clock. The turn in the opposite direction has the face looking at 1 o'clock as the swimmer leaves the wall. The head must be kept low to the waterline at this point so it can be moved quickly backward. This allows the swimmer to take a clean "bite" of air instead of choking on water splash (see Fig. 10-11).

After all three major components of the turn have been completed, the push-off into streamline is exe-

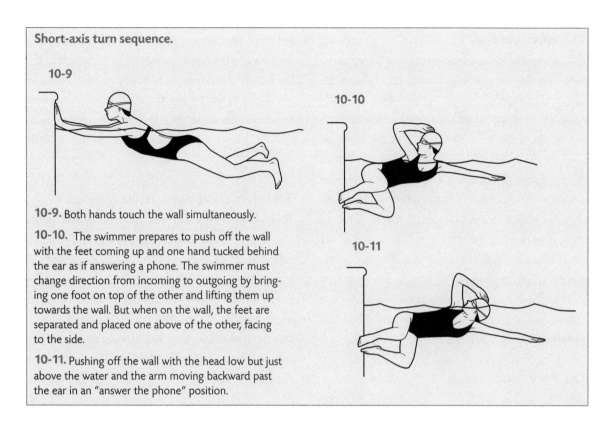

Short-axis turn sequence.

10-9

10-9. Both hands touch the wall simultaneously.

10-10

10-10. The swimmer prepares to push off the wall with the feet coming up and one hand tucked behind the ear as if answering a phone. The swimmer must change direction from incoming to outgoing by bringing one foot on top of the other and lifting them up towards the wall. But when on the wall, the feet are separated and placed one above of the other, facing to the side.

10-11

10-11. Pushing off the wall with the head low but just above the water and the arm moving backward past the ear in an "answer the phone" position.

cuted according to the stroke being swum. Turns should be practiced as correctly as possible throughout the training session so that the sensation of crisp, clean, fast turns is imprinted on the neuromuscular system. That way the swimmer's instinct will be to do correct turns, even when air is in short supply and fatigue is leading the mind to make bad choices. It is not the practicing that makes perfect; it is the nearly perfect practicing that makes the *race* nearly perfect.

Finishes

I like to analyze things backwards sometimes, especially in swim racing. I go from the finish backwards to the start. I am constantly emphasizing the importance of the finish. Much of the power swimming segments of my practices have to do with handling fatigue and great discomfort, yet holding the finish as

if the whole race depended upon it. Many times it does! I ask many of my swimmers when they first come to me, "How long in yards or time do you honestly think you can swim fast in abject pain?" Most get it wrong, saying anywhere from the whole last lap (short course) to about 15 seconds (long course). Once I reinforce this concept during repeated training bouts, they come to the realization that to give me what they first suggested is very difficult. It is very difficult to swim fast when your very existence seems near to demise. To have this sensation extend for more than just a few seconds seems an eternity, unless the swimmer is properly trained for such. The main rule of import, though, is that the swimmer should never look at the wall in the finish of any stroke. It should be emphasized daily that the red zone (from the flags into the wall) is holy ground, and swimmers should treat it with the respect it deserves.

The Freestyle Finish

For freestyle, three things must come to mind in proper sequence as the swimmer goes under the flags: (1) extra kick, no matter how much the body hurts; (2) no more breathing, with the eyes focusing first on the turning T at the bottom of the pool and then on the target cross on the finishing wall; and (3) the lunge to the wall, looking in the opposite direction of whichever hand touches. If the right hand comes up to touch the wall, the swimmer is looking to the left, and vice versa. This simple yet extremely important maneuver can allow the swimmer to touch the timing pad or wall 8 to10 inches sooner at the very end than someone who doesn't lunge because he is (incorrectly) looking at the wall and touching square to it.

The Backstroke Finish

In the backstroke, a little more calculation and concentration has to come into play. Either counting strokes from the flags into the wall or knowing the relative distance from the flags to the wall can guide the experienced swimmer to a strong finish. The whole reason for the flags is to signal the backstrokers when the wall is coming up, so when the swimmer coming hard to the finish sees the flags, he should be able to gauge how much longer it is to the wall and extend perfectly (if the gods of swimming are kind that day). A helpful maneuver is to dive downward as the wall approaches. When a swimmer is a bit shy of the wall and comes up a little short at the end (which often happens, as the backstroker becomes wall-shy after a few hand and arm slams at the finish), this submerged movement together with some extra kick can save the race by driving the body to the final touch with very little wasted glide.

Butterfly and Breaststroke Finishes

With both butterfly and breaststroke, the head should face down toward the bottom of the pool as the last stroke is taken in order to allow the greatest extension to the wall with the least resistance. But there is a difference in the rules for finishing the two strokes. The flyers have an advantage over the breaststrokers in that the former can take two kicks to the wall if the last stroke comes up short. This is because there are two kicks allowed per racing stroke cycle in butterfly. Believe me when I tell you that the second kick can make a difference at the end.

The breaststroke has only one kick in the complete cycle, and it must come after the arm movements, according to the rules. So if breaststrokers come up a bit short, they have to move their hands somewhat before they can take the kick; they cannot take two kicks in a row. Competitors in these events must see the wall coming up during the finishing cycles of the race to gauge correctly where to execute the final stroke, rather than waste time gliding into the wall, only to lose to someone who nails the finish.

Part Three

Training to Win

Chapter 11

Coaching a Year-Round Program

I abhor waste in anything, especially in all aspects of swimming—from cellular adaptation and muscle fatigue to breathing techniques and stroke form. Athletic movement at the highest level is governed by the dictum "Economy of Effort." Knowing how to save energy and spare vital sustenance is key to finishing strong... in other words, knowing how to close the race. And when it comes to vigorous training, I am positively zealous in my conviction that less is almost always better than more. Do not take this to mean that I am not an advocate of a sufficient amount of intense training. There has to be an adequate base of condition from which to build, but most coaches think that the method to develop this adequate base is through immense yardage. Knowing the body and how it adapts to physical stress, I see much better results quicker by choosing the correct adaptive sets to swim and by altering the stresses through which they are swum. It is rare that I put my athletes through repeats of more than 300 yards or meters; no need. The enzymes that we want to stress and adapt are brought into play well within the repeats of this distance.

I could never produce fast people in the water unless my swimmers pushed themselves way out of their comfort zones and then some. But I seek economy of effort in all things. That is probably why I became a sprint or "power swimming" coach. The types of repeats I select almost always differ from one another for various physiological and psychological reasons. Sprinters definitely do not like to constantly repeat things over great distances. I also strongly believe that intensity is much more important than volume. There are no "garbage yards" when swimming for me. Definitely there are some "baggage yards" for the swimmer to carry through in a series of swims to intensify the training effect of moving fast through the water, but in my program, no marathon efforts are necessary, nor are they sought. Rarely do my senior level power swimmers do more than 4,500 yards per session. If the training bouts are well planned, there really is no need to go more than that. My mid-distance people (200 strokers and 200 and 500 freestylers) will do up to 5500 yards in a training bout, but with a corresponding attendance to more leg work.

I try to stress no more than two energy systems per session, and I believe in only one training session per day. More than that and the fatigue factor becomes too great an obstacle to my training formula. The most important part of the training cycle is the rest and recovery. I would much rather have my swimmers ready for the next day's training bout more rested and recovered than have them in a constant state of fatigue, at risk for injury, illness, and burn-out from struggling with any intellectual or social responsibilities they may have. I see "two-a-days" having possibly only one general benefit: they may help the competitor to handle prelims and finals in the same day during a multi-day meet. But I cover this need by having my swimmers do

much more quality work throughout the year than most coaches, so they are well prepared for the "combat of racing" when the time comes. Several energy systems need to be adapted to their maximum potential if the swimmer is to rise to a high level of competition. Adapting only a few at a session, and in the correct cyclic manner entailing days, weeks, and months, is in my opinion the best way to guarantee their optimum development within the reasonable amount of yardage we do.

Any extended training program must take into account both short-course (25-yard/meter lengths or competition-sized pools) and long-course (50-meter lengths or Olympic-sized pools) swimming. Masters swimming even has three competition seasons, with the addition of short-course meters, inserted right after the long course. In addition to the obvious difference in pool length, several physical and psychological aspects differentiate the types of competition.

Short and Long Course

In its physical aspects, short course is more about the walls, and long course is more about the swimming. We usually see the different strokes swum with more intensity and quickness in the shorter pool. With the understanding that appropriate turns off the walls are extremely helpful in keeping pace throughout the swim and that the extra push off the walls will contribute greatly to the general speed of the whole race, the streamlines off the walls take on extra importance and are second only to the start off the blocks for speed during the race. (A 50- or 100-meter swim of any stroke, for example, will always be faster in short-course meters than the same distance in long-course meters because the former has more turns, with the corresponding extra speed off the walls.) With long course, the strokes are usually adapted to be longer and smoother since it is more swimming and is less about turning and streamlining off the walls than in short course. Distance-per-stroke is key. Analysis of many Olympic medal winners in all strokes and over all the distances has proved that faster swimmers take fewer strokes, but the distance covered per stroke is greater, so the overall speed of the race becomes faster.

Physiologic comparisons show that long-course meters are about 15% more taxing on the body than short-course yards by way of oxygen consumption and lactate buildup. In addition, between the walls in a long-course pool, the legs play more of a role in movement through water than they do in a short-course pool. So, depending upon the venue being used for competition (long course or short course), where and how the swimmers train is extremely important. I have seen swimmers who didn't have access to a long-course pool forced to compete long course against those who had trained for it. Most of the time, it was quite obvious that the short-course swimmers were at a definite disadvantage, both physiologically and psychologically.

Getting Prepared

A year-long extended training program usually has only one break of more than a few days' duration: a couple of weeks at the end of long-course season from mid-August through the first week in September allows the swimmer to recharge emotionally and physically, rededicate efforts, and rethink realistic goals for the upcoming season. Several options present themselves: travel with family and friends, sightseeing, cross-training (hiking, biking, rowing, etc.), or simply resting and letting everything "heal up." But this shouldn't last more than 2 to 3 weeks

at most, to prevent excessive dilution and diminution of the mixed (aerobic and anaerobic) training effect gathered during the whole year. Many studies have looked into the effects of extended "down time" and confirmed that after the fourth week of detraining, many of the physiological benefits gained through prolonged intense training become noticeably depleted.

The older the athlete and the higher level the athlete, the more depleted the training effect becomes relative to what was achieved at peak. Personally speaking, that is why, as a Masters swimmer, I try not to stay out of the water for any extended period. It hurts too much to fight to get back into shape. Physiologically, because the oxidative enzymes (providing the air and endurance to race) lose their training effect more quickly than the glycolytic enzymes (providing the energy and power to race with little regard for oxygen), after 2 to 4 weeks of being out of the water, it is expected that the resting athlete will lose more endurance than speed over time. Expressed in another way, detraining has a greater effect on the aerobic (endurance) system over a relatively short period (that 2- to 4-week time segment) than on the anaerobic (power swimming) system. A third way to approach this effect is to say that the fast-twitch muscle fibers (for power and sprint swimming) hold onto their adapted training effect longer than the slow-twitch fibers (endurance swimming).

Philosophy of Training and Coaching

Since there are so many variances and nuances as to methods and modes of swim training, what follows presents my take on making swimmers fast in the water. The responsibility of training and coaching athletes who have committed to swimming as their main interest in sport should be taken very seriously. Just like a captivating book by a top author unfolds to keep the reader wanting to turn pages to learn more, I try to create training sessions that generate the desire to return to practice each day to learn more about swimming fast. I bring up the most important question an athlete can ask: what have I done today to get better?!

Continuity and appropriateness are very important in that after several days of intensively training the various enzyme energy systems, the propulsive swimming muscles, and the psychological aspects of meeting demanding and discomforting challenges in the water, appropriate recovery sessions become necessary and are used to create large (macro), medium (meso), and small (micro) training cycles throughout the year. These will be explained so the reader can see the big picture of how an extended training program produces the desired adaptations that build upon past efforts to produce even greater results.

There is a major difference in training when I am coaching late adolescent to senior-level swimmers as opposed to Masters swimmers. United States Masters Swimming (USMS) was a concept, then a program started in America by Dr. Ransom Arthur around 1970 to promote a healthy lifestyle centered on swimming, which has proven to delay or even reverse some of the effects of aging on the body. USMS has grown to over 40,000 active members across the United States and, as a major proponent of health and vigor as we age, has spread worldwide. It is also a mind set. Masters people choose to take a healthy bite out of life every day and think and act young and vigorous.

Though many of the Masters show remarkable trainability and think and act much younger than their years, Father Time does press against them as he does everyone. The physiology of aging comes into the picture with these athletes and must be understood, respected, and dealt with appropriately. Extra precaution is advised when one is putting the aging body through vigorous stress day after day. Besides the articular (joint) stresses that the aging body has to endure (which sometimes don't heal as quickly from overuse or intense use), in vigorous athletes older than 50, intense training can often tease out the possibility of irregular heartbeats like atrial fibrillation and premature ventricular contractions (PVCs). PVCs are often benign and pose no danger to a training athlete, but the condition needs to be analyzed by qualified medical personnel to ensure that the "sudden death in athletes" syndrome isn't given cause to occur. To elicit satisfactory training adaptations, even with remarkable physical specimens who show tremendous courage and tenacity (like many of my Masters people), adequate rest and recovery must be instituted at correct moments and in appropriate amounts, and the athletes must be cautioned to listen to their bodies and react to discomforting symptoms appropriately. Also, I strongly recommend that all Masters swimmers have the blessing of their physicians to undertake a prolonged vigorous training schedule. What you did as a youth, no matter how high you rose in the sport, will not guarantee a perfectly safe environment as you age. Caution and the opposite of stupidity must control the total immersion of the body into a continuous, vigorous training regimen. It helps to be surrounded by appropriately like-minded peers, especially as it gets scary in the water with challenging swim sets. Once caught up in the training element, no one wants to be the "wimp of the lane."

Training young, aggressive swimmers can be a dream if the coach and the athletes are on the same wavelength. The coach has to make it clear to everyone (athletes, parents, assistants, and himself most of all) what he wants to make out of the time shared at the pool. The coach's personality usually influences the team's personality. How can a team have a personality? Easy. Winning attitudes: goal attainment, trying to be a little bit better than Nature's potential offered up, analyzing what it takes to be a champion, showing courage in the face of fatigue and pain. And, above all, owning up to one's inadequacies and not blaming others for what you caused to happen. Getting past the person in the mirror before blaming others is key to reality in all things important. Of course, the unfortunate flip side to this is the aggressive, unsportsmanlike, win-at-all-costs personality that many coaches exhibit around the water. Maybe they don't realize what gross negativity they effloresce, but their swimmers will pick up on this as sure as Monday follows Sunday and will brand the program something to shun rather than join.

Just as kids subtly learn approaches to life from their parents (though they hate to admit it), they also pick up subtle (and sometimes not so subtle) approaches to challenges and competition from the coach. Every program is a reflection of the head coach. A mixed showing by a team at important competitions tells me that the coach, or coaching staff, sent mixed messages to the athletes. The coach, or coaches, probably "played" to the more talented (as is often the case) and left the others to deal with their own responsibilities to prepare for competition. An overall team improvement at meets (which is something marvelous to experience) is much harder to come by. It means that the coaching staff had to take the time and make the effort to have their "positive message of preparedness" cascade down to all members of the program, definitely not an easy task with many swimmers of varied ability and emotional fragility. The one characteristic that should not vary throughout the team, though, is the desire to improve. The coach either works this desire or ignores it—either way, it is he who makes or breaks the program. It's nice to have a great facility, a cooperative administration, a large talent base, and supportive parents, but it all comes down to what the head coach is all about. Can he relate to people? Is he empathetic to the daily challenges life brings on top of what needs to be done in the pool? Is he a master at unlocking the cell, since we are all prisoners of our minds? I think you see what I am getting at: As the coach goes, so goes the program. A great coach could produce quality people in a bathtub. Find a great coach and almost always you find a great program.

Early Season

In North America, the extended swim program usually starts in the early fall. And this is usually short course, either meters or yards. If the swimmer is a year-long, full-time aquatic athlete, he or she most probably just endured long-course season over the summer months. After a few weeks of R & R, short-course training beckons the swimmers back to the pool. It is at this very important starting point in the extended training cycle that the emotional/psychological components kick in: nothing but positive thoughts and attitudes should fill the air. Any negativity must be acknowledged and neutralized quickly. The idea that the body follows the head is not just a physical phenomenon, it is an emotional absolute. The mind needs to willingly lead the way back *almost every day* to a very physically demanding environment.

Initiating the early-season training brings into play the balanced importance of land-based and water-based activities. Just getting into the water is not enough. The body, if we want it to be able to move water quickly (forcefully) and not get injured doing same, must be prepared with the use of latex tubing, appropriate stretching, and time in the weight room with the same dedication given the aquatic training. (Weight lifting for swimmers will be discussed in detail in Chapter 15.)

It is the custom for many coaches to involve the returnees with long extended swims as organized training sessions unfold for the new year. There is some logic to this. Good to stretch out, good to aerate the body and get it used to the water in a not-too-threatening (painful) environment. The intensity of swimming here should be moderate at first, progressing into stronger swims after a few weeks. No paddles. I don't believe in their use even though I have two patents on adjustable-resistance paddles. In addition, I feel the paddles distort the feel for the water, interfere with proper technique stroke after stroke, and place inordinate amounts of stress on the shoulder girdle. Their intended use is to make the pull stronger, mostly in freestyle, but since I design most of my sets to mix freestyle with the other strokes in varying proportions, paddle use would simply get in the way. I want my swimmers to get strong in the weight room and by moving more quickly through the water, but I don't want them to experience an altered feel for the water due to swimming and/or pulling with paddles. Any preconceived benefit for paddle use also does not warrant the potential risk of joint overuse and tissue breakdown at that site. Any good intentions from pulling with paddles and a pull-buoy come up short compared with separate strength/power training and strong swims.

Above all, I don't want to make my practices an exercise in tedium. Monotony kills enthusiasm. Variety in challenge usually stimulates it. Early in the season is the time many swimmers need psychological enhancement; many will question why they are back putting themselves through the same tough grind they just endured. While their friends were probably enjoying their summer days away from the grind of school, the serious swimmer was up very early, usually immersed in cool water, and certainly out of his comfort zone virtually every day. Most develop a tolerance/acceptance to this regimen, and a select few even welcome it. But all need to be coddled somewhat emotionally and shown gratitude by those in a position of authority (the coaches), shown that they understand the sacrifice, devotion, and dedication to something that has not promised them any guaranteed success and engulfs them daily in great discomfort.

Though I have been challenged many times on my philosophy of less is more, mega-yardage and grossly extended swims just don't have a place in my armamentarium of training. When I am challenged about my methods, I like to think of the famous quote from Albert Einstein, which, though strong in its message, does have relevance: *"Great spirits have always encountered violent opposition from mediocre minds."* Physiologically, there is little need for truly extended swims. The enzymes that need to be adapted for increased aerobic capacity are stressed and induced to increase in number and ability to function within the abovementioned 300-yard/meter distance. Repeats of 300-yard/meter swims and kicks in various combinations and speeds with and without fins have served my purpose of preparing my athletes for the vast majority of competitive events (500 free and all the 200's on down) with a decent aerobic base from which we build speed. This distance is long enough to get what I want out of the training but not so long as to make the swims boring or tedious to the point where the athletes begin to lose focus. It is around this point in the training, early on when I have everyone's attention and enthusiasm, that I have shared this truism many times over the years: "If you do everything I say and follow all that I suggest, there is still no guarantee of your success in swimming; but if you *don't* do all that I teach, I will guarantee that you fail." The serious, dedicated swimmers usually remember this and try to make me eat my words.

Right along with the swimming stretch-outs, I institute a good amount of kicking with and without fins...at least 1,000 yards per practice, all types and in various sets. Nothing extremely demanding at this point, but the legs do need less rest after each effort than the whole body would after repeat swims. Pain isolation in the legs is usually easier to handle than with the whole body when pushed. Yet, since the legs are the single largest mass of muscle to be used at any one time, the cardiovascular stress is great enough to elicit a positive training effect. With my Masters people, the use of fins seems to be the great equalizer. Various abilities and age groupings seem to blend more into a tighter unit when it comes to repeat efforts. It is quite probable that the loss of leg, ankle, and hip flexibility with aging and the consequent decrease in range of motion are greatly helped by fins. Whatever the reason, using the fins for the majority or even all of the kicking is by no means a detriment. It is important to get past the mis-thinking that fins are somehow "cheating" and that using them is short-changing the athlete. Whatever it takes to train and swim fast legally and safely is where we want to go.

And, of course, at this juncture in the macro training cycle (the main season's worth), I emphasize technique, technique, technique. It's not practice that makes you perfect; practice just makes whatever you're working on permanent. It is *perfect*

practice that makes you "perfect." If you practice something incorrectly, you will not likely improve. It is many times harder to try and rid the athlete of bad habits than to institute correct ones. The coach and athlete have to take the time and expend the energy to correct poor neuromuscular adaptation (bad technique) in such a way as to "push it out" of the athlete's physical responses. This is hard on everybody, so it is most important that proper movement through water becomes automatic, especially when much harder training is expected down the road, and, of course, when it comes time to race.

It is also during this time of mild to moderately challenging swims that I emphasize the key factor of where the seat of propulsive movement really emanates: in all the muscles of the body's core, which also involves the hip girdle. For the long-axis strokes (freestyle and backstroke), the simultaneous rolling of the hips and the whole body side-to-side throughout each stroke is essential for slipping through the water more efficiently and for mobilization of more muscle groups and power to help propel the body forward faster and longer. For the short-axis strokes (breaststroke and butterfly), the core movements have the hips moving up-and-down and rely on the supportive muscle groups (obliques, lower back, upper and lower abdominals) for power and stamina for power and stamina.

Three weeks into the season, and we should expect early physiological and physical adaptations to the above training of the connective tissue surrounding the joints, of the muscles themselves, and of the cardiovascular systems to have taken place. This could also be the time when the body rebels against the training effect. Aches and pains and generalized discomfort can come and go or linger for hours and days. The coaches should be aware of this normal adaptive transition and should counsel the athletes as such. If everyone knows what to expect and how to deal, then any doubts or insecurities can be obviated early on.

The Next Level

Now we ratchet it up a couple of notches and push the cardiovascular system a bit more, seeking a higher level of aerobic capacity. The "honest" part of the seasonal work cycle begins here and now. Training routines have been set, and the body has been "trained to train." What we want to do at this point is to push the swimmers to move faster through the water and to begin to develop the pacing needed for specific events, yet, above all, still maintain their smoothness in a somewhat relaxed manner. Constant reminders from the coach should bring forth the message that trying too hard can become counterproductive.

Not losing the focus on desired goals becomes most important in this stage of training. It is during this phase of the short-course training season that I try to get my swimmers to work not only on their main strokes and events, but to become more aware of their weaker aspects of swimming and correct deficiencies in all the strokes, starts, turns, and finishes. Yes, I said starts, turns, and finishes. I don't wait until just before important meets to have segments for diving practice off the blocks and working the walls. It is so much better to dive a little almost every practice so as to experiment and see what works and to make what works well absolutely automatic at the sound of the horn. I have calculated that with practicing starts at the end of most sessions, my swimmers get at least 500 more dives per season than other teams.

During my time as coach, it has been my experience that two or three pressing workouts followed by an easier recovery session allow the body to gather up lost energies and adapt more quickly to a higher level. It must not be felt that a recovery workout is a waste of time; on the contrary, this is the perfect time to have the athletes revisit proper technique on all the strokes and turns needed during competition.

The Taper

The taper period is somewhat like a witch's brew: it has often been saddled with mystery, superstition, hypothesis, confusion, and tradition. I prefer to use another approach. The use of the physical and biological sciences has opened up other avenues that I choose to follow. I have been correct on many more occasions than I have been wrong, and I will continue to utilize the science of swimming and the physiology of aging in training my age-group, senior, and Masters swimmers during this most important of phases.

Before the taper segment proper comes the pre-taper period. This can take up to 2 weeks of training, depending upon number and type of events to be raced. This period has importance in that it begins to get the swimmers focused on going fast and pulling a lot of water—*power swimming*, I call it. The training distance is somewhat reduced but by only a few hundred yards. What is inserted is more rest to allow faster "broken swims" for the desired competition events, more push-pace into race-pace over shorter yardage, which is repeated only a few times in each training session.

Whether I am swimming the yards myself or putting my charges through their paces, I have found that this period of training causes quite a bit of physical discomfort. Maybe it is because psychologically one begins to realize that "the big dance" is just down the road, and racing jitters start to set in. Though the mental component can play a part, I tend to think it is mostly physical: delayed onset of muscle soreness (DOMS) and other bodily insults.

Usually a good amount of muscular discomfort sets in overnight into the next day, and the swimmers become anxious about this unwanted feeling so close to competition. They want to feel good about racing, not all beaten up. But experience has shown that this negativity shouldn't, and usually doesn't, last. Those ready and willing to present their assault on speed approach the true taper phase by letting everything fall into place according to plan. Experience helps a lot here; it's a good time for the veterans of the team to calm the newbies and an even better time for the coach to do the same.

What a shame to work so hard, so long, and not "hit the taper." Well, it happens, and all too often. The athletes swim what they are told; that is their responsibility. The coach decides what is swum and how and who swims it; that is the coach's responsibility, and it is a big one.

Depending upon how much yardage was endured weekly during the main training season, what events will be raced, and the individual physiology of each athlete, my formula for taper will have a greater rather than lesser effect of producing power and speed. For those training at or near the maximum I recommend (around 4,500 yards per session for seniors and 3,500 yards for Masters), the taper can work wonders. If less yardage is swum as a matter of routine, the taper will still have positive effects, only less dramatic ones. In general, sports physiology dictates that those who are heavily muscled, natural power swimmers (strong sprinters), and/or over 35 years of age, need a 3-week taper. With this in mind, I utilize my "rule of thirds" when formulating my taper sets and yardage. What this actually means is that during the three-week period, a specific amount of yardage is dropped off consecu-

tively each week, but the attendance to racing detail increases.

Yardage is reduced appropriately by one-third the total *daily* amount by week's end; that is the important part—by week's end. Each day may not have exactly one-third removed but by week's end the daily training yardage is down fully one-third. If we started off at 4,500 yards, then 1,500 yards will be removed from the total daily session by the last day of the first week. Now we are down to the 3,000 yard mark a session. A 3,500-yard Masters practice will diminish to 2,350 yards by the last day of the first week. It is also at this time that many swimmers complain of not feeling right. The faster swims, as in the pre-taper period, can bring on lingering DOMS. The psychology of racing may also begin to affect the overall well-being of the athlete, making him "antsy" because the reality of having to prove himself against peers when the *power of the moment* is at hand places a lot of pressure on performance. Warm-ups and recovery swims become very important to prevent injury and help the mind set itself for the next bout of fast swimming.

It is also at this time that fine-tuning the target events at the big meet begins to take over the big picture. If we are talking a 200 and/or a 100 of something, then these two distances become the center of focus. A single completed distance, followed by adequate rest, is done at *push-pace* to experience the beginnings of discomfort, both aerobic and muscular. The use of fins here is still OK, especially if super-strong swims are desired as a marker from which to compare pretty-close-to-race sensations with time swum. We do this a lot. Broken swims and mixing of freestyle and the target stroke are also instituted, in a serious effort to compare physical sensations with time swum. The fins come pretty close to mimicking the results, as if they simulate the situation using a high-tech competition bathing suit, having the adrenaline of competition, and being further into the taper. A good effort here is one that builds more on psychological than on physical factors. Did I feel good swimming fast? Did I hold stroke even though I was hurting toward the end? The same effort needs to be carried into the second week of taper.

The rule of thirds continues with a further reduction in training yardage during week 2 of the taper. My senior swimmers are now down to 2,000 yards (3,000 minus 1,000) per session by week's end. The Masters will have their distance reduced from 2,350 to 1,600 yards per session. Warm-ups and recovery swims are still very important and are extremely relevant for preparation for and recovery from competition swims at the meet. To be thoroughly prepared is to be correctly prepared. I leave nothing to chance. All the details of race preparation and the actual race itself are gone over many times. Visualizing in the mind's eye various parts of the race(s) now becomes an important element to include before leaving the wall for a simulated competitive effort. Seeing yourself performing something "perfectly" just before you actually attempt it goes a long way to reinforcing proper technique.

The last week of taper (thank God!) sees a further reduction in yardage. The senior swimmers are down to about 1,400 to 1,500 yards by week's end, and the Masters will do about 1,000 to to 1,100 yards. Most of this is centered on taking the technique efforts from the week before and inserting them into sprint builds across the pool. We need to be able to swim fast yet "perfectly." The swimmers must understand the concept of *working hard to make it all look so easy*. We have been doing starts, turns, and finishes all season long, but now these movements take on an importance such that they must be performed as perfectly

as possible the first time; *reacting to the movement, not thinking about it, is emphasized*. No time to think in a race: react correctly or feel bad at the end. No room for errors here. If a mistake is made during the taper, it must be corrected immediately and positively reinforced. Having your swimmers go to the blocks to put it all on the line at one particular moment is asking a lot of them. There are so many things that can go wrong. We prepare and we hope, but we have to have it all unfold before our eyes to build on the experience. If it should be a great effort, we need to savor it but never take it for granted. We simply get ready for the next time when the challenge to put it all on the line again is placed before us.

Long-Course Season

In most states, usually several weeks elapse after short-course championships until the start of the long-course season. This is usually by default rather than choice. Most 50-meter facilities are outdoors and run by park commissions, townships, or local communities. In most states, outdoor Olympic-sized pools, prized as they are by coaches and competitive swim programs, are usually not made available for daily use until the arrival of warm weather. In the overall yearly extended training program, this leaves a relatively short time (6 to 8 weeks) in which to train long course for that venue's championships—not nearly enough as I see it. The states in the Sun Belt that switch over early to 50-meter training have a distinct advantage in that they can go to long course as early as April rather than wait till mid-to-late June, because the outdoor pools, which are used all year round, are usually heated and the weather is accommodating. Those prized programs (usually at colleges) that have ready access to an indoor Olympic pool also join the Southern facilities with an early-on-use advantage. No brains needed here to see that these situations provide a distinct advantage over the others by allowing a much more extended long-course training season.

To get the best out of a less-than-ideal situation, it would be wise for the coach to utilize the weeks before long course to present an environment where there is a buffer between intense competition seasons. This "clinic season," as I call it, can be looked at as going to "swim school," affording the athletes valuable time in the pool without getting beat up for learning and mastering the best techniques for fast swimming. When the emphasis is placed more on technique than on intense training, this perceived oasis from the surrounding desert of pain goes a long way to soothing and healing the body and the mind. Topics discussed both around the pool and in a classroom stress correct technique and the big picture of swim racing, and explain the psychology of competition and all the other important elements *outside the pool* that should be considered by serious athletes. The clinic segment even allows time, if you plan for it, for new swimmers to come and try out your program without the pressures of training for competition.

When it is time for long course, certain preparations must be considered by the coaches. They should realize and share the fact with the swimmers that training in a 50-meter pool is at least 15% harder on the body than short course. I said at least 15%. With a lot of stroke work, it goes up to around 20% more taxing. The body areas that will feel the strain the most are the legs (in the backstroke, breaststroke, and butterfly) and the respiratory system. A hard-push long course is much more demanding than in a 25-yard pool. For one thing, the yardage mounts up more quickly when swimming long course. "Down and back" short course is 50 yards; the same in the "big pool" is 100 meters, with fewer

walls from which to push off for help. Earlier I made the distinction between the two venues that "short course is about the walls, while long course is about the swimming." Of course the turns must be mastered for each event (except for 50s of each stroke) if you want to have a good swim, but the real emphases on moving through water Olympic style are: (1) keeping the strokes long and smooth and (2) controlling the breathing. The seemingly nonsensical statement that with long course you must hurry up and slow down rings true every time. Every stroke has its portion of glide and streamline—the time in the stroke when "making friends with the water" is the smart choice. Knowing how much harder long course is than short course will make the swimmers appreciate the techniques learned during the clinic sessions, we hope. The essence of long course lies in having the confidence to keep the strokes long and strong and knowing when to build pace as the race progresses, especially when fatigue sets in and breathing becomes labored.

The smart play in training long course is to break down the pool into segments similar to those of the short-course pool, since the latter venue is what most swimmers are used to. The extended distances can be psychologically handled better if there is a similarity from which to draw. We simply break the distances up mid-pool to simulate the different segments of short-course training and racing. A good example is the 100-meter swim of any stroke. I approach this event by breaking down the distance into quadrants (25-meter segments). The concept of easy speed (going as fast as you can while controlling your breathing) becomes even more important when training 50 meters because of the physiological demands of more swimming and the psychological challenges reacting to this. Lose the breath, lose the race. Control the breathing, and you are still in control of your swimming destiny for that event.

Since the long-course season is much more compact than the short-course season, everything has to be trained with more urgency. There is no luxury of time. Every day demands more from the coaching staff and the swimmers. Everyone has to be ready to go each training session. Training schedules must be constructed accordingly to allow the swimmers to more quickly adapt to the increased demands of 50-meter swimming. Since most programs are outdoors in the summer months, the vagaries of the weather, which sometimes can present formidable obstacles, must be taken in stride and chalked up to the extra challenges that long course provides. Where cycles of conditioning and race preparation ran in three- or four-week segments during short course, truncated allotments are presented for the long course. Everything must be compacted in such a

way as to still provide a workable taper. Only here that dwindles down from three weeks to 7 to 10 days.

With long course, the psychological boosting from the coaching staff is as important as the yardage handled each day. The 15% to 20% greater demand in the big pool must be respected yet met each time out in such a way that the swimmer adapts almost without realizing the day-to-day effort. The use of fins is a must to help in this adaptation, even more so than in short course.

I also suggest that the coaching staff pit one training lane against another appropriately. Maybe weaker swimmers will use fins for a prescribed distance against the "horses" in the next lane swimming unaided. This is both challenging to the faster people and boosting to the slower people; even though they have the aid of the fins, their ability to keep up with, or even get to the wall before, the faster people does wonders for the psyche.

CHAPTER 12

Warm Up, Stretch Out, and Cool Down

Unless you are an experienced athlete, there is a good chance your warm-up/cool-down ritual is lacking in execution and content. It could be missing the necessary movements to prepare the body for upcoming vigorous exercise and to allow it to recoup after vigorous exercise. A car engine shouldn't be revved up right off the bat and driven because it needs to warm up and circulate the lubricating oil first. This allows the life-blood of the engine to travel through and bathe all the parts that need protecting. Otherwise you prematurely age the components of the engine.

The reason for the human body to have a warm-up period is similar but with the potential for much more serious consequences if not provided. There are procedures that need to be performed appropriately in order to protect, enhance, and preserve vital body parts and function that engage in vigorous exercise. Not affording due respect to these preparatory and conditioning procedures is just asking for trouble no matter what the age of the athlete. Inhibited performance would be the least of the problems; debilitating injury or serious or fatal physiologic consequences concern me more. Logic and experience would dictate that some preparatory procedures be done to "alert" the body to upcoming vigorous exercise. I am sure those engaging in strong physical activity that pushes the body way out of its comfort zone will most likely remember any deleterious effects they experienced by not taking the time to warm up or cool down properly.

The physiology of aging dictates that the older the swimmer, the more warm-up/cool-down he needs. The more muscle (at any age), the more warm-up/cool-down. Breaststrokers, butterflyers, and individual medley swimmers seem to need more warm-up and cool-down than freestylers and backstrokers.

Warm-Ups

As with most processes in the body, there are oppos-ing or balancing systems to help keep the body able to handle whatever is thrown at it. The body's inter-nal physiologic environment is controlled by the *autonomic nervous system*, which allows it to handle the transition from rest to vigorous exercise. At rest, the *parasympathetic system* controls much of the body's autonomic functions including respiration, heart rate, blood pressure, muscular strength, and tension. During increased activity, the *sympathetic system* takes over. The first part of the warm-up, what I call the "loosening-up" phase, allows for a smooth transition so the parasympathetic system can release its hold on the vital organs before the sympathetic sys-tem activates. To wake up the muscles, I recommend 10 minutes of easy to moderate activity—often a slow version of the stroke to be practiced that day. At prac-tice sessions I also recommend the use of a kickboard at this time. The swimmer kicks on his side using fins, holding the kickboard parallel to the water's surface out in front with one arm stretched over the rounded end. The swimmer should be looking back over the opposite shoulder (where she has been, not where she is going). This procedure stretches (1) the shoul-der girdle (in a neutral position that does not cause an impingement on any of the internal structures there); (2) the neck muscles (which can tighten from tension and stress); and (3) the upper back. The arms on the kickboard are switched each length for eight lengths short course or four lengths long course. The loosen-up could be as short as 400 yards/meters or as much as 800 yards/meters, depending upon muscle tight-ness and how long it takes to feel loose and relaxed in the water.

Of course, the colder the water, the more the warm-up. There have been times when I have had

to first soak up heat by taking a hot shower to raise the body's core temperature sufficiently before get-ting into excessively brisk water, especially when competing outdoors and at the mercy of the weather. Loosening up in warm water (above 84°F) is actually ideal (though it probably would not be for actual racing). Less yardage needed, muscle-friendly ambiance, psychologically soothing surrounding medium; all perfect for a nervous or anxious swim-mer to be immersed in before the slings and arrows of a tough workout or a competition are flung.

After the loosen-up, which is at the discretion of the coach and the swimmer, I set the warm-up for the day, usually between 800 and 1,200 yards or meters. Various sets are used in varying distances and speeds, starting off slowly, sometimes with "short stuff," and then progressing to longer swims at moderate effort. Then we prepare the heart and lungs a bit more as we move on to push-pace with "broken" swims. And then there are days where the option of doing longer swims at moderate pace will properly prepare the body aerobically for what comes next. All this brings about the body's readiness to handle the intensity of the main set or any upcoming competitive swims. Some of my fair-skinned swimmers act as beacons; when they show a reddish glow on the upper back, they are ready—their musculature has been warmed sufficiently by induced blood flow to the area.

At competitions, the above protocol should be followed sans kickboard, since training aids are not allowed at meets. If the warm-up lane is crowded, try to find a more open place to swim so the easy stretch-out swims leading into push-pace can be held to pro-vide the benefits listed above to adapt the body to fast swimming. Many competitors like to do a sprint lap or two off the blocks to sort of leave a "memory" of fast movement for the neuromuscular system before rac-ing, but this can build up lactic acid higher than resting levels, as can the above warm-up ritual. I advise at least a 20-minute complete rest-down to give the body time to eliminate any lactic acid buildup and bring all things back down to resting levels. This should be factored into the warm-up schedule and the day's agenda when you are preparing to race. If you race in an early event, then enough lead time should be factored in to allow for appropriate rest-down. Get into the water early, warm up, and then get out and let the body recover for your upcoming first event.

Starting off the pre-race warmup with a 200 yard freestyle simply gets the body moving in swimming fashion. This is the time to "make friends with the water" and concentrate on developing a good "feel" for the water. Whatever strokes will be raced at the meet, they are mixed with freestyle as the pace is built up to "easy speed." If only freestyle is being contested, I suggest one-arm fly be mixed with free to enhance body movement, relax the lower muscles of the back, and to make the freestyle itself feel smooth. Six 50's alternating free/stroke and stroke/free on an easy interval are swum, building slightly from easy speed into push-pace. Working streamlines and push-offs will reinforce what will be needed when racing. Some stretching of the shoulders and legs should be done in between sets to ensure an enhanced range-of-motion. As mentioned above, a few sprint starts off the blocks are important, especially to power swimmers. Feeling fast in warm-up goes a long way to feeling fast as you step to the blocks.

Sample Warm-Ups

Two sample warm-up procedures before a training session are:

Warm-up 1

- Swim 400 yards of loosen-up: mixed swimming and kicking with and without fins. This includes using the kickboard to help stretch the neck, upper back, and shoulder girdle muscles.
- Swim 8 x 25 yards (no fins) freestyle alternated with stroke (on 30 sec). We work the push-offs into streamline for both freestyle and strokes.
- Now we descend in time but ascend in energy used in the next three sets, each becoming 5 seconds faster than the preceding.
- Swim 4 x 50 yards (no fins). Odd swims: 25 yards freestyle (flip-turn), 25 yards stroke (on 60 sec). Even swims: 25 yards stroke, 25 yards freestyle (on 60 sec).
- Swim 4 x 50 yards in the reverse order from above, only 5 seconds faster (again, no fins). Odd swims: 25 yards stroke, 25 yards freestyle, but make sure to add the red-zone finish (on 55 sec).
- Swim 4 x 50 yards (once more, no fins). The first two 50s are 25 yards freestyle (flip-turn), 25 yards stroke; the second two 50s are reversed but another 5 seconds faster (on 50 sec).
- Swim 4 x 75 yards (with fins): 25 yards freestyle + 25 yards kick + 25 yards stroke (on 1:15 or 1:20 or 1:30) depending upon ability to hold the pace.

Total yards = 1,500

Warm-up 2

- Swim 400 yards of loosen-up (with fins): 100 yards kick, 100 yards freestyle, 100 yards one-arm butterfly, 100 yards dolphin breaststroke.
- Swim 200 yards backstroke with fins.
- Rest 30 sec.
- Swim 200 yards one-arm/alternate arm butterfly with fins.
- Rest 30 sec.

- Swim a 200-yard individual medley (no fins) starting off with 50 yards of one-armed butterfly (as we always do in warm-up), followed by 50 yards backstroke, then 50 yards breaststroke, concluding with 50 yards freestyle.
- Swim 4 × 50 yards (with fins): each 50 is composed of 25 yards underwater streamline kicking + 25 yards swim of choice (on 1:20 or 1:30)

Total yards = 1,200

Warm-Up for Asthmatics

There is a small but growing segment of the swimming population that benefits greatly from a certain type of warm-up. The true asthmatic and/or exercised-induced asthmatic needs to lessen the concentration of certain irritating chemicals released into the bronchiole tree that bring on labored breathing early in vigorous exercise. What works here, even if the swimmer is appropriately medicated against asthmatic attack, is to first do a few hundred yards/meters of easy swimming and then to push the pace for at least six short bursts of 25-yard builds with 30 to 45 seconds of rest per length. If the body handles this well, fine; either the medications are doing their job of protecting the asthmatic swimmer or it could simply be a good day medically to race or push through a workout. The symptoms sometimes induced can be daunting and anxiety-provoking for the uninitiated asthmatic athlete, but he or she must realize that such symptoms are not dangerous, simply a coughing or tightness in the chest that will soon dissipate. The swimmer then goes back to some easy swimming to relax and, if desired, can do a few sprint builds to "wake up the muscles" for racing. The combination of reduced or eliminated asthma-inducing chemicals and the protective medications can truly allow great things to happen in the water.

Speaking of asthma medications, if inhalers are used, they should be given about an hour before the respiratory demands of racing; this provides enough lead time for the medication to settle in and protect the bronchiole tree, even if the drugs are touted as being able to work more quickly. Experience has shown all too often that the medications may not have enough time to work properly if taken as usually prescribed: 15 minutes before needed. If other medications are needed to provide a combined protective effect, they should also be taken long enough beforehand to allow their full protective effect.

Stretch-Outs

Cold makes everything tight. And tight is not conducive to fast, powerful movement. Cold muscle fibers need warming before they are put to work. The smart way that I suggest and that works for my swimmers is to have them take a several-minute hot shower and stretch there before getting into the water. If this is not practical, then some easy swimming and kicking starts off the training session to first heat up the fibers. Then the swimmers work on what they feel needs stretching. So how important stretching is? Will stretching actually help the muscles deliver more power? Does it prevent injury? I get these questions all the time. My answers are always the same: I feel stretching is absolutely essential. It increases the range of motion and the force with which muscle moves by improving the fibers' ability to contract. It also protects and prepares the muscles and their corresponding connective tissue.

This is an important point: As crucial as stretching is to training, you should never try too hard to elongate muscle tissue. Some days an athlete is more limber, some days less so. You should stretch comfortably, never letting anyone physically (hands on) assist you, which can lead to muscle, ligament, and tendon damage. You, alone, must control the intensity of the stretch. Nature has provided a safety mechanism to protect the body. It is called the *stretch reflex*. If you stretch the muscles too far or with too much force—by bouncing (ballistic stretching) or having someone else pull too hard or too far on a joint, for example—the body senses a potential problem, and a nerve reflex responds by sending a signal to the muscle fibers to contract and prevent perceived damage from over-elongated muscle fibers and their connective tissue to the bones (tendons). Obviously, this is counterproductive, making the muscles tighter, rather than looser.

Holding the stretch is the next important element of this procedure. Again, the body tries to resist stretching, but if we gently cajole it into relaxing the muscles and connective tissue, the fibers will eventually elongate. This takes on average about 30 seconds to get the results we want. In a cold environment there may be times when one stretch is not enough. No problem; you can simply stretch a muscle or muscle group several times after about 30 seconds rest in between stretching bouts. In fact, I recommend stretching several times a day to keep the muscles relaxed and elongated, especially as the weather cools.

It is always better to under-stretch than to over-stretch. Elongating the muscles should feel good, not torturous. Always be at a point where you could stretch a little further, but never get to the point where you have gone as far as you can go. It is important to listen to your body. If tension builds in a muscle or you begin to feel pain, your body is trying to tell you that something is wrong. Back off on the stretch and let it feel right (see Figs. 12-1 through 12-3 for several stretch sequences).

Bouncing or intense movement in a muscle group undergoing the stretch procedure is just asking for trouble. Stretch first, and then move. We want static stretching, not ballistic stretching!

12-1. Stretching sequence for arms and shoulders.

12-1a. In a standing or sitting position, interlace your fingers above your head. Now, with your palms facing upward, push your arms slightly back and up. Feel the stretch in arms, shoulders, and upper back. Hold stretch for 15 seconds. Do not hold your breath. This stretch is good to do anywhere, anytime. Excellent for slumping shoulders.

12-1b. Hold your left arm just above the elbow with your right hand. Now gently pull elbow toward opposite shoulder as you look over your left shoulder. Hold stretch for 30 seconds. Do both sides.

Note: The stretching illustrations in this book are excerpted from the Swimming Stretches Poster ©1992, by Bob Anderson, illustrated by Jean E. Anderson, Stretching Inc., Palmer Lake CO 80133. www.stretching.com

12-1. Stretching sequence for arms and shoulders, *continued.*

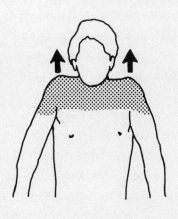

12-1c. With arms overhead, hold the elbow of one arm with the hand of the other arm. Keeping knees slightly bent (1 inch), gently pull your elbow behind your head as you bend from your hips to the side. Hold an easy stretch for 30 seconds. Do both sides. Keeping your knees slightly bent will give you better balance.

12-1d. Shoulder shrug: Raise the top of your shoulders toward your ears until you feel slight tension in your neck and shoulders. Hold this feeling of tension for 3 to 5 seconds, and then relax your shoulders downward into their normal position. Do this two to three times. Good to use at the first signs of tightness or tension in the shoulder and neck area.

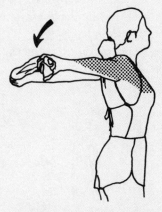

12-1e. The next stretch is done with your fingers interlaced behind your back. Slowly turn your elbows inward while straightening your arms. An excellent stretch for shoulders and arms. This is good to do when you find yourself slumping forward from your shoulders. This stretch can be done at any time. Hold for 5 to 15 seconds. Do twice. Then repeat stretch 12-1a.

12-1f. Hold a towel near both ends so that you can move it with straight arms up, over your head and down behind your back. Do not strain or force it. Your hands should be far enough apart to allow for relatively free movement up, over and down. To isolate and add further stretch to the muscles of a particular area, hold the stretch at any place during this movement for 10 to 20 seconds.

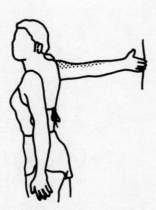

12-1g. Left: To stretch the front of the shoulders and arms you can use a wall, doorway, or fence. Face the wall, and then put your right arm behind you at shoulder height against the wall. Keep your right shoulder close to the wall as you slowly turn your head over your left shoulder to look in the direction of your right hand. Looking over your shoulder should create a stretch in your right arm and shoulder. Hold a comfortable stretch for 15 to 20 seconds. Do both sides. **Right (variation):** Also do the stretch with the arm bent at approximately a 90-degree angle. This will help further prepare the shoulder and arm for the movements required in swimming.

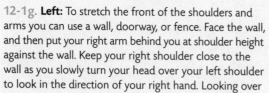

12-1h. Place both hands shoulder-width apart on a fence or ledge, and let your upper body drop down as you keep your knees slightly bent (1 inch). Your hips should be directly above your feet. To change the area of the stretch, bend your knees just a bit more and/or place your hands at different heights. Find a stretch that you can hold for at least 30 seconds. This will take some of the kinks out of a tired upper back. The top of the refrigerator or a file cabinet is good to use for this stretch. *(Remember to always bend your knees when coming out of this stretch.)*

12-1i. From the position illustrated, with your palms flat and fingers pointed back toward your knees, slowly lean backward to stretch the forearms and wrists. Be sure to keep your palms flat. Hold a comfortable stretch for 20 to 30 seconds. *Do not overstretch.* Stretch for a good feeling. Enjoy stretching. This particular stretch is also helpful to help heal tendonitis of the inner elbow (medial epichondylitis).

12-2. Stretching sequence for legs and hips.

12-2a. To stretch the upper hamstrings and hip, hold on to the outside of your ankle with one hand, with your other hand and forearm around your bent knee. Gently pull the leg as *one unit* toward your chest until you feel an easy stretch in the back of the upper leg. You may want to do this stretch while you rest your back against something for support. Hold for 30 seconds. Make sure the leg is pulled as one unit so that no stress is felt in the knee.

12-2b. Sit with your right leg bent, with your right heel just to the outside of your right hip. The left leg is bent and the sole of your left foot is next to the inside of your upper right leg. (Try not to let your right foot flare out to the side in this position.) Now slowly lean straight back until you feel an easy stretch in your right buttock and hamstrings. Use hands for balance and support. Hold an easy stretch for 30 seconds. Do not hold any stretches that are painful to the knee.

12-2c. After stretching your quads, practice tightening the buttocks on the side of the bent leg as you turn the hip over. This will help stretch the front of your hip and give a better overall stretch to upper thigh area. After contracting the butt muscles for 5 to 8 seconds, let the buttock relax. Then continue to stretch quads for another 20 to 30 seconds.

12-2d. Next, straighten your right leg. The sole of your left foot will be flat on ground resting next to the inside of your straightened leg. Lean slightly forward *from the hips* and stretch the hamstrings of your right leg. Find an easy stretch and relax. If you can't touch your toes comfortably, use a towel to help you stretch. Hold for 30 seconds. Do not lock your knee. Your right quadriceps should be soft and relaxed during the stretch. Keep your right foot upright, with the ankle and toes relaxed.
Repeat stretches 12-2a through 12-2d for the other leg.

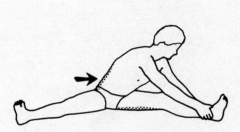

12-2e. Sit with your feet a comfortable distance apart. To stretch the inside of your upper legs and hips, slowly lean forward *from the hips*. Be sure to keep your quadriceps relaxed and feet upright. Hold for 30 seconds. Keep your hands out in front of you for balance and stability or hold on to something for greater control. Use good posture with this stretch. Concentrate on keeping the lower back flat as you do this stretch. Do not strain.

12-2f. To stretch your left hamstrings and the right side of your back, slowly bend forward from the hips toward the foot of your left leg. Hold for 30 seconds to each side.

12-2g. Put the soles of your feet together with your heels a comfortable distance from your groin. Now, put your hands around your feet and slowly pull yourself forward until you feel an easy stretch in the groin. Make your movement forward by bending from the hips and not from the shoulders. If possible, keep your elbows on the outside of your lower legs for greater stability during the stretch. Hold a comfortable stretch for 30 seconds.

12-2h. Sit with your right leg straight. Bend your left leg, cross your left foot over and rest it to the outside of your right knee. Then bend your right elbow and rest it on the outside of your upper left thigh, just above the knee. During the stretch use the elbow to keep this leg stationary with controlled pressure to the inside. Now, with your left hand resting behind you, slowly turn your head to look over your left shoulder, and at the same time rotate your upper body toward your left hand and arm. As you turn your upper body, think of turning your hips in the same direction (though your hips won't move because your right elbow is keeping the left leg stationary). This should give you a stretch in the lower back and side of hip. Hold for 15 seconds. Do both sides. Don't hold your breath; breathe easily. **Then repeat stretch 12-2g.**

12-2. Stretching sequence for legs and hips, *continued.*

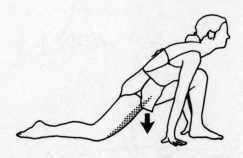

12-2i. Sit on the soles of your feet, with your toes pointed behind you and lean backwards. Do not let your feet flare to the outside. If your ankles are tight, put your hands on the outside of your legs on the floor and use your hands for support to help you maintain an easy stretch. Do not strain. Hold for 15 to 30 seconds. The further you lean back, the more you flex the ankles.

12-2j. As shown in the drawing above, move one leg forward *until the knee of the forward leg is directly over the ankle.* Your other knee should be resting on the floor. Now, without changing the position of the knee on the floor or the forward foot, lower the front of your hip downward to create an easy stretch. This stretch should be felt in front of the hip and possibly in your hamstrings and groin. This will help relieve tension in the lower back. Hold the stretch for 30 seconds. Do both legs.

12-2k. With your feet shoulder-width apart and pointed out to about a 15-degree angle, heels on the ground, bend your knees and squat down. If you have trouble staying in this position, hold onto something for support. It is a great stretch for your ankles, Achilles tendon, groin, lower back, and hips. Hold stretch for 30 seconds. *Be careful if you have had any knee problems. If pain is present, discontinue this stretch.*

12-2l. Left: The calf is composed of two muscles: the gastrocnemius, more to the outside or surface, and the soleus, deeper inside the gastrocnemius or below it. To stretch your calf, stand a little ways from a solid support and lean on it with your forearms, your head resting on

your hands. Bend one leg and place your foot on the ground in front of you, leaving the other leg straight, behind you. Slowly move your hips forward until you feel a stretch in the calf of your straight leg. Be sure to keep the heel of the foot of the straight leg on the ground and *your toes pointed straight ahead.* Hold an easy stretch for 30 seconds. Do not bounce. Stretch both legs.

Right: Now, to stretch the soleus and Achilles tendon, slightly bend the back knee, keeping the foot flat. This gives you a much lower stretch, which is also good for maintaining or regaining ankle flexibility. Hold for 15 seconds on each leg. This area needs only a *slight feeling of stretch.*

12-3. Stretching sequence for neck and back.

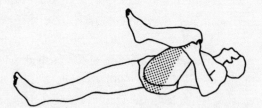

12-3a. Straighten both legs and relax, then pull your left leg toward your chest. For this stretch keep the back of your head on the mat, if possible, but don't strain. Hold an easy stretch for 30 seconds. Repeat, pulling your right leg toward your chest.

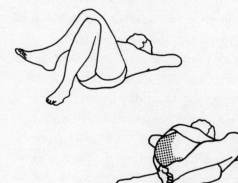

12-3c. Bend your leg and, with your opposite hand, pull that bent leg up and over your other leg as shown above. Turn your head to look toward the hand of the arm that is straight (head should be resting on the floor). Make sure the back of your shoulders are kept flat on the floor. Now, using your hand on your thigh (resting just above the knee), pull your bent leg down toward the floor until you get the right stretch feeling in your lower back and side of hip. Keep feet and ankles relaxed. Hold a comfortable stretch for 30 seconds, each side. **Then repeat 12-3a.**

12-3b. From a bent knee position, interlace your fingers behind your head and lift the left leg over the right leg. From here, use your left leg to pull your right leg toward the floor until your feel a stretch along the side of your hip and lower back. Stretch and relax. Keep the upper back, shoulders, and elbows flat on the floor. The idea is not to touch the floor with your right knee, but to stretch within your limits. Hold for 30 seconds. Repeat stretch for other side.

Cool-Downs

Cool-downs, also called warm-downs or "recovery" efforts, are just as important as warm-ups to help the body adapt and recover for the next set or racing event and to prevent injury. Recovery can be passive, gently active, or moderately active. It has been shown many times that active recovery, even gently active, is much better than doing nothing but trying to catch your breath (passive recovery).

There are two types of recovery movements that work. In one, you do not move from the wall, but rather bob up and down, allowing the heart to rise above the waterline and go below it. In synch with this, you breathe in when the heart is above the waterline and blow out when the heart is below the waterline. This physicality works to blow out the built-up carbon dioxide forcibly. Physiologically, this does three things that are important for recovery: it lowers blood pressure, it slows the heart down, and it lessens the respiratory rate. This is what works if repeat sets or intervals are being done with little rest and recovery. Getting as much control over breathing as quickly as possible is the key to repeat faster swims. Absolutely no talking during this time; the only concern to the athlete now is to gain as much air back as possible, as quickly as possible.

When recovery swims are allowed after a strong effort, ideally the swimmer should first move easily through the water to try to "come quickly back down to earth" (that is, where the air seems more plentiful). Then the swimmer should move through the water fast enough to utilize the built-up lactic acid as fuel (re-oxygenation through the liver), but not so fast as to create more, and to help the muscles contract enough to push the lactate out of the fibers into the circulation, to be carried away from the area of buildup more quickly than would happen with the much slower mechanism of simple diffusion. This swim occurs at about 60% effort, a little bit more than half full-speed. With experience, swimmers develop their own sense of correct recovery speed.

The strokes done in racing or the pushed swims should be used along with freestyle during the recovery. Since lactic acid builds up right at the site of the specific muscles used but takes time to dissipate away from these sites, the recovery process is speeded up if the exact muscles and movements used during the intense swims are put through the warm-down procedure. It has also been shown that stretching is even more important in recovery or warm-down swims than in warm-up.

Warm-Down Protocol

The warm-down protocol for a faster recovery and injury prevention for races of 100 yards and longer is similar to the warm-up at the beginning of the meet:

- Swim 200 easy yards of freestyle and stroke by 25-yard lengths of each, to get the air back (blow off CO_2).
- Swim 4 x 50 yards at 60% effort: 25 yards freestyle + 25 yards stroke that was just raced (if butterfly, one-arm butterfly *always* in a warm-up and cool-down) on 1:10 or 1:15 min.
- Swim 4 x 50 yards at 60% effort: 25 yards stroke + 25 yards freestyle on 1:10 or 1:15 min.
- Swim 200 yards straight of freestyle/stroke by 25-yard lengths of each.

CHAPTER 13

Training Sets for Speed

I use four main types of paced swimming during my training sessions, each involving different enzymes and physiology for the training effects we want to bring to the blocks: pace, builds, push-pace, and race-pace. There is an additional speed that is important, and it is the slowest. I call it recovery. This brings the swimmer back down to earth and helps the body recover more quickly (active recovery) than if he just rested on the side of the pool (passive recovery). This easy-swim time is absolutely necessary to prepare him for his next strong effort. My philosophy mainly consists of getting the swimmers uncomfortable—asking them to hold stroke and kick at a strong pace and then build up to an all-out effort towards the finish. Not only am I trying to induce the body's reaction to vigorous movement through water and have the swimmer adapt to the different degrees of discomfort, I am also conditioning his psychological response to same. Dealing with great discomfort emotionally while trying to put forth a strong effort is the key to fast swimming.

Getting the swimmer uncomfortable brings in what I call "baggage yards." Not "garbage yards," just piling on more yardage that most likely will not produce a desired training effect of any consequence. I stress the body and then cause the appropriate enzymes, buffers, and other physiologic elements to adapt to allow fast swimming. I favor several methods of training my swimmers, of course, but there is a training effect that brings together all that I seek quickly: "add-ons" and "tag-alongs." I have also found over the years that if my swimmers push hard in the main set for three-quarters of the race distance (75's for the 100 yard/meter events, and 150's for the 200 yard/meter events), they still stress the appropriate enzymes for extended speed. Psychologically and physiologically I can get them to swim through more quality repeats this way.

This chapter gives several examples of power swimming workouts. You will notice that the grand total yardage is much less than is seen in traditional training sessions. The yardage can vary from a max of 5,000 yards down to 3,000 yards; no need for us to go more than this. The main set of this workout is made up of what I call "lightnings," broken 300-yard/meter swims. The "lightning" designation comes into play at the 100 yard/meter segment. Ideally it should be pushed hard enough for the swimmer to feel as if he were struck by lightning. If we want to challenge the swimmer aerobically, the swimmer gets 20 seconds of rest after the 150 and then 10 seconds of rest after the 100. If we want the swimmer to be able to push the pace harder, then the swimmer gets 5 seconds of rest per length swum to allow for a bit more recovery between swims. This factors out to allow 30 seconds of rest after the initial 150 yards/meters and 20 seconds after the 100. I came up with the lightning to get all three types of pacing in; it provides a good mixture of swims and is the best way I know to get swimmers to a higher level of condition quickly while yet making them push hard enough to also train for speed. If done honestly, the "baggage" 150, being strongly paced, brings the swimmer to discomfort. The push-pace 100 brings out the courage and drive needed to produce fast people, and the race-pace attempt for the final 50 not only trains my people for speed but also trains them to handle the finish—I feel it's the ideal swim set. Do several lightnings in various ways, and you have a great main set from which to train fast.

Power Swimming Workouts

I'm only including loosen-up, warm-up, and various main sets. But the reader should know that there are several post-main sets where kicking is stressed, breath control and streamlining sets performed.

Warm-Up

Loosen-up: Swim 1 x 400 yards easy-paced mixed swims and kicks.

Prescribed warm-up

- Swim 8 x 25 yards (no fins) freestyle (on 30 sec).
- Swim 4 x 50 yards (no fins) freestyle to stroke push-pace (on 50 sec).
- Swim 4 x 75 yards (with fins). Each 75 is made up of one lap of each free/kick/stroke (on 1:15).
- Swim 3 x 100 yards (with fins) free/stroke/ free/stroke by 25's (on 1:30 or 1:40).
                Total = 1,400 yards

Main Set I

Power swimming: 6 lightnings, the first 3 lightnings without fins and the second 3 with fins.

Lightning 1 (no fins)

- Swim 75 yards stroke and 75 yards freestyle.
- Rest 20 to 30 sec.
- Swim 50 yards stroke and 50 yards freestyle.
- Rest 10 to 20 sec.
- Swim 25 yards stroke and 25 yards freestyle.
- Rest 1 min.

Short-hand designation: 75 st + 75 free (30)// 50 st + 50 free (20)// 50 st/f (stop).

Lightning 2 (no fins)

- Swim 75 yards freestyle and 75 yards stroke.
- Rest 20 to 30 sec.
- Swim 50 yards freestyle and 50 yards stroke.
- Rest 10 to 20 sec.
- Swim 25 yards freestyle and 25 yards stroke.
- Rest 1 min.

Shorthand designation: 75 free + 75 st (30)// 50 fr + 50 st (20)// 50 f/st (stop).

A Note about Terminology

I realize that not all of my readers will be acquainted with the swimming shorthand given in this chapter for workouts and sets. In the sets described below, slashes are placed between each 25-yard (or meter) pool length; for example, "50 yards freestyle/ stroke" means that the first 25 yards is freestyle and the second is *any other stroke*. "On 50 sec" means that you start each interval 50 seconds after you started the previous one. So if you are swimming a "broken" 200 yard distance, and you start the first 50 yards at the 60 mark, or as we call it, "the top" (of the pace clock), you start the remaining three 50-yard segments at 50 seconds, then on the 40-second mark, then on the 30-second mark respectively. The amount of rest between each interval depends on how fast you cover each 50-yard segment. In other words, if you swim an easy pace and finish swimming 50 yards in 45 seconds, you will only have 5 seconds of rest—sometimes a good thing if we are working to make pacing more automatic and easy to hold. The opposite of broken in swimming is "straight or continuous." St = stroke

Lightning 3 (no fins)

- Swim 150 yards freestyle.
- Rest 30 sec.
- Swim 100 yards stroke.
- Rest 20 sec.
- Swim 25 yards freestyle and 25 yards stroke.
- Rest 1 min.

Shorthand designation: 150 free (30)// 100 st (20)// 50 f/st.

Lightning 4 (with fins)

- Swim 150 yards stroke.
- Rest 20 to 30 sec.
- Swim 100 yards freestyle.
- Rest 10 to 20 sec.
- Swim 50 yards stroke.
- Rest 1 min.

Shorthand designation: 150 st (30)// 100 free (20)// 50 st (stop).

Lightning 5 (with fins)

- Swim 75 yards kick and 75 yards freestyle.
- Rest 20 to 30 sec.
- Swim 50 yards kick and 50 yards stroke.
- Rest 10 to 20 sec.
- 50 yards, 25 kick to 25 swim choice.
- Rest 1 min.

Shorthand designation: 75 k + 75 free (30)// 50 k + 50 st (20)//50 k/swim.

Lighting 6 (with fins)

- 150 yards kick.
- Rest 20 to 30 sec.
- Swim 100 yards choice.
- Rest 10 to 20 sec.
- 50 yards, 25 kick + 25 swim choice.

Take an easy 100-yard recovery swim.

Shorthand designation: 150 k (30)// 100 swim (20)//50 k/swim + easy 100.

Main Set II

You will do shorter but faster swims over 75 yards: 3 sets of 4 x 75-yard swims = 900 yards. Every one of these swims is serious (I use the expression, "with bad intentions"); the swimmer *must* be at least in push-pace mode. This is very demanding on the muscles. That is why the set has only 900 yards.

Set 1

Swim 4 x 75 yards (no fins):

- (75) stroke on 1:30//.
- (75) free/stroke/stroke (on 1:30)//.
- (75)free/free/stroke (on 1:30)//.
- (75) all free (stop).

Rest about 2 to 3 min, depending upon age and ability.

Set 2

Swim 4 x 75 yards (with fins):

- (75) all kick on 1:15 //.
- (75) kick/free/stroke (on 1:15)//.
- (75) kick/kick/stroke (on 1:15)//.
- (75) all stroke (stop).

Set 3

Swim 4 x 75 yards (no fins):

- All free on 1:30//.
- All stroke on 1:45//.
- All free on 1:30//.
- All stroke (stop).

Take an easy 100-yard recovery swim.

Main Set III

Here we use 100-yard swims mixed with kicks. Mixing kicks with swims and requiring hard effort is much better as a training element for speed than using the legs alone for kick sets. Fins are used in this set to hold speed for both swimming and kicking and to force the legs to work harder.

Swim 10 x 100's. In the first five swims, the first length of each 100 yards is done at easy speed; then the swimmer builds the rest of the 75 into a fast red-zone finish. The last 5 x 100 swims have the swimmer holding a strong 75—then finishing as strong as possible. I call this type of swimming "It is all about the last lap!" All 10 swims are done fast and with fins.

1. Swim 25 free + 75 stroke on 1:45 or 2 min.
2. Kick 25 + 75 swim free on 1:45 or 2 min.
3. Kick 25 + 75 swim individual medley (IM: butterfly, backstroke, dolphin breaststroke) on 1:45 or 2 min.
4. Kick 25 + 75 one stroke on 1:45 or 2 min.
5. Swim 25 yards free + 25 kick + 50 stroke on 1:45 or 2 min.
6. Swim 75 free + 25 stroke on 1:45 or 2 min.
7. Swim 75 stroke (IM order) + 25 free on 1:45 or 2 min.
8. Kick 75 + 25 stroke on 1:45 or 2 min.
9. Kick 75 + 25 free on 1:45 or 2 min.
10. Kick 25 + 50 free + 25 stroke (stop).

Take an easy 100-yard recovery swim/kick.

Main Set IV

Here we train for 200 yard events, be it stroke, freestyle, or IM. The swims are paired according to what strokes are used. The first part of every swim is a straight 200 yards done with fins for pace swimming; this is followed by 4 x 50 (broken 200) of mixed swims at push-pace effort, with no fins. This is a relatively long set of 2,000 yards/meters, since 5 x a pair of 200 yards is done to train various strokes, the cardiovascular system, the enzymes necessary to energize the effort, and the specific musculature to power it through.

1A. **With fins:** Swim 200 yards main stroke at paced effort (no freestyle, no IM). Rest 1 min.
1B. **No fins:** Swim 4 x 50 yards at push-pace: all free// stroke/free// free/stroke// all stroke (on 50 seconds).
2A. **With fins:** Swim 100 yards free (baggage) + 100 yards stroke at a strong pace. Rest 1 min.
2B. **No fins:** Swim 4 x 50 yards at push-pace: all free// all stroke// free/stroke// stroke/free (on 50 seconds).

3A. **With fins:** Swim 100 yards strong kick (baggage) + 100 yards IM at a strong pace. Rest 1 min.

3B. **No fins:** 4 x 50 kick/swim// swim/kick// all kick// all swim (20 seconds rest after each 50).

4A. **With fins:** Swim 200 yards all free as such: (100 yards pace swim + 100 yards push-pace). Rest 1 min.

4B. **No fins:** Swim 4 x 50 yards at push-pace: all free (on 55 sec)// all free (on 50 sec)// all free (on 45 sec)// all freestyle. These exercises with diminishing times are called "descends."

5A. **With fins:** 100 yards kick (baggage) + 100 yards swim stroke or freestyle at a strong pace. Rest 1 min.

5B. **No fins:** Swim 4 x 50 yards at push-pace: free/stroke (on 50 sec); keep the pattern; can change the stroke.

Take an easy 100-yard recovery swim.

Main Set V

This is an accommodation set that can be utilized to train for both the 200 and the 100 of anything. Everything is centered around 150's; doing this we are pushing the pace for all the swims, since my rule of "less yards means faster swimming" comes into play. Each 150 yard swim starts off with an easy speed 50, then a build 50, and finally a push-pace 50 into a strong finish. We do 6 x 150 yards, the first 3 without fins, the second 3 with fins. We are trying to hold the distance-per-stroke throughout the set if possible.

1 Swim a continuous 150: 50 yards stroke + 50 yards free + 50 yards stroke, build the pace, trying to keep distance-per-stroke (DPS). Rest 1 min.

2. Swim 50 yards free + 50 yards stroke + 50 yards free (straight swim); build the pace (DPS). Rest 1 min.

3. Swim all freestyle, building by 50-yard intervals; roll and reach; hold the pace (DPS). Rest 1 min.

4. 50 kick + 50 free + 50 stroke (straight swim); push each 50 (with fins). Rest 1 min.

5. 50 kick + 50 stroke + 50 free (straight swim); build the pace (with fins). Rest 1 min.

6. Swim 50 choice of anything + 50 kick + 50 choice of swim; build the pace (with fins) (stop).

Take an easy 100-yard recovery swim.

Main Set VI

Here I use the "add-ons" and "tag-alongs"; the tag-alongs have greater yardage. These phrases simply mean that after a lead-off prescribed swim followed with appropriate rest (five seconds rest per length swum), an add-on swim at push-pace or better 25 50 yards/meters is added on to work the finish while in discomfort. A tag-along is a great addition, either 75 yards/meters or 100 yards/meters.

- No fins; swim 100 free/stroke/free/stroke (by 25's) 20 seconds rest + 100 stroke/ free/free/stroke tag-along (1 min rest).
- With fins; 75 fast freestyle (15 seconds rest) + 75 stroke push-pace tag-along (1 min rest).
- No fins; 100 free/stroke/free/stroke push-pace (20 seconds rest) + 50 free/stroke "add-on" (1 min rest).
- With fins; 75 stroke fast (15 seconds rest) + 50 free "add-on" walk or bounce in the water back to starting wall for active recovery.
- No fins; 50 freestyle (10 seconds rest) + 100 free/stroke/free/stroke (1 min rest).
- With fins; 50 fast kick back dolphin (10 seconds rest) + 100 free/kick/stroke/kick + 100 easy recovery to end set.

Leg Work for Breaststrokers

Since the breaststroke is the most demanding stroke on the legs, I suggest additional training breast kick with waterproof medicine balls in deep water to improve endurance, power, and to create "fast legs" from the knee down. Though hardly any yards are swum, the legs are worked harder and more specifically than in any swim set, so the legs should be loose and warmed up. Also, be aware that a given weight is perceived to be heavier while you are in the water than on land. A typical 7-pound medicine ball on land may not seem much, but almost instantly that 4:1 ratio of how much anything in the water is that much harder than on land creates what feels like a 28-pound cannon ball overhead. And after about 15 seconds of hard kicking with the ball overhead, it starts to get heavier, or at least seem so.

Bout I: A 7- or 9-pound medicine ball is held out of the water in front of the swimmer at eye level. The swimmer kicks breaststroke in place in quarter-circle segments, in each quadrant taking 15 to 30 seconds; then he takes a 90-degree snappy turn to either the right or left. When 2 to 3 minutes of snappy turns have been completed, rest for 1 minute. Repeat three times.

Bout II: The squad forms a circle in the water. While kicking the breaststroke, each member must throw the ball to another member to the right or left, trying not to hold the ball for more than 1 second. After several rounds, the ball is thrown in the reverse direction. Then the squad rests for 1 minute and repeats the kicking bout.

Bout III: Breaststrokers break into groups of four. Each swimmer should form one side of an imaginary square. *Two* medicine balls are used simulta- neously. The swimmers toss the ball back and forth quickly to the opposite side of the square. Concentration and timing must be established to prevent the balls from hitting each other and prevent the balls from hitting the swimmers. Continue for 60 seconds before resting and repeating.

Bout IV: While on deck, the coach or a teammate throws the medicine ball to the swimmer kicking the breaststroke. The swimmer tosses it back, having to angle up to the person on the deck, moving away from the deck with every successive throw to increase distance and the force needed to complete the throw. Complete ten tosses before resting; then get closer to the wall and repeat to make a total of three rounds. (I have had a few strong, determined kickers who could do 100 catches and tosses, but it took time to build up to this.)

Bout V: Put away the medicine ball. Now it is "water-walking with no fins." This is the absolutely most inefficient way to move through water. The energy it consumes per unit time is tremendous. With the knees lifted as high as possible and the hands fisted or clasped to prevent the natural tendency to scull the water, the swimmer first kicks leaning forward pushing backward with the bottom of his feet. Upon reaching the wall, he does the same only on his back, everything being reversed in movement (the bottoms of the feet pushing the water again backward away from him. This really stretches and strengthens the hip flexors and all the attendant muscles of the hip girdle and the legs.

After all this strenuous kicking, the swimmers *must* take the time to warm down their legs and loosen them up. I did my job if they can barely walk to the locker room. When they ache and groan, I know the sessions did what they were intended to do.

CHAPTER 14

Training with Fins

Over the years, thousands of swimmers have gone through my age-group, senior, and Masters programs. Thousands more have attended my clinics and racing camps, and hundreds have trained with me privately. And they have all had to train with fins.

I may be unique in my desire to make fin-swimming such an important part of training. I rely on fins to a large degree to help me teach and coach everyone who comes under my eye so they can negotiate movement through water more easily. I respect all my swimmers enough to allow them to feel for themselves what it means to slip through water, to have more propulsive forces than drag forces, and to have the correct body line while swimming. All these sensations are magnified with the use of fins. They help the athletes attain a higher level of condition all the while; in addition, the all-important ankle flexibility is being worked on every minute of their use.

I don't mean short fins, cut-off fins, the extra long, extra stiff scuba-diving fins, or even those made of flimsy soft rubber. *I am talking specifically about flexible fiberglass or fiberglass/plastic combination blades as long as 18 inches, with neoprene inserted down the middle of the blade and a full-foot neoprene bootie.* I am now into the fourth generation of fin design that I use and recommend, and I think they are the best training tool I have (see Fig. 14.1).

I Chance to Meet a Russian Coach

A little background is in order to show how and why I became a devotee of fin training. Some years ago I was vacationing in Fort Lauderdale with my family, and as a professional courtesy, my 10-year-old daughter, Lee, was allowed to train with the resident swim team in Boca Raton, called Mission Bay. While she swam in a side pool with the age-groupers, the USA National Team was practicing in the main competition pool under the watchful eye of Mark Shubert. They were there preparing for the upcoming World Championships in Spain. In fact, the place was packed with talent, since the Russian National Team was training there, too.

Naturally, I made my way over to the main pool to watch the talent. Coach Shubert came over to me and, after learning that I too coached swimming, kindly let me remain on deck to watch his swimmers. One didn't need a special coach's eye to see what "world class" meant. But the one thing that stood out most was the fact that many of the Russians had special fins on and they were moving through the water like dolphins. Only a few of our swimmers had fins, and they were the soft, floppy, all-rubber kind I had used as a kid.

I have the permanent mental imprint watching our best flyer, Pablo Morales, who had just set the 100-meter world record two weeks earlier, look so much slower and less forceful with his flimsy fins next to the Russians with their new style of snappy fiberglass "kickers." The difference was so dramatic and my interest was so piqued

that I had to investigate the new style of footgear.

By pure chance (or maybe Providence chose to take a hand), I was able to strike up a conversation with one of the Russian national coaches who spoke some English. He asked me some questions about American swimming and America itself. I, of course, pumped him for as much information as I could in a few minutes about this dramatic new fin design. He was the one who had developed the design and protocol for their use; it was this project and the attendant problem-solving that allowed him to earn his Ph.D. in physical exercise at one of the Russian sports colleges.

Four years later, I was coaching a middle-level team in northern New Jersey, turning a mediocre program into the front-runner in our division. The other division in our league also had a strong team that we hadn't met yet. They were from Staten Island, New York. And guess who ran the program…Yes! It was this Russian coach and his wife. I had heard about a tough foreign coach producing some fast kids, but I had no idea who he was. As it turned out, he had come to America right after the 1988 Olympics. He recognized me from across the pool during team warm-ups at our championship meet, which was held in his pool that year. When I remembered who he was, I hugged him instinctively. There was a lot of mutual respect—but I really wanted to beat him. I was lucky that day, but it was close! For the next 10 years our teams beat each other up whenever we met.

Fin Conditioning

Fins are my best "assistant coaches." They get my swimmers to a higher level of condition by forcing them to swim faster, which means pushing against more water all the while, and at the same time they increase the flexibility and strength of both the legs and ankles. They also help me help the swimmers to understand stroke technique and body position in the water much quicker and more thoroughly than I could without them, even when fatigue sets in.

The elongated yet flexible fin blade allows for a longer "hull" in the water so, obeying the rules of laminar flow and hydrodynamics, movement in general is magnified and becomes that much easier. A swimmer wearing fins, even if his feet were tied with no kicking allowed, would take, on average, two freestyle strokes less per 25 yards just by being longer and more streamlined in the water. Simply

having the fins on and pointing them to the back of the pool forces the legs, and particularly the ankles, to increase their flexibility and their efforts during every kicking motion. This increased demand sets up the connective tissue around the ankle (ligaments and tendons) to be stretched into a more flexible condition, kick after kick, becoming stronger at the same time. We see a double training effect building here: increased strength and flexibility, two very important conditions for the swimmer, since if the feet are not pointed strongly back because of inflexible ankles, they will point to the bottom of the pool and act as parachutes by grabbing too much water and hindering streamlining. Also, any strength gained in this area allows for more powerful kicks all the time for all the strokes.

The heart and lungs don't know the swimmer is using fins; they only respond to the increased stresses brought about by their use. With fins on, I

14-1. Four generations of fin design.

expect faster swimming, since the intervals with fins are set to be much more demanding. When you move through water faster, you pay the price with more resistance to overcome. This trains the lungs to take in more oxygen and requires the body to utilize it more efficiently with each breath; it also demands the heart to beat faster and with more force to circulate this oxygen to the powering muscles, and it forces the body to adapt to this oxygen demand further by producing more hemoglobin in the circulating blood to actually carry the oxygen. The largest mass of muscle (the legs) used at any one time in swimming is forced to convert the mechanical advantage of the fins into forward propulsion. And this is a good thing, since I don't think enough emphasis is placed on the legs, especially toward the end of a race. I use various training sets to stress both swimming and kicking separately, and then I combine the two within a set to force the body to endure race-pace efforts that mimic the combat of competition.

Fin Usage for Each Stroke

In three out of the four racing strokes, the legs provide a minor (though important) percentage of forward thrust; only the breaststroke requires the majority of forward propulsion from the legs. My daily use of fins provides the quality work that I want to get in to keep the legs from deserting the body as fatigue begins to overtake the swimmer. Even with the breaststroke, one dolphin kick per stroke (the kick that is used in breaststroke drills with fins since the standard breast kick can not be performed safely with fins due to too much tension on the knees) can benefit the athlete who uses fins because it first enhances the body's ability to move in a smooth undulating fashion, which is the correct

way to race breaststroke most efficiently. It also works the hamstrings, which is the most important muscle group in breaststroke. Why do I say this? Because in breaststroke, unlike the other racing strokes, *you can only go as fast as your kick.* Since the hamstrings need to contract first to bring the ankles and heels up to the buttocks to initiate each kick, they need to be powerful enough and with appropriately increased endurance (especially in long course) to keep priming the kicks for forward thrust. Using the fins to practice the dolphin kick either on the belly or the back stresses the hamstrings so they gain strength and endurance (see Figs. 14-2 through 14-5).

Breaststrokers head the list in the relative importance of kick to stroke, because they generate from 50% to 70% of their forward propulsion with an efficient, powerful kick. There are balanced breaststrokers, those with enough upper-body strength and efficient sculling efforts to provide a decent front-end stroke segment to match the back-end stroke segment, the kick. But most of the superior breaststrokers I have seen rely on their legs for most of their forward propulsion and especially to bring the race home.

Next in line for relying on the kick is the butterfly. Here, about 30% of the forward propulsion is generated from the hips down through the legs, assuming correct timing and streamlining. Third is the backstroke, which gets about 20% from the legs. And finally, interestingly, freestyle—the fastest stroke in competitive racing—uses the least propulsion from the legs: about 10% for sprinters (six-beat kick) and 5% for the distance people (two-beat kick). But do not lose respect for the legs or overlook their need to be trained, because at all levels of competition the legs can make the difference as the race nears its end. It's the legs that get you to the wall. The kick to the finish, no matter what the event,

Dolphin-breaststroke drill with fins.

14-2

14-3

14-4

14-5

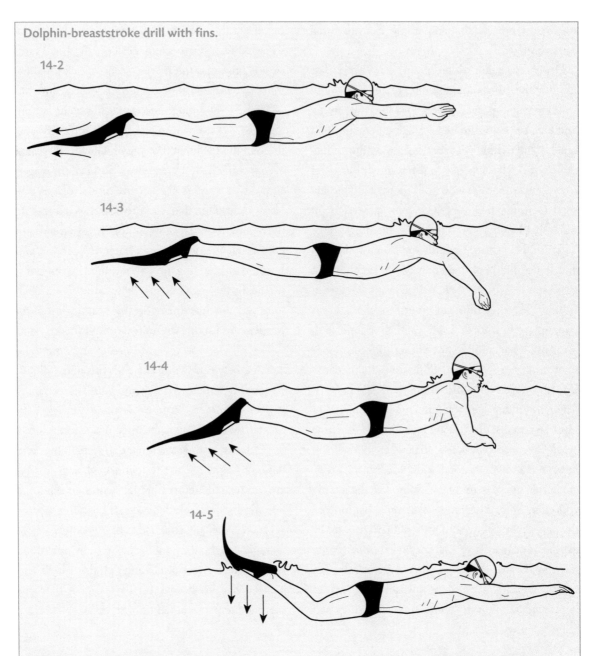

14-2. Finishing the streamline position and starting to grab water, the swimmer sweeps out with hands, with the legs, feet, and fins pointed back to extend body length.

14-3 and 14-4. As the arms grab water and begin the squeeze, the legs and feet are forced up to initiate the dolphin kick.

14-5. As the legs and fins kick downward, the arms are thrust forward with force to form the streamline position; the swimmer looks down to allow water to go over the head with less resistance.

might just provide that something extra to bring home a medal.

Depending upon which group of swimmers has my attention, the emphasis on fin usage shifts. With young age-groupers, I want a lot of fin swimming and kicking. I want to develop good body position quickly and reinforce it every day. I want the youngsters to feel what it is like to slip through the water smoothly yet with power, and I want them to get used to using their legs. The only movement in water that I work without the fins is the breaststroke kick, and I have specific drills and exercises both in and out of the pool that stress and strengthen the target muscles there. Of course this group does swim without fins; they must, in order to feel what it is like to have to work to catch water, grab hold of it, and push it backward before letting go. But most of their yardage is swum benefiting from the mechanical advantage of the fins.

For my older age-groupers and into the senior level swimmers, the use of fins usually elicits a groan, because they know that what follows will bring sets of definite total body discomfort if they are honest about training fast. Some like the feeling and enjoy going fast. Some like going fast but not the pain that it brings. But most of them eventually get the idea that if we use fins and do the quality sets that I have set up to stress scientifically the various muscles, organs, and physiologic enzymes to prepare them for the combat of racing, they will

benefit from swimming less total yardage, eliminating what I call "garbage yards." Usually, 4,500 yards or less brings all the training adaptations I feel are necessary for a day's practice in order to swim fast.

There are training days that I designate as "fin days" for all my swimmers: fins on for everything done in the pool that day: swims, kicks, underwater breath controls, and streamlines. Some of my biggest turnouts at Masters practice are on these days, and I can understand that. Many Masters swimmers are older and some lack the strength, experience, or confidence to move through water the way they and I would like. Using fins allows them to improve physically and psychologically to handle new challenges, sometimes racing to the wall against faster people who I have swimming without fins.

This all works as long as I create an appropriate balance between swimming with fins and without. The less experienced, less confident, and generally weaker swimmers do more sets and yardage with fins so they can keep up and train more closely to the faster, younger, stronger athletes. The more difficult swims are mostly performed with fins, as are the "rescue swims" that let swimmers continue training as inevitable fatigue sets in. Some people get psychologically attached to the "cheaters," as we jokingly call the fins, but that is an individual thing (the use of fins is not cheating at all). These "fin addicts" absolutely love fin days, and if that gets them to the pool, that's fine with me.

CHAPTER 15

Resistance Training

I never met a swimmer who was too strong. In fact, most are not strong enough. Those who understand the importance of being able to move water quickly will see that they need to become first as strong, and then as powerful, as possible.

There is no question that power swimming is one of the most technique-laden sports. Mastering the movements can take years, and there are no shortcuts to proficiency. Though some may learn correct movement through water faster than others, those who are stronger and more powerful will simply swim faster sooner. The added strength and power gained from an appropriate resistance training program will also go a long way to preventing injuries.

As I developed my own philosophy of coaching over the years—that of a "power swimming" or sprint coach—I came to realize the importance of the ability to grab hold of the water (the "feel") and move it quickly on demand (power). Remember, water is 1,000 times more dense than air, and its physical properties act to resist the swimmer more the faster he tries to move through it. My approach to coaching fast swimmers requires that they work hard to experience the three most important elements needed to move through water quickly: (1) technique, (2) strength into power, and (3) condition. Most coaches would probably place strength and power last, convinced that speed comes from condition. While there is no arguing about the importance of being in swim shape, if the athlete cannot move a lot of water quickly for an extended period, he will not be a strong contender in this sport. Distance-per-stroke (quickly) is always the defining measure of fast swimming.

Lifting heavy weights elicits the response of many muscle fibers contracting at the same time, producing the adaptive effect of creating greater force. Lifting lighter weights with more repetitions produces less force but elicits the effect of endurance, since it requires fewer muscle fibers to contract simultaneously but does so over an extended time; some fibers can relax and wait their turn. Nature provided this mechanism for our survival, ensuring us both the speed and the endurance to run for safety so we could escape being dinner for saber-toothed tigers and the like.

Power in its essence is strength over time. How *quickly* (time factor) can you make the strength factor move and produce the results we want? The swimmer must be able to move water quickly and hold it over an extended period of time, a correspondingly longer period of time compared to similar-distance events on land (you remember the 4:1 ratio). Endurance now plays into the mix. An example: a 100-meter freestyle requires the speed and power of a 100-meter dash, but demands that this output last for the time it would take to endure the 400-meter run. Add to this the fact that the faster you move through water, the more the water resists, and you can see the specialized muscular training needed to swim fast.

Strength for Swimming

The logical approach to strength gain starts with ensuring that the body is prepared to handle the rigors of progressive resistance training. At first, lighter resistance with more repetitions enhances the effect of creating endurance. But it also provides an added benefit: it allows the connective tissue surrounding joints and where muscle connects to bone (tendons) and bone connects to bone (ligaments) to

Cullen Jones

A good example of the benefits of weight lifting, among many others, is a young man very close to my heart, Cullen Jones. Jonesey was a NCAA champion, World University Games Champion, USA National and Pan Pacific Champion, member of the world record-setting 4 x 100 free relay, and the fastest swimmer in the world in 2006. Not bad for a kid who came to me as a skinny 14-year-old. He was all arms and legs and thrashed about the pool in ways that reminded me of a stork, which I nicknamed him. Cully always had the gift to sprint; what made him world class, aside from his growing to 6'6" with the perfect torpedo build, was the 30 pounds of muscle he attached to his bones. Now he has the power to move as much or more water per second than anyone on the planet.

adapt to handle increased pressure from increased resistance; this adaptation is a smart, logical way to help prevent injuries. Once the body has adapted and a strong foundation is developed, increased resistance can safely be added.

The best plan to produce a balanced effect is to cycle the two approaches in 3- to 4-week segments. The first three to four weeks of an extended training season in the weight room are taken up with extended repetitions (30 for each prescribed exercise) done one per second but with easily-handled resistance — not too light, of course, which would be a waste of time, but enough to be able to be moved with no excessively demanding physical exertion. After this adaptive period, increased resistance can be added with correspondingly fewer repetitions.

Circadian Rhythms

Circadian rhythm adds another dimension. It has a definite effect in how the body reacts to moving resistance and to how it reacts to the corresponding form of training. There are several physiologic parameters related to strength that peak at certain times during the 24-hour cycle of a day, all of which allow the body to perform better as it adapts to gaining strength, as shown in the chart on Peak Times for Some Body Functions.

As we can see from the chart, body temperature rises naturally between 5 p.m. and 6 p.m. (I remember my mom, saying when I was ill as a child, that if my temperature rose to 100 degrees at dinner time, I was still sick; if 99 degrees or less, then I was on the mend. Someone must have told her that way back when.) Between 5 and 6 p.m, the muscles are more easily warmed, so they can handle physical movement more efficiently. *But note:* No matter what time you train, it is very important to make sure the muscles are warmed so they won't tear. Skeletal muscle in the average athlete becomes about 10% stronger around 6 p.m. This contributes to the fact that most swimmers do better in evening competitions when the finals of serious competitions are held. In addition, perceived exertion seems less between 6 p.m. and 7 p.m. Since the workout feels easier, one is psychologically able to push harder to get more out of the workout.

The ideal way to allow the body to adapt to progressive resistance training is to start with latex tubing, also called surgical tubing. Starting with tubing carries greater benefit because no actual weight is lifted *per se* (as with free weights or machines) that could hurt the spine or other supportive structures. Also, you can adjust (increase) resistance quickly and easily by tightening the tubing or moving away from the point of attachment. This adaptability can prevent overstressing the muscles or joints if they have not recovered sufficiently from a previous exercise bout. Though free weights are good in that they cause associated muscle groups to fire to help keep appropriate body position against gravity while performing resistive movements, for swimmers, this plays a secondary role in developing swim-associated strength into power. Work with tubing is good, since the use of latex more closely reflects the gravity-free environment of water, and the actual resistive move-

Peak Times for Some Body Functions and Their Effects

Body Function	Peak Time	Effect
Grip strength	6 p.m.	You'll be as much as 10% stronger on the racquetball court, in the weight room, or pulling water quickly in a swimming sprint
Perceived exertion	6 p.m. to 7 p.m.	Your workout will seem easier, so you'll be able to push harder for longer through various sets
Reaction time	6 p.m.	Early evening may be prime time to hit a fastball, or react to the starter with a quick time off the blocks
Body temperature	5 p.m. to 6 p.m.	When body temperature peaks, muscles work better, because they're warmer

ments with latex simulate swimming movement more closely than work with free weights or machines.

I like latex tubing so much that I even have swimmers as young as 8 years old start by using the lightest resistance bands under close supervision as their main source of out-of-water exercise. Eventually they graduate to heavier bands and body-weight movements against gravity to get stronger, until about 13 years of age, when they add (appropriately, of course) the rigors of the weight room. Not only does this add another dimension to their training, but the younger ones feel more like the older ones, doing extra work to get as strong as possible.

The supportive connective tissue is made stronger with gradual increases in resistance training (no more than 10% per week). This go-slowly-and-carefully approach reduces the chance of injury in the weight room, especially with younger teenagers or older Masters swimmers too eager to get big and strong. The smart athlete takes more time to build gradual but solid strength throughout the year with a carefully planned regimen of weight training, rather than seeking quick results and risking serious orthopedic injury.

Basic Weight-Lifting Protocols

As a general rule of thumb, if the aquatic athlete is under 45 years of age and does not consume too much physical energy at work or with family or social life, then a visit to the weight room three times weekly is appropriate. This is almost a requirement for high-school, club, and college-level swimming. The weight-lifting bouts must be separated by at least 48 hours to allow for some recovery and muscle buildup after they are broken down from the previous resistance bout. Athletes over 45 years of age, regardless of lifestyle, should limit serious weight-lifting to two sessions weekly, separated by at least 48 hours. (If, however, swimmers have missed in-pool training during the week, they may carefully add an extra session of weight or latex training if they feel up to it; sometimes a missed training session is just what the doctor ordered to prevent staleness and/or injury).

In addition to the weight room proper, swimmers should do dry-land exercises five times weekly, either on deck before swim practice or at home before a trip to the weight room or pool. A dry-land workout includes exercises that move the body against gravity using its own weight or with added resistance: crunches, leg lifts, push-ups, pull-ups, latex pull-downs, pulls-across, squeezes with arms and legs, and so on. I have conditioned myself to perform between 300 and 600 crunches each morning, adding weight from 10 to 45 pounds after each 100. One full abdominal crunch should last two seconds (1 second up, 1 second down) with a rest of 30 seconds between 100s. Core strength is so vital that five times weekly is not too much.

The dry-land exercises should either be done on the clock (in 30-, 60-, or 90-second bouts) or with high repetitions (pushing to get at least 100 or multiples of same per exercise) to enhance the endurance of the muscles. I also suggest that dry-land sets, whether calisthenics or latex tubing, last as long as the particular race you're training for. If, say, a 200-yard freestyle swim lasts about 1:45, then pull-downs with latex for the triceps could be done for between 1:45 and 2 minutes.

Early-Season Workouts

As mentioned above, to help acclimate the body to safely engage in resistance training, early in the competitive season (for at least the first 3 to 4 weeks), swimmers should use lighter weights and higher reps, rather than trying to move heavier and heavier weights with fewer reps, again with adaptation and endurance in mind.

As the season progresses into the second month, one of the three weekly lifting bouts should use heavier weights according to the military protocol.

Military Protocol. With this routine, we still get in our 30 reps, but they are broken up inversely by increasing resistance: the more the weight moved, the less the number of repetitions.

- Start with a weight that the athlete can move quickly and powerfully for 12 reps; rest 30 seconds.
- Add 5 or 10 pounds, depending upon the exercise and the athlete, and do nine reps; rest 45 seconds.
- Add another 5 or 10 pounds and do six reps; rest 60 seconds.
- Finally, add as much weight as the athlete can move forcefully (but we still must obey the one-second-per-movement rule) for three reps.

It is more important to be able to move a moderately heavy weight forcefully through a range of motion than to struggle with too-heavy a weight. If the lift cannot be performed in control in one second, then the weight is excessive.

If scheduling requires lifting and swimming on the same day, it is my view that it is better to lift *after* swim practice rather than before; otherwise you may have a distorted "feeling" in the water while moving through the strokes. Many programs start their training session for the day with the weight room, and this works for many young, eager, focused athletes. But I have noticed over the years that if there is questionable enthusiasm or compromised energy for whatever reason, best to get them in the pool first. The problem arises with this protocol: when and if they are so worn out from aquatic training, will they voluntarily enter the weight room afterward? With sprinters and older Masters swimmers, if swim practice includes "power swimming," weight lifting just before swimming will keep them from responding as they should. Unless there is dedicated time several hours before swim training (allowing the muscles to somewhat recover if properly refueled), less is more in a case like this; better to bag the weights in favor of the pool.

Mid-Season Workouts

As we approach the middle of the competition season (the third month), the emphasis should shift from endurance to power. But workouts should still include some timed bouts of resistance training to "remind" the muscles how long they need to fire intensely for a specific event, and the training schedule should be modified to take event-specific preparation into consideration.

Neuromuscular adaptation: these two words say it all when it comes to describing what we want from the athlete to master his sport. The concept of training the body to correctly respond to whatever demands his sport lays out is what extended training is all about. Movement must be repeated in such a way that the nerves and the muscles react instantly and correctly to the ever-changing demands placed upon the fast-moving body. For fast swimming, these words describe the concept that speed requires constant focus on moving smoothly and strongly through the water without fighting it. Two out of the three weekly lifting bouts should be centered on moving heavier weights with force (one movement out per second, one movement back per second). The third bout should still use high reps to remind the muscles of the need for endurance, even in the "power" events.

If two weight workouts are done per week, then one is done with heavier weights for power and one

Different Kinds of Muscle Fiber

The different types of muscle fibers can be altered in their function by the stresses they are forced to adapt to. Red slow-twitch fibers (with blood supply) seem to handle resistive stress quite well; they get stronger (but no faster in their firing capacity) along with increasing their endurance properties. The two types of fast-twitch fibers (white, very fast, no blood supply and red, medium-fast with blood supply) seem to have what we might call a love-hate relationship with progressive resistance adaptation. At first they crave it and adapt well to produce more power quickly, but as resistance training continues and swim training gets more intense, more of the red medium-fast fibers take over since they are more rugged (they have some endurance due to a blood supply to help in fueling and waste removal) and are better suited to handling weight stress. We see some decline in the very-fast white fibers (which are suited for all-out speed) to produce more of the medium-fast red fibers. What does all this mean? We can lose some extreme quickness to gain more extended speed. This is the target condition for events longer than 100 yards, but not for the 50- or 100-yard competitor. But all is not lost if we allow enough time for ALL the fibers to heal up. Those gifted with an abundance of all-out fast-twitch white fibers will see them overcompensate and produce more power than ever for championship efforts if the taper is sufficiently long and executed with the science of physiology geared for the individual athlete.

keeps the lighter weights with more repetitions to help maintain endurance.

Major Competitions

As we approach the big competitions (5 weeks out), lifting becomes secondary in importance, as most of the swimmer's energy should be devoted to the pool. For junior and senior level athletes, we drop down to two sessions per week of heavy lifting, separated by at least three days (Monday–Thursday, Tuesday–Friday). Masters swimmers who have been lifting twice weekly should retain this protocol until the start of the 3-week taper. Once we have set foot on holy ground (the taper period), lifting is reduced to once weekly. The one session of heavy lifting per week at this point is to remind the musculature of its job to produce power upon demand. I recommend that swimmers take specific energy supplements before weight-lifting bouts throughout the year, but especially at this point. (See Chapter 22 for information on suitable supplements.) The muscles' energy stores must be topped off every day as we approach the taper. As lifting becomes less important and fast swimming becomes more so, we hope for the fast-twitch muscle adaptation to take over.

All weights stop 10 days out from the big meet. (Some coaches may think this is too long to go without resistance training. I believe more in muscle recovery and its importance on training fast in the pool). In most instances this is sufficient time for the musculature to heal, repair, and maximize whatever power has been developed by the swimmer's genetics and hard work and yet retain the generated power from the weight room for the big meet.

CHAPTER 16

Training the Mind

Everything we do runs through the mind: what we perceive and what we believe. Fish are prisoners of their environment: they have to swim. We are prisoners of our minds: we *choose* to swim. But knowing how to make the mind work for us instead of the other way around can mean the difference between who is ready to race and who is just filling up the other lanes when the starter says, "Take your mark."

The psychology of racing gets to the very essence of why we race: all the training and preparation in the world mean very little unless the mind is ready to lead the body into combat. Thirty percent of the brain is dedicated to vision, actual and virtual. What the mind "sees," it wants to make happen. Spend enough time visualizing positive things and at least part of the fantasy can become a reality.

The best state of mind in which to swim a race is relaxed but controllably on edge. This takes experience and lots of practice. It is amazing how perceptions in the mind can bring about responses in the body. When it is time to compete, your body usually responds with an increased pounding of the heart, rapid but irregular breathing patterns, a rise in blood pressure, muscles on the brink of intense contractions—the total sensation of approaching combat. All this must be controlled before competition begins, then released under control throughout the race.

The Power of the Moment

Probably the most difficult task in competitive swimming is to bring all the elements of preparation, experience, desire and focus together at the precise moment needed to perform. Swimmers don't get do-overs; they don't have half-times in which to regroup. There is no changing sides of the court after intermittent contests to make everything seem as even as possible. You get to the blocks, you take the commands to get ready, and you go. It is extremely difficult to react instantly and perfectly to the command to race and to follow through to the best of your ability, training, and psychological makeup. But it can be done. The best swims for the biggest meets require careful preparation of the mind: swimming the event in visualization; preparing all the necessary rituals to get ready to race; controlling the anxiety rather than letting it control you; and preparing for any adverse circumstance that may arise. All must be gone over and given the respect they deserve.

No time to think on the block; not supposed to, really. All the thinking should have been done before; done during training, done during warmup, done while waiting for your event to come up. As you are stepping up to the block, you need to react, not think. You need to get so focused that no distractions are allowed to encroach upon the task at hand, and this takes practice. Training yourself to focus upon demand is key to producing up to your potential. And with every event, you need to refocus as strongly as possible. If things don't come out as planned or desired, you have a whole five minutes to cry over it. Then it is on to the next contest.

Everything in life that is worthwhile requires *focus*. No matter how talented, how intelligent, how desirous of a positive outcome—without focus, you will get less than your best. OK, so how do you get focus? What I have been doing up to now is treating focus like a noun. It needs to be a verb. It requires action to put it in play. We can provide help in all sorts of ways. There are psychological "tricks" that help the mind concentrate on the task at hand. After all, isn't that what focus really is: concentrating on the here-and-now? Not an hour ago, not 10 minutes in the future, but *right now*—the power of the moment.

Tools for Focus

Mint

Various types of *mint* have come into vogue in academic circles to enhance psychological arousal under pressure. Teachers, becoming aware of this mental boost, have been giving their students mint-flavored candies or breath mints before and during achievement tests. The stuff works. In hundreds of youngsters, peppermint has drawn the greatest positive response of all the mint flavors, enhancing focus and the ability to bring answers to mind under pressure. It acts on the arousal center of the brain, which is stimulated by the mint scent. I will try most anything to help my athletes focus, so my swimmers have been taking peppermint lozenges the last few years as their events are called to the blocks. Between 5 and 10 minutes before racing, they chew a couple of Lifesavers. There is a relatively new delivery system for mint that I feel works the best: Listerine mint strips. These instantly dissolve on the tongue. Placing three or four consecutively on the tongue as the preceding one dissolves away as the swimmer approaches the blocks is the protocol I suggest. I feel it makes a difference. A few deep breaths once the mints are on the tongue, and the intense cooling sensation enhances the effect. And it gives the swimmers one more thing to do to help them believe they have an advantage over their competition—a psychological boost in itself.

Color

The stimulation of our senses is a powerful tool to arouse us psychologically. Since, as I mentioned previously, the brain devotes a large portion of its capacity (30%) to vision, I figured this is an important area for stimulation. I have worked with the *psychology of colors*, taking hints from advertisers (billboard signs and logos) and actual companies (supermarkets and other retailers who color-code different sections of their stores to influence the psychology of awareness, which in turn influences buying). Color is likely to have the most influence on a swimmer as he is preparing to race and during the race itself. What the eyes are looking through at those moments may supply the needed impetus to react and focus. I've tried several types of colored goggles and found that the visual enhancement from bright amber lenses really gets the mind going. Knowing that traffic lights use amber to warn of a pending change from green to red, I figured the amber must put the emotional psyche on alert, and I have found that it does.

Breath

Most land-based athletes don't realize the importance of breath control. They train, huff and puff, and breathe to recover as best they can while performing their events. They are not usually coached to control their breathing before racing, while racing, and for recovery afterward; what comes naturally is what will have to suffice for the duration. But a swimmer needs breath control; he will live or die by it in his races. He should have been trained constantly to control the air exchange before competition, during it, and for the recovery afterward.

However, most swimmers I have seen have not been taught how to breathe under stress; they seem to be breathing just to stay conscious. What they need to do is breathe to *relax*, breathe to *gain inner strength*, and breathe to *become focused*.

If you take the time to watch a nervous athlete closely and home in on the breathing pattern, most often you will see shallow breathing for four to six breaths, and then actually breath-holding for 3 to 6 seconds. The breath-holding occurs because the athlete is distracted enough to disrupt what should be automatic behavior. If the athlete would take the time to breathe in slowly and deeply through the nose, letting the belly protrude ("belly breathing," which allows the diaphragm to drop down and expand), consciously hold the breath for 3 seconds, and then exhale slowly but fully through the mouth, an almost immediate sense of relaxation would envelop the whole body. I have my swimmers do this in modified form, as described in the chapter on starts, while the swimmer is behind the block. It's a last chance to get a few good air-exchanges in, which also enhances immediate focus for the moment.

I think of swim racing as a form of controlled violence, similar to a thoroughbred race: the horses are set up behind the starting gate, the gate flies open with the ring of a bell, and they are off! But relaxation is still needed amid the mounting stress that competition can bring.

I frequent what may be the most famous surf shop in the East, Ron-Jon's in Cocoa Beach, Florida. They have a huge selection of wildly designed T-shirts that are real eye-catchers. The best design they have, in my opinion, captures the true spirit of mental training under stress: a surfer with good form, in control, on top of a powerful wave with these words printed on the shirt: *The Power of the Moment!*

PART FOUR

Health, Nutrition, and Performance

CHAPTER 17

Keeping the Athlete Healthy

When lecturing on public health, I often start out with the statement: "If you all knew what was out there waiting to get you, you would all go hide in a cave...until I told you what was in the cave." This means that there is really no place to hide against sickness, injury, or worse. It is our responsibility to be constantly vigilant regarding our own welfare and health, and what we do as young people all too often can present itself years later as cause and effect.

A lot of public health is logic. People need to be exposed to this logic in such a way as to convince them to incorporate it into their lives. A coach-and-athlete combination who abides by the rules of good public health will most probably have a training advantage over those who don't. To quote an oldie: "An ounce of prevention is worth more than a pound of cure," every time.

Lesson number one is to try and put balance in one's life. To give vigorous athletic training equal billing with the rigors of today's demands in the classroom, the workplace, and society, the successful athlete has to be aware of all that can tear at him, both physically and emotionally. Just as a successful competitive swimmer must learn to "make friends with the water" and move through it with an economy of effort that belies the ease spectators see, so must the athlete move through life. Those athletes engaged in long-term training toward a specific goal must be aware of, and avoid, all possible roadblocks to their efforts to improve. The ability to train hard every day requires devotion to making the right choices every day—not an easy task for most young (and, sometimes, not so young) healthy people.

Most take good health for granted. (Don't we all until it leaves us?) These people seem to think they are "bulletproof" and that they can expect their bodies to respond to every demand quickly and successfully. The thought of getting sick or injured just isn't as tangible as it should be. My goal—and experience has burnished this in my mind—is to educate all my athletes to the point just shy of being obsessive. However, as important as it is to know when to push yourself, it is equally important to know the difference between working toward goals and putting yourself in harm's way.

Overreaching versus Overtraining

Those who know physiological adaptation to training know that the most important part is the R & R (rest and recovery) between exercise or competition bouts. What goes on here can make all the difference in performance, both in day-to-day training and at the big meets. *Overreaching* and *overtraining*

describe the syndromes (the signs and symptoms) of pushing too hard and/or too often. The main difference between the two is the length of time and the degree to which performance is hindered. This is an important distinction. It is not the overt symptoms the athlete exhibits that define the condition, it is the degree to which performance is diminished. The same symptoms can be experienced with both conditions, but it may take only a few days to a few weeks to recover to full performance after overreaching, whereas it can take weeks or even months to come back from overtraining.

In addition, different athletes react to the stresses of vigorous training differently. Some athletes exhibit some of the symptoms of overtraining, yet are able to race well. Some exhibit few or no symptoms during practice sessions but race poorly. It takes a wise athlete and an understanding coach to spot problems that relate to performance upon demand.

Clues that a swimmer may be overtraining are several: the overt physical signs of excessive stress manifest as irritability, difficulty sleeping (often being too tired to sleep properly), walking around with constant body aches, decreased ability to concentrate, susceptibility to colds and other illnesses, and a change in eating habits. According to the International Center for Aquatic Research (ICAR) at the Olympic Training in Colorado Springs, Colorado, to be considered "subjectively stale," as the condition is described, an athlete has to present with at least three of the above.

There are also internal physiological parameters that mark an unrelenting stressful condition. Analysis of the athlete's blood would show muscle damage, including a rise in enzymes that would otherwise be contained within the muscle cells proper (such as an increase in creatinine phosphokinase or lactic dehydrogenase) and an increase in urea. An elevated concentration of the hormone cortisol is a classic stress marker, along with a rise in white blood cell concentration, which can signal that the body is fighting off an infection.

In addition, the effects of overtraining in the pool under the "bad intentions" of hard intervals or racing produce a reduction in aerobic capacity. This can manifest itself as an out of air feeling too early in a practice or during a race. We see a shift to anaerobic physiology rather than a reliance on the aerobic physiology built up during training.

We must not forget the mental and emotional consequences. As overtraining controls our physiology, the mental energy seems to wane. This is a result of two things: absolute brain energy depletion (poor glucose supply to the brain because glucose is in such high demand by the muscles) and the *knowledge* that the body is going to make energy demands that cannot be met. A dedicated athlete does not suffer from short-term memory loss; what hurt yesterday and the day before will most assuredly hurt today, maybe even more, with a cumulative effect. As I said before, fish are prisoners of their environment: they have to swim to survive. We, on the other hand, are all prisoners of our minds: we choose to swim. One of my coaching heroes, former Olympic Coach Jack Nelson, esteemed now-retired head coach of the nationally known Fort Lauderdale Swim Team, is justly famous for his motivating slogan: "Access to Success Is Through the Mind."

Student athletes should take note of this: since glucose is the only fuel the brain can utilize to function fully, it becomes a matter of necessity to replenish glucose supplies right after practice. In fact, it has been shown physiologically that there is about a 2-hour window where (depending upon how one replenishes with the correct food choices)

eating can measurably affect the re-supply of glucose and glycogen to meet the energy requirements of a demanding life. Since carbohydrates usually form a chemical in the brain called serotonin, which has a tranquilizing effect, they need to be balanced with some protein and fat, which produce epinephrine (adrenalin) and norepinephrine (noradrenalin). These act as stimulants and can counteract the drowsy feeling one may get from an intense carbohydrate load. And all athletes who choose to take part in vigorous exercise and constant training must ingest a sufficient and appropriate energy supply to power the brain, the muscles, the immune system, and all the vital organs, all of which must work overtime to prevent overtraining. (For more on nutrition, see Chapter 20.)

If symptoms of "too much" begin to cloud the days, then immediate rest from all vigorous specific training is a must. What works for the older athlete is usually a week off from everything and a change of schedule to allow for mental healing. After a week, some easy cross-training can be instituted, such as leisure bike-riding or relaxed walking in pleasant sensory surroundings—just about anything that gets the swimmer away from the pool. No guilt should be felt for missing practice; an imbalance in the athlete's schedule brought this about in the first place, so some short-term rehab is in order.

Infectious Diseases

In addition to the mental and physical effects of overreaching and overtraining, vigorous training also involves the risk of immunologic breakdown, which leaves the athlete open to infectious diseases. When the swimmer is exhausted from training hard and working in close physical proximity to the rest of the team, it is easy to become sick and to suffer from it.

There is a 3-foot rule in public health: if you can separate yourself from someone who is sick with a cold or other upper respiratory infection (URI) by at least 3 feet for the short time that you may share proximity, your chances of coming down with the infection are reduced. I want to emphasize the fact that a short time of exposure means just a few minutes at best. Double the distance, and you cut the risk to at least a quarter. If you are walking behind someone who is sneezing or coughing during cold season, take a detour off to the side so as not to breathe in his trailing effluence, spreading germs. If forced to share space with someone exhibiting symptoms of a cold or URI for longer than an hour, try to get as far away as practical and have as many people fill in the space between you two, and, if at all possible, open the windows to circulate fresh air. Spraying a Lysol-type product through the air in a contaminated space will help to reduce virus and bacteria load. The air ducts and accompanying filters in the home and car should be sprayed at least once a week. Years ago it was discovered that the infecting bacteria for Legionnaires' disease in hospitals found a "home" in the hot water pipes and air ducts heating the rooms. A cough or sneeze in a car can cause several thousand infecting organisms to linger for days in the A/C ducts, a major cause for relapse or reinfection.

At the pool, we can take a logical approach to prevention. Even though swimmers are surrounded by water, they, too, can sweat. In fact, most swimmers, if they don't replenish liquid during practice, will lose up to 2 pounds of weight. This is water weight equivalent to about two pints (32 oz) of fluid. Replacing this is not only important for more effecient muscle contraction during practice but also vital for overall well-being. Logically, and with good public health in mind, if there are any swimmers

exhibiting URI symptoms, they should not be at practice, infecting the rest of the team. To help control infectious spread, swimmers should not all be bunched up in the same tight area after each set; they should be spread out a bit and breathing in different directions. Remember, even a 3-foot separation can make a big difference.

In terms of the viruses and bacteria that cause the vast majority of URIs, there are three main components to consequential infection: (1) the infecting load or total amount of initial exposure; (2) the length of time exposed; and (3) the condition of the body and its immune system at the time of exposure. The absolute simplest yet most important procedure to keep the spread of infection down is to prevent potentially contaminated hands from coming in contact with mucous membranes (eyes, nose, and mouth). Carrying gel-type disinfectants to use on the hands before eating out (if no access to a rest room), for example, is a smart move.

Another simple but very important procedure is to blow the nose after exposure to airborne germs, or better yet, at the end of every day, to help eliminate many of the infecting organisms caught in the nasal passages and in the upper respiratory tract before they can "dig in," since it takes up to several hours for most infecting organisms to penetrate the mucous linings of the body. The body's coating of mucus, which it produces to lay down a protective layer over all the linings opening to the environment, gets thicker as it dries out, so I recommend blowing the nose while taking a hot shower, as the moisture from the hot water works to hydrate and loosen. You should also keep hydrating the body with fluid intake throughout the day, and, as we will discuss in Chapter 19, you should never wait to get thirsty to drink. It is extremely important to keep up hydration when the seasons change from the humid summer to the cooler, drier fall and winter months. Regular intake of sufficient liquid is especially important in extreme climates—both hot and cold—since they can each dry out the body's port-holes to its surroundings. If the relative humidity in your home is less than 50% during the dry, cold winter months, then the air is too dry.

Chlorinated water is very drying and irritating to all mucous membranes, but it is not just the chlorine. It is more what chlorine has combined with—body fluids interact with free chlorine to produce hypochlorites. This is what we smell at pools and what burns our eyes and makes us cough. Symptoms include sensitivity to the smell of chlorine, burning eyes, and coughing with exertion at some pools. Along with lack of rest and overtraining, reactions to chlorine can put the swimmer in a run-down, less protective condition. The thick mucus that is caused by a negative reaction to chlorine is not helpful at all to the body and hinders its ability to breathe, especially under duress. To help correct this and some of the other negative effects on the respiratory tract, I highly recommend using a hot steam vaporizer in the bedroom each night. The benefit comes from a sterile, soothing, warm mist that helps heal an irritated respiratory tract and ward off infection. In addition, each morning, the room should be aired out and sprayed down with a product like Lysol to prevent mold growth on rugs, drapes, blankets, and blinds. It is worth all this extra work to prevent illness that could prove detrimental to a swimmer who needs to train hard and breathe unimpaired.

Pain versus Discomfort

It is important for a swimmer to do everything possible to prevent overtraining, overreaching, injury and illness, and a major element in this prevention is the ability to differentiate between pain and discomfort. This might seem to be a trivial distinction; in reality, it is what makes successful athletes in any sport. There is obviously a difference between pain and discomfort, usually a question of degree and amount, but it is up to the individual athlete (and his coach) to know where the boundaries lie and what the consequences are if they are crossed. We must also add the concepts of present-time and delayed-onset pain or discomfort to the mix to provide a more complete and accurate picture of what is happening as an event progresses.

Every athlete worth his sweat gets better only by forcing the body through the rigors of the sport-specific training and any appropriate cross-training. This produces discomfort, both immediate and delayed. Sometimes an athlete will be in all-over pain and sometimes it will last for quite a while. While many athletes need to have this feeling to be sure they are training at a level that will produce results, the discomfort may cause others to drop down in intensity and stay within their relative "comfort zones." Experience in a particular sport will usually help the athlete learn to deal with this reaction in an adaptive and positive way. An athlete *should* move in and out of the comfort zone; this is sound physiological practice and creates the flexibility necessary for continual adaptation and improvement.

The mental and emotional aspect of this reaction to training is centered around the perception of the progression from discomfort into pain, and this is something that must be successfully dealt with if the athlete is to progress. In no other sport is the perception of hurting all over and being "out of air" more manifest than in swimming. As was pointed out earlier, humans evolved as be land-based animals; moving vigorously on land produces a sense of training stress that becomes associated with the sport in a way Nature intended. The athlete adapts, and condition and performance are improved. But moving vigorously in a medium 1,000 times more dense than air (water) brings additional stresses on the athlete. We have seen that the harder and faster one swims, the more the water resists. Running out of air on land is one thing; running out of air in the water is much more daunting. Any sensation that the air supply is or will be compromised while in water will almost always bring in emotional as well as physical factors that the athlete must address. I tell my swimmers, "If you think you can, or you think you can't...you are right!" The athlete has the choice to deal with discomfort, knowing that he or she will benefit in the end from being made to feel that way.

Pain, on the other hand, is where good medical and physiologic sense take over and respect what the mind and body are signaling. Pain is Nature's way to protect the body from imminent damage or greater damage later on. There is nothing wrong with backing down from pain, especially if it becomes local-ized, intense, and unremitting. Training past this kind of pain can cause injury and set the training schedule back. If the pain is skeletal-muscular, conditioning and/or rehabilitation may bring the athlete back. If the perception of pain in an otherwise sound athlete keeps interfering with performance, then the mental or emotional aspect must be addressed and a cause sought out and corrected. Often it takes a sports psychologist or other expert to get to the root problems and place things in proper perspective. When I see that a particular barrier can and needs to be surmounted to get to the next level of training adaptation, I have to emphasize the fact that I believe in the athlete and feel certain, with all my knowledge and experience, that he or she can rise above and control their improvement. I kid with them and say, "You need to take Dumb Pills," or anything that will prevent negative feelings from arising when we all know better. Most of the time I want my swimmers to think about a lot of things in practice, all geared to help them improve. But on occasion the Dumb Pills are necessary to stop thinking too much and just swim.

Chapter 18

Preventing and Treating Injury

It is much better to prevent than to treat injuries, but if treatment is necessary, in athletic training it pays to seek out the root cause as quickly as possible. In swimming this may not be as easy as one would assume. For example, there can be several reasons for the most common problem in swimming, so common it has its own syndrome: swimmer's shoulder. The second most common malady named with a body part is breaststroke knees.

Most physicians see the athlete after the injury, too late to prevent anything. With luck, they see the athlete in time and have appropriate knowledge and ability to do some good. In any case, time, effort, and consistent energies will be needed to effect improvement that is sufficient and quick enough to get the injured athlete back on track, none the worse for the experience. But there is a dictum in medicine and especially in sports medicine: "the body never forgets." The older the athlete or the more severe or chronic the injury, the less likely it is that total healing will occur.

Spotting trouble before it gets out of hand, if within the realm of appropriate training and competition, is not only the responsibility of the actively training athlete and his coach, it is the only sane way to approach high-level sports, or any level of sport, for that matter.

Swimmer's Shoulder

Injuries or weakness in other body parts can be nemeses for the various strokes in competitive swimming, but the shoulders are by far the most important areas at risk for injury among aquatic athletes who train vigorously on a regular basis.

The cause or causes of swimmer's shoulder can be either endogenous (from within the body) or exogenous (arising from a source outside the body). The possibilities range from lack of flexibility, strength, and endurance in the supporting musculature of the shoulder to an unfortunate genetic body type in the shoulder girdle proper, which allows for impingement of tendons—all endogenous. Faulty technique or overuse in a particular repetitive athletic movement, on the other hand, would be considered exogenous.

Swimming in general promotes flexibility, but those who compete as triathletes, for example, and overemphasize running and biking tend to concentrate on stretching and strengthening only their lower extremities. As a result, most runners and bikers have relatively weak upper bodies that also lack flexibility. This double whammy can easily contribute to shoulder problems and hinder the development of good technique in the water.

Training for Shoulder Safety

To train all the competitive swim racing strokes most efficiently, one needs to incorporate more than just the shoulder muscles into training. The body's core muscles must be trained as a group: abdominals, external and internal obliques, and lower, middle, and upper back muscles, which include the latissimus dorsi, trapezius, and rhomboids (see Fig. 18-1a and b). Muscles trained as a group enable the body to roll side-to-side in a level position through the water for long-axis strokes (freestyle and backstroke) and to make the smooth and rhythmic undulation (dolphin-like) from the hips for short-axis strokes (breaststroke and butterfly). In this way, the pressure is taken off the shoulders, and the large muscle groups can help move the body through the water more efficiently. Once this side-to-side rolling motion or up-and-down hip motion is mastered, the swimmer can get more distance-per-stroke and slip through the water at an energy savings that is astounding.

In addition, it is most prudent to develop the smaller but very important supportive muscles in the back of the shoulder, the rotator cuff. The four muscles that make up the rotator cuff are, from bottom to top of the shoulder girdle, the subscapularis, the teres minor, the infraspinatus, and the supraspinatus (see Fig. 18-2a and b). It is this last muscle's tendon that takes the brunt of "hits" when the head of the humerus (upper arm) is forced upward into the shoulder girdle against a bony prominence called the acromion processes. (The acromion is the bone you feel when you pat yourself on the shoulder.)

A good example of this occurs when a swimmer "bounces" off the wall in open turns. Both shoulders would be expected to take the "hit" when the arms are jammed against the wall, as they should be for a quick, crisp turn in breaststroke, butterfly, or individual medley transition, and then the power arm (the arm that goes over the water) gets a second "hit" because it is used to push the body off the wall with more force as the body changes direction. If someone is turning from right to left, as is usual with right-handed swimmers, the right shoulder is the one at risk. This second "hit" seems to produce the greater compression damage over time, as it gets repeated over hundreds into thousands of times during a training season.

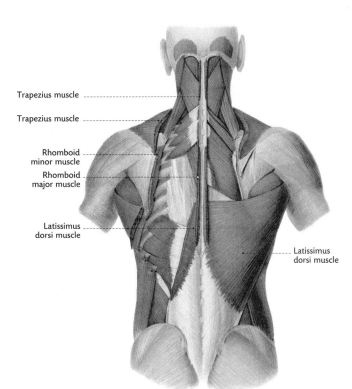

Trapezius muscle

Trapezius muscle

Rhomboid
minor muscle

Rhomboid
major muscle

Latissimus
dorsi muscle

Latissimus
dorsi muscle

18-1a. Core musculature of the back: the rhomboid, trapezius, and latissimus dorsi muscles.

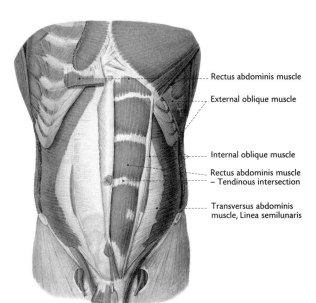

Rectus abdominis muscle

External oblique muscle

Internal oblique muscle

Rectus abdominis muscle
– Tendinous intersection

Transversus abdominis
muscle, Linea semilunaris

18-1b. Core musculature of the abdomen: the transversus abdominis, rectus abdominis, internal oblique, and external oblique muscles.

This compression from excessive movement of bone against muscle and tendon can be decreased by strengthening the musculature within and around the shoulder girdle. Impingement of this muscle and its associated tendon can also occur with repeated overhead movements in freestyle, butterfly, and in backstroke if there is naturally (genetically) not enough room for all the structures to move freely without rubbing against each other, or with overuse and the inflammation and swelling that follow.

Specific shoulder strengthening exercises with latex tubing and light weights done on a regular basis (three times weekly works well) should prove effective for preventative strengthening of both the shoulder girdle proper and the rotator cuff underneath, as well as for rehabilitation of an already inflamed condition. Flexibility exercises should be introduced as well. This has a twofold benefit: (1) to break up any adhesions that may develop as the body's response to inflammation and injury and (2) to increase the range of motion. It is so much easier to move through water with an increased range-of-

motion (ROM) from the shoulders that increased distance-per-stroke is almost a given. Also, the potential for muscle tears is greatly reduced if we stretch the muscles gently but thoroughly, holding each stretch for about 30 seconds before vigorous exercise. It is much easier to stretch muscle fibers, which are designed for elongation, than the corresponding connective tissue (tendons) which are not. (For more on stretching, see Chapter 12.) Anti-inflammatory medication should be considered to help reduce any swelling already in place and to prevent it from increasing.

Breaststroker's Knee

The second area of the body that is most vulnerable to overuse injuries is the knee. Repetitive strain injuries happen when the body cannot take the constant repetitive movements that cause inflammation, damage, and impairment to proper functioning of any muscle group or joint. Swimmer's shoulder is the most notorious; what we might call

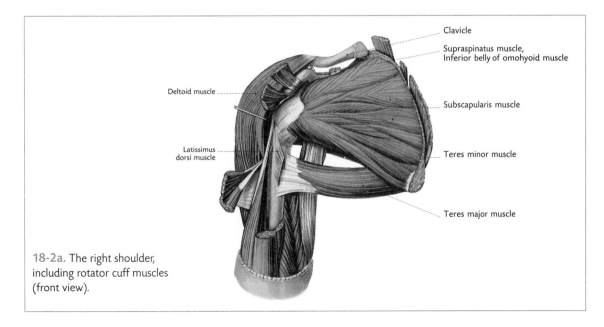

18-2a. The right shoulder, including rotator cuff muscles (front view).

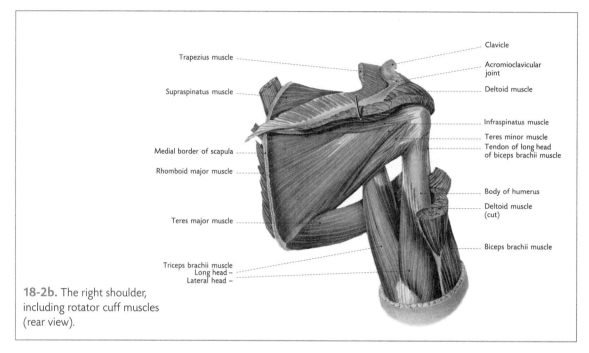

Trapezius muscle

Supraspinatus muscle

Medial border of scapula

Rhomboid major muscle

Teres major muscle

Triceps brachii muscle
Long head –
Lateral head –

Clavicle

Acromioclavicular
joint

Deltoid muscle

Infraspinatus muscle

Teres minor muscle

Tendon of long head
of biceps brachii muscle

Body of humerus

Deltoid muscle
(cut)

Biceps brachii muscle

18-2b. The right shoulder, including rotator cuff muscles (rear view).

"breaststroker's knee" falls into this category of injuries, right behind the shoulder in frequency.

It is widely assumed that swimming is the almost perfect non-impact athletic endeavor in an anatomy-friendly gravity-free environment. And this is exactly the problem. The body has a tremendous ability to adapt to its surroundings, though in some cases it may take as long as 2 or 3 years. The more the body swims, the more it gets used to gravity-free conditions—not having to deal with the pounding and stresses gravity can produce on the body day after day.

Cross-training on land can thus set the swimmer up for a fall by placing too much pressure on the rather delicate joints of the ankles, knees, and hips. All too often, swim coaches have their athletes do various vigorous activities on land (running steep banks of steps, long runs up and down hills, continuous-walking deep-knee bends, and the like); these coaches are so convinced this cross-training will produce a positive holistic effect that movement on land becomes a mandatory part of their

swimmers' daily training. This routine may work for some, even more than some, but in the long run (no pun intended) this practice is putting the swimmer in harm's way. The only exception to my premise is the obvious training of triathletes, which, by the nature of their chosen events, must bridge the gaps among watery (gravity-free), mechanical (bicycle), and gravity (land-based) environments.

Unfortunately, epidemiological studies indicate an increased incidence of osteoarthritis—the wearing away of bone, cartilage, and other joint elements—in all age groups, particularly the damage that is now being seen in many of the articular (joint) areas of the body. Remember this rule of trauma and overuse: *The body never forgets.* Trauma, no matter how seemingly trivial, can leave its "footprint" on the body, and the older the athlete, the less able he will be to remove these markers of damage and fully repair the physical insults.

With each step taken on land, the moving body puts pressure about equal to three times its total weight on the knees and hips. Add weights to knee-bend exercises or movements and the pressure can mount to 13 times body weight. The soft cartilage actually needs some of this pressure to squeeze it and push out the fluid that bathes the surrounding area. As a sponge is squeezed, once the pressure is released, the surrounding nourishing liquid is absorbed back into the cartilage tissue, bringing in nourishing substances that allow it to thrive and function properly. That is all well and good, as Nature has adapted humans to functioning on land, but within limits of intensity and endurance. If land-based exercise is not overdone and if no trauma is sustained, the knee can function as designed for many years.

Water, on the other hand, is not supposed to place the joints in this type of peril. But the knees still endure a slow, continuous barrage of mechanical insult with increasing intensity as swim training is increased over time. Intermittent discomfort can lead to continuous pain and then damage, often becoming permanent. Some athletes are blessed with

cartilage and connective tissue substance and design that adapts appropriately to the mechanical stresses place upon them, but most are susceptible to varying extents. Add the stresses of land-based movements, and many a promising career can be placed in jeopardy or at the very least pain and discomfort endured as daily burdens—not something to look forward to before coming to the pool. Chronic pain usually leads to permanent injury and dysfunction. Pain should be respected for what it does: alarm the sufferer. Have the pain treated to prevent its recurrence, and dysfunction may be prevented.

Of all the racing strokes, it is breaststroke that forces the knees to endure the greatest tension. The stroke requires the legs to snap crisply together through a motion that is truly not joint-friendly. The greatest stress is placed on the medial (inner) aspect of the knees as they whip toward each other to produce forward propulsion. In addition, the torque (twisting) effect upon the knee joint at each wall for each open turn can place the knee in

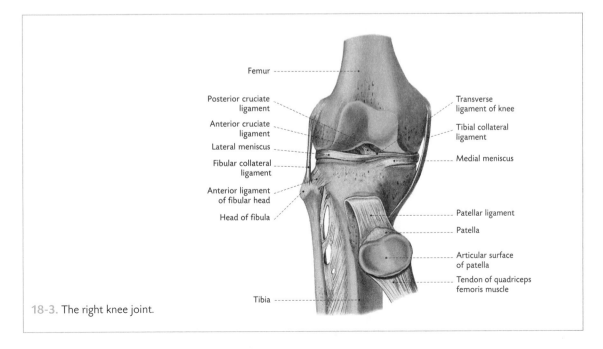

Femur

Posterior cruciate ligament

Anterior cruciate ligament

Lateral meniscus

Fibular collateral ligament

Anterior ligament of fibular head

Head of fibula

Transverse ligament of knee

Tibial collateral ligament

Medial meniscus

Patellar ligament

Patella

Articular surface of patella

Tendon of quadriceps femoris muscle

Tibia

18-3. The right knee joint.

a position that stretches and twists the ligaments, tendons, and menisci within the knee capsule to cause inflammation, swelling, and osteoarthritis. The menisci are fibro-cartilaginous, crescent-shaped discs at the inner (medial aspect) and outer (lateral aspect) areas of the knee joint that act to separate the cartilage ends of each bone and cushion their movement (see Fig. 18-3).

Pain with any type of movement is a sure sign of trouble. Normal movement of the knee (mostly up and down or with some slight side twisting) should be smooth, pain-free, and silent. I mention "silent" because a clicking or grinding noise emanating from the knee joint as it moves through its range of motion—called crepitus—is sometimes benign, sometimes a harbinger of trouble, especially if accompanied by pain. Sometimes you can actually feel the grinding more than hear it by placing your hand over the knee (or any joint for that matter) as it is moved. Normally, as Nature has intended, the

How to Distinguish Meniscal from Patellar Syndromes

What you notice	Meniscal	Patellar (kneecap)
Symptom site	Localized on side of knee	Pain in front of knee; pain right under kneecap
History of locking	Sometimes locks with pain	Grating, ratcheting, no locking
Weight-bearing activity	Pain during activity	Pain after activity, sometimes for hours
With "cutting" sports	Pain with rotation	Less pain, diffuse if any
When squatting	Pain going down in a squat	Pain coming up from a squat
When kneeling	Rarely painful	Pain with direct pressure on knee
When jumping or pushing off walls	May be painful	Definite pain, difficulty pushing off hard surfaces
Doing stairs or hills	Painful going up	Painful going down
When sitting	No pain	Pain in front of knee
Strengthening the supporting quads	Helpful but usually won't cure	Often the solution, with leg lifts
Swimming breaststroke	Pain as the legs come together as kick finishes	Pain as legs bend and heels come up to buttocks
Swimming other strokes	No real pain with dolphin and/or free or back kicks	Pain in the knee as it bends with kick
Pushing off wall in turns	Twisting off wall causes pain on sides of knee	Pain at knee with any turn leaving the walls

movement of the patella (kneecap) in its groove as the leg is extended and contracted includes the two most slippery surfaces in the human body.

Causes of Knee Pain

Deciphering knee pain, knowing which symptoms involve which internal structures, is extremely important for both coach and swimmer. The chart opposite might help in deciphering where and what the damage may be, but the sooner trouble can be properly diagnosed by the appropriate professional (usually a sports medicine or orthopedic practitioner), the sooner the proper treatment can be implemented and healing can occur or at least further damage from training can be halted.

Extensor-chain pain is by far the most common source of knee distress. Leg extension is the movement of the bent leg toward a straight position; the extensor chain is the series of muscles, tendons, cartilage, and bone that connect the thigh to the lower leg and hinge at the knee. The large quadriceps muscle attaches around the front two-thirds of the knee for natural protection, while the hamstrings attach in back of the knee. The kneecap (patella) is attached by means of its own tendon to both long bones of the leg (femur and tibia). If there is any defect (pain or diminished function) in the ability to extend the leg at the knee, the ability to explode off the starting block or spring off the walls in a streamline fashion will be hampered, as will the ability to kick with force in most positions, especially breaststroke.

As a "poor man's" guide to differential diagnosis, I will describe the most prominent types of pain, their causes, and the associated symptoms with movement. This is by no means intended to be used by coach, parent, or athlete in place of qualified professional care. This is simply a good quick outline that raises awareness and places caution at the center of the training regimen. As mentioned above, a swimmer with pain, injury, or difficulty in this area should be taken to a skilled practitioner who is experienced in treating injuries of this sort.

The meniscus gets involved when a twisting stress is placed upon the knee joint. This can happen acutely on land with a misstep or a quick cutting motion or a forceful sideways movement against the knee. It can also arise from chronic and repetitive stress on the knees (as is seen with veteran swimmers), producing slow degeneration and tearing. *Meniscal pain* is localized to the side of the knee with the tear. It allows the tear to produce a flap of tissue that can get caught and compressed between the long bones of the leg. This can give the knee the sensation of a painful "locking." This type of discomfort is usually sharp and happens with twisting and cutting movements of the knee.

A meniscus tear causes pain with a full squat, hurts when climbing up stairs, and can produce swelling at the knee. Twisting tests for a meniscus tear will produce a painful, palpable "clunk." Exercising and strengthening the joint-protecting quadriceps will help in recovery, along with appropriate rest from the offending movements, only if the tear is very small and the internal damage is minimal. But if the tear is moderate to severe, surgery will probably be needed to repair the damage.

Patellar pain, on the other hand, stems from damage to another internal structure of the knee joint. The kneecap is a wedge-shaped structure that normally slides up and down in its groove during extensor chain movements. When the kneecap tracks poorly in this groove, painful overuse problems usually result. Normal motion of the patella in the groove does not cause degeneration or pain. Pain with lessened mobility is often characteristic of patella inflammation. This inflammation is usually related to chronic stress at the site from on-land exercise or movement: leaning directly on the knees, running downhill, deep-knee bends, or squats with or without added weights. Kneeling puts direct pressure on a sore or inflamed patella and will produce definite localized pain. Jumping and landing against rigid things (ground, cement, wood flooring, etc.) will also produce knee pain.

A condition peculiar to women is the *bowstring effect of the kneecap*. This comes about when women's wider hips force the kneecap to track outward from its natural groove. Sometimes quadriceps atrophy is the culprit, allowing the knee joint to move out of line of the groove Nature intended. Pain or discomfort starts diffusely directly behind the kneecap. There is no locking of the knee joint *per se*, but a "ratcheting" sensation is felt with movement. Pain is often noticed after physical movement even if the athlete is at rest. An easy diagnostic test for patella pain involves dropping down to a full squat: there should be no pain dropping down, but rising up again will definitely be uncomfortable. The pain is felt right under the kneecap.

What helps in rehabilitation of kneecap inflammation is to strengthen the supporting musculature around the knee joint to keep the bending of the knee in proper alignment. Anti-inflammatory medication and ice after trauma, and then heat the next day or two when trauma has subsided some, can work to get the inflammatory condition under control.

Technique and Well-Timed Rest

I would have to say, and I think most who know the sport would agree, that the single most important element in injury prevention in swimming is correct technique. It helps to have been taught the right way early on; neuromuscularly, this is a big advantage. Good technique is something that should stay with you forever. Sports people call it "muscle memory"; scientists call it "neurological adaptation." Put any name to it you want, but it is the coach and athlete who must understand that this requires constant reminding and training, because the human element brings in mistakes and faults over time unless we take great care to prevent them. Call it laziness, call it carelessness, call it lack of focus: it all comes down to taking the time to do it right and not settling for just moving through water. One need not be a born swimmer: I have seen highly motivated, talented athletes who have come to swimming relatively late make it their business to learn quickly and correctly how to perform the most efficient movements through water, which seems to emphasize how much a positive attitude means.

I would be remiss if I didn't include the one thing that requires no exertion of the athlete: *complete rest*. Correctly timed rest periods allow the body to heal itself and recover sufficiently to adapt to the stresses it has been put through, and ultimately to achieve a higher level of condition all around. With proper recovery nutrition, this is what allows the athlete to rise to higher and higher levels of condition and performance.

Sun Protection

Swimmers who train outdoors need to take one special precaution: they must guard against the sun's deleterious effects on the body. The two main areas of concern are the exposed skin and the eyes. Skin cancer is becoming much more frequent and is showing up in patients still in their late teens. And cataracts (usually an old person's syndrome), the clouding of the lens of the eye due to excess cellular growth from the sun's ultraviolet rays, is also showing up more and more with early symptoms in younger people.

What most people do not realize is the double-dosing of the sun on the water: direct rays and even more dangerous rays reflected off the water. The sun's radiation emits high energy that our eyes cannot detect but that we can certainly feel. Swimmers who train in the sun with tinted goggles that are poorly made (not of a poly-carbonate substance) and not UV-coated are leaving themselves open to both cataract formation and retinal damage. Any tinted eyewear that reduces the squint reflex could allow more of the damaging rays to penetrate the back of the eye unless a protective UV coating is present. This also holds true for anyone spending time on deck—coaches, trainers, parents, siblings: around the pool, sunglasses should be the rule. Gray and smoke lenses are the best choices for protection to the eyes and allow for clearer vision.

The two types of radiation that concern us are UVA and UVB. The "A" rays penetrate tissue more deeply than the "B" and can do harm from sunrise to sunset. UVB radiation, which has the capacity to burn tissue, is worst when the sun is at its peak, usually between 10 a.m. and 3 p.m. Suffice it to say for our purposes here that the body needs to be adequately protected at all times from this danger. Since our natural UV-protective ozone layer is diminishing steadily from greenhouse gas build-up, it has come to the situation where the sun, which took one hour when I was a teenager to burn my skin, now takes only 15 minutes.

Many manufacturers have come up with sun-protective formulas that coat a swimmer's exposed skin even while he or she is in the water. No matter what the SPF (sun protection factor) or what claims the label makes, most offer no more than 90 minutes of adequate protection (less for fair-skinned swimmers or in strong sun). A reapplication will provide additional protection for only 30 to 40 minutes more. There is a definite daily amount of UV that the body can absorb; then it has to be moved inside. The protective gel, lotion, cream, or spray must be applied liberally at least 30 minutes before exposure to allow time for the active ingredients to penetrate the layers of the skin. People on deck should also *never* stay there without sporting a wide-brimmed sun-protective hat. Palm leaf is better than simple straw. Dark-colored clothing protects better than light clothing. For those fair-haired, light-eyed sun-worshipers: get wise. The sun may be good for the earth and even a little bit for us, but it can kill. The most dangerous type of skin cancer, melanoma, is on the rise to epidemic proportions; and it knows no bounds of age. The younger the person when overexposed repeatedly to the sun, the greater the tendency to form skin cancer. I speak from personal experience. I have had nine burned out and several more pre-cancers frozen, all because I couldn't get enough sun when I was a lifeguard at the local pool and the beach. Hindsight is always 20/20. Learn from my mistakes. Though we really didn't know that much in the early 1960's about the absolute dangers of excess sun exposure, now we do.

CHAPTER 19

Dehydration

If you find yourself in a state of dehydration, you have made a mistake. Whether you are preparing for intense competition, trying to meet the demands of rigorous training, or going through the all-important recovery from same, if there is simply not enough liquid in your body, then your performance will suffer and your recovery will be impaired. Even your mental acuity may be compromised.

Relying on the body's thirst mechanism is fool's play at best. One of the core dictums of sports medicine is "drink before you are thirsty and after you are not." Think about those words and make them clear in your mind. Don't wait until thirst becomes a prominent drive, and don't just drink a bit and then stop because the immediate driving thirst has been satisfied. I mention this for good reason: If you are thirsty, you are no doubt dehydrated already and have been for several minutes. Most non-athletes walk around in a state of at least partial dehydration much of the time, becoming aware that something is wrong only when they're challenged physically. And the older one gets, the less reliable the thirst alert becomes. In almost 40% of the elderly population, the thirst mechanism is so weak that it is often mistaken for hunger!

There are several seemingly sophisticated products available to help the athlete rehydrate. Many serve, or claim to serve, the purpose of fueling the muscles, providing a recovery environment for "spent" or damaged muscles, or replenishing electrolytes that have been lost through the body's heat-dissipation mechanism (sweating). But the single most important element is water.

It may seem ironic that swimmers, who are literally immersed in water for most of their training, can become dehydrated. But swimmers sweat like any other athlete who trains vigorously. Ask any swimmer who has come to the pool without the water bottle how quickly he gets cotton-mouthed. And this is made worse if the ambient air and water temperatures rise higher than they should so that body heat can't be dissipated. Swimming outdoors in a cooler, dryer environment will also parch the athlete more quickly.

Water in the Body

Water is second only to oxygen in importance to life. A healthy man's total body weight is about 60% water; a woman's is about 50%. We can survive losses of up to 40% of our body weight in fat, carbohydrate, and protein, but a water loss of only 9% of body weight can be fatal. Approximately two-thirds of the water in our bodies is contained inside our cells. The remainder is outside the cells, transporting fuel and waste to and from sites of metabolic activity.

Water within the body plays several important roles in exercise, mostly related to the blood's capacity to carry various elements (oxygen, fatty acids and amino acids, carbon dioxide and other metabolic wastes) to and from the organs' cells. Water also plays a large role in heat dissipation from muscles and the regulation of blood pressure and cardiovascular functioning.

An interesting relationship develops when the body is forced to handle vigorous exercise. Metabolic oxidation during muscular contraction actually produces water as a by-product. But this accounts for only about a tenth of the total water lost during exercise. Mainly, the body loses water from evaporation through the skin, evaporation through exhaled

Controlled Conditions

For indoor training, the optimum conditions are a water temperature of 80°F, ambient temperature of 75°F to 80°F, humidity between 60% and 70%, and a constant inflow of fresh air. Outdoors, more factors come into play. The water temperature should be around 82°F if the air temperature is below 80°F and the sun is low in the sky, not directly overhead. If the air is cooler—say, in the high 60's to low 70s—the water temperature should be 83°F or 84°F. Some may say this is too hot and that the working body produces sufficient heat to suffice for a training session, but in cooler water with cooler ambient air, swimmers with low body fat will start to shiver more quickly and waste energy. In addition, colder water increases the risk of muscle tears. Yes, the body warms itself to a certain extent with movement, but down time during recovery or the evaporative-cooling effect outdoors can allow the muscles to cool too much if the environment is chilly. A dehydrated body is more susceptible to almost any stress, including a cooler ambiance. A well-hydrated athlete is more resistant to all stresses.

air, and excretion from the kidneys and the large intestine. At rest, the kidneys excrete about 2 ounces of water per hour. The kidneys do excrete more as the metabolic rate increases, but only up to a point. If the body senses that the fluid loss is occurring too rapidly, it will compensate by producing an antidiuretic hormone, greatly decreasing production of urine. What is produced in the kidneys becomes very concentrated (deep yellow in color), odoriferous, acidic, and loaded with various endogenous minerals. In fact, if this were to become a constant condition on a near-daily basis, the athlete could wind up with a kidney stone, since many of the body's minerals precipitate out of solution in an acidic environment.

In this book, we are concerned with every factor that influences a swimmer's ability to perform. Becoming dehydrated, even minimally, can impair muscular contraction to the point that the swimmer feels heavy and slow, as if he or she is swimming in thick syrup instead of water. Like a piston in an automobile engine that seizes when it doesn't have enough oil for lubrication, the muscle fibers (myofibrils) will rub against each other excessively, producing too much friction and creating excessive heat in addition to the heat resulting from metabolism. This slows down movement, increases the likelihood of muscle-fiber spasm, and noticeably reduces power. It noticeably becomes much harder to get across the pool. Many studies have shown that dehydrated athletes cannot tolerate prolonged (greater than 60 minutes) vigorous exercise and heat stress. The heat stress factor is mitigated somewhat for swimmers because the water they are immersed in has a much better heat-drawing capacity (a greater "heat sink") than air. But as intensity of training increases, so do the effects of internal heat production, and so even a fully immersed swimmer will dehydrate during an intense practice session.

The impact of dehydration on the cardiovascular and heat-regulatory systems is quite predictable. Fluid loss decreases plasma volume; this, in turn, decreases blood pressure, which then reduces blood flow to the muscles and skin. In an effort to deal with all this, heart rate increases. Because less blood reaches the skin overall, the body retains more heat in areas with a lot of muscle activity. That's why hard-working swimmers often have flushed upper backs (and this is one of the markers I use to see who is really pushing in the water). As fluid loss approaches 2% of total body weight, both heart rate and body temperature are elevated during exercise. If dehydration progresses to 4% or 5% of body weight, the capacity for prolonged aerobic effort declines by 20% to 30%.

In athletic endeavors that require a mix of aerobic and anaerobic activity or more anaerobic than aerobic activity (like races lasting three minutes or less, which covers most traditional swimming events), the drop-off in performance is not as dramatic, but it does occur—especially if multiple events are swum over a relatively short period. And even a small drop off in performance is enough to make a notable difference in close competition.

Opposite is a chart of the body's negative responses to dehydration. Unfortunately, most athletes do not improve immediately upon rehydration; the time delay can be hours before the athlete approaches optimum training condition again. It is always much better to prevent dehydration than to try to correct it.

The Biochemistry of Dehydration

Electrolyte loss during sweating is another product of dehydration. Again, swimmers don't sweat as much as other athletes, but they *do* sweat and they do lose body fluids. Sweat is about 99% water, but it is also a filtrate of blood plasma; it contains many electrolytes, including sodium (Na^+), chloride (Cl^-), potassium (K^+), magnesium (Mg^{++}), and calcium (Ca^{++}). A drop in calcium can produce a condition called low-calcium tetany, which causes painful,

Alterations in Function and Performance Due to Dehydration

Function	Dehydration	Rehydration
Cardiovascular		
Blood volume/plasma volume	diminished	delayed correction
Cardiac output	diminished	delayed partial recovery
Stroke volume	diminished	delayed partial recovery
Heart rate	diminished/then increased	delayed correction
Metabolic		
Aerobic capacity (VO_2max)	somewhat diminished	stays diminished
Anaerobic power	somewhat diminished	stays diminished
Anaerobic capacity	somewhat diminished	stays diminished
Blood lactate, peak value	diminished	stays diminished
Buffer capacity of blood	diminished	delayed weak recovery
Lactate threshold	diminished	delayed response
Muscle and liver glycogen	diminished	stays diminished
Thermoregulation and fluid balance		
Electrolytes in muscle and blood	diminished	no change
Exercise core temperature	increased	delayed cool down
Sweat rate	diminished	delayed response
Skin blood flow	diminished	delayed response
Performance		
Muscular strength	slightly diminished	slightly diminished
Muscular endurance	diminished	stays diminished
Muscular power	diminishes over time	delayed weak response
Muscle movement to exhaustion	greatly diminished	delayed weak response
Total work performed	diminished	stays diminished

debilitating muscle spasms like "charley-horses." This can stop a practice or a performance dead in its tracks and keep a swimmer out of commission for the rest of the day. A lack of potassium and magnesium can produce muscle twitching that weakens the musculature's effort, including that of the heart muscles if enough is depleted. And the loss of salt (sodium chloride), which draws and retains water wherever it is needed in the body (the osmotic effect), can negatively influence water balance.

As the kidneys slow urine production to hold onto fluid, they produce a powerful hormone, the strong antidiuretic chemical mentioned above, called *aldosterone*. This prevents the kidneys from excreting sodium and chloride ions. The increased concentration of these ions signals the hypothalamus to produce the thirst alert so we will increase our fluid intake to dilute the salt back down to normal. But this is not an immediate response. Someone who becomes thirsty in the middle of vigorous training or competition has entered the "zone of metabolic distress," and his or her performance will most likely stay

> ## The Three Rules of Hydration
>
> 1. Your need to replace body fluid is greater than your need to replace electrolytes.
> 2. Since the thirst mechanism does not reflect your state of hydration, *drink before you are thirsty and after you are not.*
> 3. Adequate fluid intake during vigorous training reduces the risk of dehydration and energy depletion and optimizes the body's cardiovascular and thermoregulatory functions.

diminished for the immediate future. The damage is quick and lasting: up to 48 hours may be needed for electrolyte and fluid rebalancing, which is an unacceptable time delay for those training daily or racing several days in row. This is where commercial recovery drinks can be useful: They have enough salt in them, along with other ions, to actually create a slight thirst and trigger the athlete to drink more, keeping dehydration at bay.

CHAPTER 20

Eat to Compete

Putting aside the so-called breakthrough diets hyped wherever you turn today, an athlete's nutrition can be simply stated: it must be high in quality carbohydrate, moderate in muscle-friendly protein, and low in fat. It should also include sufficient vitamins and minerals and plenty of fluid. How we supply these headliners is the key to good competition nutrition.

The timing of the "refueling" episodes is also important. After vigorous exercise, depleted muscle craves sustenance. Its ability to absorb and deposit glycogen is maxed out within 2 hours of having completed exercise. The longer you wait after this window, the less the muscles will reabsorb quickly and so they will not have a full stock of energy supply for the next exercise bout. The liver, which functions to build and store energy-providing carbohydrates, also senses depletion and craves substances to implant in its tissue in the form of glycogen. Since most of the body's stores of glycogen are deposited in the liver, refueling within this two-hour window is very important.

As a rule the body can store not more than 1200 calories of blood sugar and can supply about 800 more from its own fat stores, a total of 2000 calories. These can be consumed within a single prolonged intense workout, leaving the athlete energy-depleted and unable to power a following training session. Even the brain becomes dulled if it is short-changed in its supply of glucose; therefore it is mandatory that energy drinks be consumed before, during, and after each practice to allow a seriously training swimmer to keep going.

Nutritional Needs

There are four main nutritional requirements the athlete must meet:

Water: to replace fluid lost as sweat and through intense and prolonged exhalations; needed in order to hydrate muscle fibers for smoother, more efficient contractions; to regulate heat production and allow it to dissipate through sweat and exhalation; to keep the blood volume up for adequate circulation to the working muscles and vital organs: and to aid in glycogen fixation, a process by which stored carbohydrate is able to be transported to the working muscles and liver.

Electrolytes: to replenish essential minerals (calcium, potassium, sodium, chloride, magnesium, zinc, etc.) lost in sweat. Calcium, as we discussed in Chapter 19, prevents low-calcium tetany, which can produce intense muscle spasm; potassium and magnesium are needed to help regulate skeletal and cardiac muscle firing and subsequent contraction; and salt (sodium chloride) is needed to regulate osmotic fluid effects and also to allow proper muscle contractions. Zinc is of particular importance, since it helps catalyze enzymes in the red blood cells that clear out excess carbon dioxide (CO_2) during intense exercise. And if CO_2 is reduced, more oxygen can take its place in the circulation; more oxygen means the ability to make more energy. The serious athlete-in-training should consume 15 mg of zinc daily (as opposed to a minimum of 1 mg for the average adult). Multivitamins tend to have plenty, but fortified cereals, lean red meat, sardines and anchovies, and beans are also good sources of zinc.

Quality carbohydrate in a mixture of simple and complex forms: to build up blood concentrations of glucose, the prime fuel source of muscle and brain, but also to prevent glucose spiking and the attendant insulin response, which then lowers blood sugar excessively, and to replenish the stores of muscle and liver glycogen, the body's premium-grade reserve fuel for near-instantaneous availability of chemical energy.

Quality protein: to supply amino acids that repair and regenerate muscle fibers and promote muscle growth and adaptation. Different proteins are absorbed by the musculature at different rates. This provides for an extended environment of muscle repair and replenishment. Muscle tissue is normally composed of 70% water but of only 22% protein (a pound of muscle only has 3.5 ounces of protein in it), because muscle requires lots of water to be in place to bathe the contracting fibers as they rub against each other to help dissipate heat and reduce friction. Even a small degree of water loss, then, can impair performance. We've already discussed the process of rehydration (see Chapter 19). Refueling muscles with carbohydrate is not as straightforward; it is a case once again of *what, how much,* and *when.*

Carbohydrates for Athletes

The typical American diet (in which 45% of the daily calories come from carbohydrate, 15% from protein, and 40% from fat) actually allows depletion of muscle glycogen after three days of intense training. When carbohydrates (carbs) are increased to 65% of calories (with 15% fats and 20% protein), muscle glycogen is restored within 24 hours. Carbohydrates, it has been found, are deposited into muscle faster and to a greater extent when protein is added at the same time. The proportion of each that produces the greatest benefit is a 4:1 ratio of quality carbs to quality protein. Many studies have recently shown that to maximize the rate of glycogen repletion, carbohydrate consumption should be a priority after exercise. One and one-half grams of complex carbs per kilogram (2.2 pounds) of body weight should be consumed immediately after intense muscular activity, with half that amount added every hour for about five hours. Conversely, delaying carbohydrate ingestion for several hours will actually slow glycogen repletion.

Glycogen replenishment is actually a two-phase process. In the first hour after exercise, a muscle transporter protein known as GLUT-4 opens the gates to the muscle cells, allowing glucose to flow in, thereby facilitating the rapid resynthesis of muscle glycogen. A second, slower but longer lasting process takes place, in which carbohydrate-hungry muscles become more sensitive to insulin, the anabolic hormone that helps drive glucose into muscle cells. This second phase can take as long as 72 hours post exercise to complete. But athletes-in-training can't wait this long for glucose, so they require immediate consumption of quality carbohydrates to start the GLUT-4 process right after intense exercise.

When you are figuring out carb intake, it's good to understand the relationship between glucose and fructose. Both sugars have the basic, classic 6-carbon chains, but only glucose can be readily used for energy by the muscles and the brain. Fructose's molecules have to be rearranged into glucose before the body can use it; it is drawn to the liver, where it is transformed into glucose and then into its stored form, glycogen.

The chart on page 140 shows various fruits and their glucose and fructose contents. Fruits with more glucose than fructose, like bananas, will provide more instant energy. Those with more fructose than glucose, like apples, will provide more prolonged energy. There are many with a close ratio of both sugars, like blueberries, that provide both quick and sustained energy. Fructose, it should be noted, sometimes causes a bit of gastrointestinal discomfort. The body can come to tolerate it with repeated exposure.

Protein for Athletes

The body's digestion and incorporation of protein is even more complicated than its absorption of carbohydrates. Carbs are readily stored, but the body has no "protein store" beyond what makes up the musculature, energy enzymes, and other tissues that incorporate protein in their structure and function. So protein levels are in a constant state of flux. Complex muscle tissue can be broken down to provide amino acids to the amino acid pool that then supplies protein building blocks wherever they are needed. An adequate amino acid supply is required after vigorous activity so that broken-down muscle tissue can be rebuilt quickly and strongly.

Since all protein is constructed from amino-acid building blocks that are chemically bonded together, what "blocks" we take in determines what proteins (and in what quality) we can build and/or rebuild. There are about 20 amino acids that can be utilized from digested whole foods to build and repair protein tissue. Of these, about half are *essential amino acids*, which cannot be synthesized by the body—they must be taken in from an outside source such as ingested food or supplements. There are also about 10 nonessential amino acids, which the body does manufacture. (Glutamine is the exception, as we will discuss in Chapter 21.)

Glucose and Fructose in Various Fruits*

Fruit	Glucose	Fructose
Apple	2.3	7.6
Apricot	1.6	0.7
Banana	4.22	2.7
Blackberries	3.1	4.1
Blueberries	3.5	3.6
Cantaloupe	1.2	1.8
Grapefruit	1.3	1.2
Grapes (American)	6.6	6.9
Grapes (European)	6.5	7.6
Kiwi (no skin)	5.0	4.4
Mango	0.7	2.9
Nectarine	1.2	1.1
Orange	2.2	2.5
Papaya	1.4	2.7
Peach	1.1	1.3
Pear	1.9	6.4
Pineapple	2.9	2.1
Plum	2.7	1.8
Raspberries	3.5	3.2
Strawberries	2.2	2.5
Watermelon	1.6	3.3

*Glucose and fructose values per 100 grams (roughly 4 ounces) of fruit.

The body absorbs various proteins at different rates. Whey, the straw-colored liquid that comes from the separated curd of milk during the cheese-making process, is the most quickly absorbed and is directed to the "hungry" post-exercise musculature (about 2 hours after consumption), followed by egg whites and soy (about 5 hours after consumption). Casein, the phospho-protein ingredient in milk that becomes the main substance in cheese, has a complementary effect to whey in that it is more slowly absorbed (about 7 hours after consumption) but sends a steady stream of replenishing amino acids to the musculature. With its two types of muscle-friendly protein, you could say that milk is the near-perfect competition food. Soy provides some benefit, since it is a complementary source of protein, but it is not as easily used by the muscles.

Real Food for Swimmers

Now that we've discussed some biochemistry of nutrition, let's consider some "real-time" nutrition needs and sources for swimmers. Correct calorie choices are a must, even though temptation stalks us everywhere as we patronize restaurants and wander supermarket aisles.

To figure out an appropriate calorie intake for the day without athletic training for a non-elite but determined participant in sports as he enters his 30's, we must first determine his resting metabolic rate (RMR). This is found by multiplying body weight by 10; it is the minimum number of calories needed to run all the systems of the body, basically what you need just to stay alive. (Most biological processes slow down after age 60, so caloric demands are also somewhat reduced unless the aging athlete keeps pushing activity.) Next we need to figure out how many calories are needed to get

Sample Calorie Intake

A moderately active 40-year-old 190-pound man using mixed strokes with fast interval training for an average of 90 minutes will consume about 1,100 calories during the practice session. If fins are used, add another 30% to bring the total to over 1400 calories. Then, because swimmers usually do not (or cannot) swim fast for a whole workout, subtract 10% to 20% to get a 1,200- to 1,300-calorie burn. The rate of calorie burn will continue above RMR for at least two hours after practice; this should be figured into total caloric need for the day. When we add up the values for this man, we get a total caloric need of 1,900 calories + 950 calories + 1,200 calories = 4,050 calories. These calories should be in the proportions most easily handled by the body—65% carbohydrates (2632 cal.), 20% protein (810 calories), and 15% fat (607 calories).

through the day. If the swimmer is rather sedentary apart from moderate athletic training (having a desk job, for example), take 30% of the calculated RMR and add it to the above figure. If the swimmer is moderately active outside the pool (on his or her feet, as a teacher or salesperson might be), add 50% of the RMR. And if the swimmer is quite active (in a mobile job or as an elite athlete training more than once a day), add 70% of the RMR. A younger athlete (high school into college) or an elite-level athlete into his 30's will need to supply more than listed. One thousand calories or higher per day than listed above is nothing unusual so long as body weight remains at the chosen optimal level for height and body type.

For Masters athletes, who have a tendency as they age to accumulate inches around the middle and elsewhere because of slowed overall metabolic rate, appropriate concern and effort to control body weight comes free with training. A few examples of effort-and-expenditure follow. Calories that can be burned when working out: a 150-pound, 50-year-old man in good shape, for example, burns about 10.6 calories a minute during a fast freestyle swim. A 170-pound man of the same age bracket uses 12 calories a minute, and a 190-pound man consumes about 14 calories a minute. If he is using fins, add 3 to 5 more calories per minute.

Swimmers have ferocious carbohydrate cravings, which should be satisfied to ensure adequate energy intake. Whole grain cereals and rice, whole wheat breads, quality granola bars, fruits, juices, and pastas are great sources of good carbs. A small bag of potato chips delivers nearly the same number of carbs as a slice of whole wheat bread, but with 10 times the fat. In addition, the bread has more fiber and protein and a little iron and calcium to boot. The idea is to get as many nutrients as possible with your calories.

A simple trick to estimate roughly how many quality carbs you need to ingest as an athlete is to multiply your body weight by three. This gives you the number of grams you'll need. Each gram of carbohydrate contains about 4 calories. So for a 190-pound man, this works out to 190 x 3 = 570 grams of carbs. Then 570 x 4 (calories/gram) approximately equals 2,300 calories, close to the figure we derived using the more complex percentage formula at left.

The athlete should always be open to trying something new rather than settling for the usual fast (though often tasty) food. Eating junk food is permissible once in a while, but athletes should strive to make quality food choices for optimum performance.

Many young athletes not only make poor food choices, they also don't eat a varied enough diet. Even those wanting to eat healthy often place too narrow restrictions on what they think they can eat. They become fat-phobic and reliant on food supplements at the expense of a rich, varied selection of nutrient-laden foods.

Lots of swimmers tend to under-eat because they claim not to have enough time, because they've absorbed from their coaches and teammates the message that fat people don't swim fast, or because they don't understand the concepts of energy intake and expenditure. Eating five to six times daily is the correct way to fuel up. In addition to breakfast, lunch, and dinner, a mid-morning snack and a pre-practice snack with hydration can make all the difference in the workout. Having a small, high-quality carb-and-protein meal to aid in recovery and refuel brain and body within an hour after the workout is extremely wise. Also, energy bars that contain a good balance of carbs, proteins, and fats are great to have on hand at all times, and nowadays they taste pretty good, too. Keep them in your locker, swim bag, or car wherever you go.

Sample Meal Plan

A sample meal plan for an adult in regular training requiring 4,000 calories a day is:

Replacement drink to be taken to practice: 24 oz of liquid made up of 12 oz grape juice and 12 oz Powerade®: 300 calories (7% of daily total), 55 grams carbs, 0 grams protein, 0 grams fat. Powerade is selected because it has malto-dextrin as one of it main energy sources. This provides an extended-release form of carbohydrate which is mixed with fructose and sucrose in the formula to provide a balanced supply of energy.

Breakfast: 1 1/2 cups grape juice, 1 cup strawberries, 1 1/2 cups Total® cereal, 1 cup 1% milk, 1 roll, 1 teaspoonful Smart Balance® spread, 1 tablespoonful strawberry jam: 651 calories (16% of daily total), 127 grams carbs, 19 grams protein, 10 grams fat.

Mid-morning snack: 1 bagel, 1 teaspoonful Smart Balance spread, 1 tablespoonful jam, 8 oz Powerade, 8 oz grape juice: 400 calories (10% of daily total), 80 grams carbs, 7 grams protein, 6 grams of fat.

Lunch: 1 lean roast beef sandwich, 8 oz cranberry or grape juice diluted with equal amount of water, 1 medium banana, 2/3 cup potato salad, 1 peach or nectarine: 900 calories (22% of daily total), 144 grams carbs, 25 grams of protein, 26 grams of fat.

Mid-afternoon snack: 3 pretzels, 16 oz Gatorade®, 1 cup of grapes: 345 calories (9% of daily total), 80 grams carbs, 5 grams protein, 2 grams fat.

Dinner: 1 1/2 cups of chicken chow mein, 1 cup of rice, 12 oz iced tea, 1 orange, 1 cup 1% milk: 800 calories (20 daily total), 90 grams carbs, 60 grams protein, 18 grams fat.

Evening snack: 1 banana, 1 cup 1 percent milk, 1 cup non-fat frozen yogurt, 16 oz Powerade: 600 calories (13% of daily total), 98 grams carbs, 12 grams fat.

The list on pages 143–144 tells *what* to eat *when*. It offers up several meal choices that can be timed in relation to workouts. One important item should be noted: Whenever an energy source is consumed

Ed Nessel's Energy Drink

I've concocted an energy drink that tastes great, has about 600 calories total, 40 grams of high-quality mixed proteins (whey, casein, soy, egg), only 5 grams of fat, and plenty of healthy stuff like fiber, vitamins C, E, and B-complex, and other antioxidants. If I am going to the weight room to put in an honest hour there, I take this drink about an hour before I leave home. If I am training in the pool that day, I take this within an hour of getting home so I know the nutrients will get to my muscles quickly and help regenerate my energy stores.

Here's my recipe. Blend for 30 seconds and enjoy! Makes a few glasses' worth of high-octane fuel.

- 1 cup egg substitute such as Egg-Beaters®
- 1 cup vanilla soy milk
- 1 cup frozen strawberries
- 1 cup red grape juice
- 1 banana
- 1 cup nonfat flavored yogurt
- 2 scoops vanilla-flavored whey protein

before a workout, it should consist of whey protein mixed with other appropriate ingredients in shake form.

When to Fuel and Refuel the Machine for Serious Training

Though proper eating is vital for those wishing to push their bodies to perform well in their chosen sport, correct supplementation is a very important add-on. Some foodstuffs are absorbed more quickly and thoroughly than others (e.g., whey protein); some are needed to refuel "hungry" body parts throughout the day (dairy, egg and soy proteins). Others are added to aid the psychology of consumption (dark chocolate). It is absolutely true: many athletes emotionally need certain foods and tastes to soothe their psyches after pushing so hard in training. Circadian rhythm also dictates certain needs in athletes, who are used to training at certain times. Grape juice should be consumed before and during vigorous exercise to help prevent platelets from sticking, which allows the blood to circulate more quickly to the muscles that need to be fueled. The list below gives you an idea of what to eat when.

1. **If you train mornings before 10 a.m.**
   1A. *Preworkout fueling 30 to 60 min. before training:* Most intake should be in liquid form: 12 oz Accelerade® liquid or power mix of the same into liquid; 1 banana or 2 slices watermelon; or small bowl oatmeal with skim milk and banana and 12 oz whey protein + Eggbeater® + soy milk mixture; bring 32 oz of energy drink or grape juice/Powerade mix if workout is longer than 60 min.; consume throughout.
   1B. *Breakfast within 1 hour of workout:* 3-egg equivalent of Egg-Beaters omelet + mushrooms and onions if tolerated + Canadian bacon; 12 oz fresh juice; coffee or tea to taste; 12 oz Endurox®.
   1C. *Midmorning snack:* Flavored liquid or solid yogurt; choice of fresh fruit, preferably in the berry family; at least 12 oz of Fusion® juice, a concentrated mix of fruits and vegetables.
   1D. *Lunch:* Caesar salad with tomatoes, onions, grilled chicken, turkey or omega-3-rich fish (tilapia, salmon); or tuna salad

sandwich on whole wheat; or sardines and anchovies over a salad; 24 oz of liquid from juice, skim milk, and/or green tea.

1E. *Midafternoon snack:* Nuts, either peanut butter on crackers or a few handfuls of almond/cashew/raisin mix; can take 2 to 3 squares of dark chocolate; 12 to 16 oz coffee, tea, and/or juice.

1G. *Dinner:* Grilled fish, chicken, or fresh turkey, or 12 oz lean red meat; creamed spinach or green beans and corn; choice of tomatoes, onions, peppers, or a mix of same with olive oil dressing; sherbet or nonfat ice cream.

2. If you train at lunchtime between noon and 2 p.m.

2A. *Breakfast:* Flavored oatmeal with mixed fruit; liquid yogurt; energy drink of mixed proteins.

2B. *Mid-morning/pre-workout snack*: About 1 hour before training: 12 oz Accelerade liquid or powder into liquid; or a tall glass fat-free chocolate milk; glass of grape juice.

2C. *Lunch:* Following workout within 1 hour: tall glass of juice; 12 oz Endurox; western omelet; chocolate milk; 12 oz fruit-flavored sherbet.

2D. *Mid-afternoon snack:* Couple of handfuls of mixed nuts with dark chocolate M & M's.

2E. *Dinner:* Hearty bowl of soup; sliced lean roast beef open sandwich; sweet potato + mixed greens and/or carrots; mixed salad with plenty of tomatoes, flavored with olive-oil-based salad dressing; fat-free ice cream or sherbet.

3. If you train after work, between 5 and 8 p.m.

3A. *Breakfast:* Mixed grain cereal with berry fruit + skim milk; whole grain toast + jam + peanut butter; coffee/tea to taste.

3B. *Mid-morning snack:* 12 oz mixed protein + yogurt energy drink.

3C. *Lunch:* Soup; chicken breast sandwich with tomatoes; roll and butter; juice; coffee or green tea.

3D. *Mid-afternoon snack:* Tall glass of apple juice; 3 to 4 squares of dark chocolate; banana.

3E. *Pre-workout snack:* 12 oz Accelerade or equivalent amount of skim chocolate milk; glass of grape juice.

3F. *Dinner:* Within 1 hour of training session: grilled salmon or tilapia or sirloin steak; sweet potato + mixed vegetables; 12 oz Endurox drink.

CHAPTER 21

Helping the Body Heal

We all know the body can handle many types of stresses. Nature has provided for this or else none of us would grow out of adolescence, let alone age into maturity. A highly trained athlete can usually handle the physical stresses demanded by his sport to a greater extent than the so-called "weekend warrior." But there is one circumstance that has nothing to do with athletic prowess or good coaching or even high-minded determination, and it can make or break a competitor. That circumstance is physical trauma, whether from an accident, an overuse injury, or reparative surgery.

You've already read it: the body never forgets. Sooner, sometimes, rather than later, we blow a tire, we get a flat. We are forced off the road and have to stop and make a repair to get going again. The above is intended only as a metaphor for what our main focus is: the human body. The blown tire cannot repair itself, but much of the body can. And with the proper help, it can be on the road to meeting the desired and anticipated goals of success in swimming.

The "never forgets" part can come into play sooner and with more negative impact if we don't respect certain biochemical and physiological and sound public health tenets.

How the Body Heals

The body's first response to physical trauma is to isolate and then adapt the affected tissue to try to lessen the extent of damage. Then regeneration begins, which takes time and energy, nutrients and hydration, rest and recovery. The most critical nutrients involved with healing include protein, enzyme cofactors, glucosamine, omega-3 fatty acids, zinc, vitamins A, C, and E, and iron. The fact that these substances can all be purchased over the counter affords the athlete and coach the opportunity to help the healing process along.

When the body is injured, its normal functions can become compromised. Depending upon the severity and the extent of physical trauma, the body's need for high-quality protein is substantially increased. The immune system is extremely dependent upon quality protein to manufacture all the important elements for keeping infection and inflammation from getting out of control. Several studies have shown that about 25% of hospitalized patients and as many as half of general surgery patients exhibit protein malnutrition. This can significantly lengthen the time of healing by allowing inflammation to linger and possible infection to fester. Also, the building of new blood vessels (*revascularization*) and the actual remodeling of tissue can both be delayed and impaired. Anyone undergoing major surgery can attest to the body's need for help in recovery, having experienced a dramatic loss in energy and a sustained increase in overall weakness.

Protein Supplementation

Much of this can be alleviated by the simple intake of quality protein starting about a week before elective surgery and adequate fluid intake before and after surgery. Prime sources of protein include fish, lean meats, eggs, or a quality vegetable protein such as soy. Soy is also available in powdered form that can be mixed in drinks or in yogurt. Several individual amino acids can provide an additional protein benefit. Increased intake of sulfur-containing amino acids such as *cysteine* and *methionine* (as found in eggs, for example) can shorten the inflammatory stage and lessen the amount of protein destroyed during inflammation.

The amino acid *arginine* functions as an antioxidant to kill bacteria and increase T-cell-mediated activity (from the thymus gland), which, in turn, also enhances immune function. Supplementation with arginine (found in many foods, including wheat, nuts, chocolate, red meat, and poultry) has been shown to increase significantly the amount of collagen deposited into a wound site during the healing process.

Glutamine is the most abundant amino acid in skeletal muscle protein, and as such, its uptake during stress tries to exceed that of any other amino acid. Because it is an effective nitrogen donor (all amino acids must have the element nitrogen as part of the molecular structure) and a precursor for protein synthesis, glutamine is also extremely important in helping to rebuild wounded tissues. The body can synthesize glutamine in small amounts for when it is at rest or moving gently. However, depending upon how vigorous the stress or intense the trauma, the body's ability to produce glutamine in joints and skeletal muscle can fall short of need. Endogenous sources (from within the body) are soon depleted by various causes: generalized sepsis (infection), extensive burns, major injury, surgery, intense exercise, and overtraining in athletes. Exogenous sources of glutamine (from outside the body by way of diet or supplementation) are needed to help in the healing process and overall recovery. It is now classified as a "conditionally essential" amino acid, meaning that as the need for it increases, the supply must come from outside the body in greater amounts.

Mineral Supplementation

There are a few front-liners among minerals whose absence when the body is physically stressed can inhibit the repair process. *Zinc* is a very powerful ally in supporting immune function and the healing process. We know that zinc levels decline dramatically under physical stresses, and we see that zinc wants to concentrate in wounds during the period of collagen synthesis and help strengthen new tissue. Those who are zinc deficient may suffer a compromised immune system response, which can delay closure of wounds and ulcers and cause the connective tissue (collagen) that does form to have a weaker tensile strength. The simple application of zinc right at the wound site in either spray or ointment form can reduce the size of the wound and shorten healing time even in patients who are not zinc deficient. Zinc is also useful when taken internally; I recommend that any athlete undergoing intense training take a vitamin supplement that contains it.

Iron is the other essential mineral nutrient that aids new cellular growth and wound healing. The enzyme *ribonucleotide reductase*, which requires iron as a co-factor, is essential for DNA synthesis. Since cells cannot divide without prior DNA synthesis, iron deficiency can impair the proliferation of all cells, some of which are involved in wound debridement (removal of dead or dying cells and other contaminants from the site of trauma) and healing. Iron-deficiency anemia can be a concern for menstruating women, and anemic patients of any age will also exhibit delayed wound healing.

Some salts of iron are absorbed better than others, and some are more irritating to the gut than others. Consult a knowledgeable pharmacist to help you make the best selection. For example, I like ferrous gluconate (Fergon™) because it is one of the least irritating iron salts to the gut, the quality of the supplement is good, and it allows good absorption through the gut to provide higher levels of iron in the blood and tissues where demand exists. As a rule, it is best to take vitamin C along with the iron supplement to ensure the proper oxidation state of the mineral for best absorption. Care must be taken, though, with children, the average male, and women not menstruating with regard to iron. This is not a harmless supplement. If more is ingested than needed over an extended period of time, a very serious inflammatory condition can arise in the liver which is as bad as it sounds: *hemochromatosis*.

Some minerals are needed only in small concentrations to have a positive effect on many metabolic processes. We call these *micronutrients*. *Copper* and *manganese* are examples; they act as co-factors for enzymes involved in collagen synthesis. If, for some reason, a deficiency existed for either of these two minerals, the overall healing process would be compromised.

Vitamin Supplementation

Vitamins, especially A, C, and E, play a significant role in recovery and wound healing. Giving *vitamin A* for 7 days after surgery increases lymphocyte (infection-fighting) activity and collagen synthesis and enhances the integrity of new scar tissue such that its "bursting strength" is increased. Large doses of A (more than 100,000 IU per day) can reverse post-surgical suppression of the immune system and speed up healing, but doses at this level can only be taken safely for no more than a week. During the recovery period from severe injury or infection, vitamin A in doses ranging from 10,000 IU to 25,000 IU per day can be safely used for a few weeks' duration. The reason for caution with this vitamin is that it is fat soluble and is readily stored in the body. Toxic levels that can hurt the joints and increase pressure on the brain are more easily reached than with water-soluble vitamins, which are more readily excreted daily through the kidneys.

The water-soluble *vitamin C*, meanwhile, increases the strength of new collagen formation and the rate of healing, enhances the immune system, and helps fight general infections. Severe traumas such as burns, fractures, or major surgery cause a substantial decrease in plasma vitamin C levels. The stresses associated with injuries and wound healing dramatically increase the body's overall need for C. Amounts as high as 1,000 mg (one gram) per day can safely be ingested for a few weeks. Studies have shown as much as a 42% reduction in blood vitamin C levels by the third day following major surgery if extra C is not ingested.

The caution here, even though the vitamin is excreted daily, concerns the kidneys. Since about 50% of vitamin C degrades to a molecule called oxylate, there is always the potential for kidney stones in the form of *calcium oxylate*, the most insoluble substance known in physiology. As soon as calcium and oxylate come together in solution, they immediately precipitate out in the urine as the salt calcium oxylate, first as gravel and eventually as stones as the gravel binds together. Adequate hydration with non-calcium and non-oxylate-containing liquids (water is best) will usually dilute the urine enough to help prevent this type of stone formation. Cranberry juice, for example, contains soluble oxylates; this is not a good choice to take with a lot of vitamin C because of the above potential reaction.

Vitamin E supplementation also enhances immune function and increases resistance to infection. But special benefits come from E's ability to help prevent the excessive free-radical destruction that seems to surround wounded tissue, thus reducing secondary damage and improving the healing process. Topical vitamin E has been touted as preventing or at least lessening scar formation if applied directly to a wound. Scar formation may be more a function of genetics than of vitamin effect, but it *has* been shown that vitamin E can lessen collagen formation and, thus, *keloids* (an excess laying down of dense fibrous tissue over a wound that bulges outward to augment the appearance of a scar). Location on the body and genetics play a strong part in keloid formation, though, suggesting that there may be something of a cosmetic effect with E. If the strength of wound closure is important, topical E should probably be avoided.

Other Supplementation

There are four ancillary substances that have been found to help the body deal with inflammation and damaged tissue. The first is *glucosamine*, a natural compound produced in the body that acts as a vital precursor of important large molecules needed to maintain the healthy function of connective tissue and joints and to help heal damage. The substances that glucosamine produces are glycoproteins, glycolipids, and glycosaminoglycans or mucopolysaccharides—large biochemical descriptions of the components of the various tissues that make up ligaments, cartilage, synovial fluid, mucous membranes, and blood vessels. In cases of serious and extensive trauma, whether from an accident or from overtraining, the body's store of glucosamine or its ability to produce same may not be sufficient to meet the demands of tissue under repeated physical stress or trying to heal. The benefits of glucosamine are so well known that it can now be found on the shelves of pharmacies, health-food stores, and supermarkets. It has no disturbing side effects, so for those needing recovery and regeneration from the body's response to intense training, injury, or trauma, glucosamine should be a mainstay.

A second group of substances whose benefits are becoming better known are *omega-3 fatty acids*. Found naturally in several species of fatty fish, these are very powerful antioxidants that head right for damaged or over-stressed areas and act to reduce or prevent inflammation. They also act to help keep a healthy blood lipid profile (cholesterol and triglycerides) and are integral components of cell-wall architecture. A deficiency of omega-3s compromises the transport of important substances across cell membranes, which can also contribute to poor wound healing. Omega-3s can act as blood thinners, so caution should be considered if you are taking aspirin or other anticoagulant medication. Many fish are great sources of this antioxidant, for example: tilapia, salmon, herring, sardines, anchovies, and other deep and cold water fatty fish.

The third ancillary substance is the enzyme *bromelain*, which is found naturally in tropical fruits, the highest concentration being in pineapples. Bromelain aids digestion, and we all know how important this is under the stress of competition; it helps the athlete handle food and beverage intake much better and acts to settle the stomach down. Bromelain also has the innate ability to attack dead and damaged tissue and aid in its removal and resolution. Though I have known about bromelain in tropical fruits for years and its effects on the body,

it took the 1996 Olympics in Atlanta for a team (the German national swim team) to bring the enzyme to many people's attention in concentrated capsule form. The original product, called Wobenzym, was taken daily by the German swimmers to aid in their recovery from day-to-day training and racing.

The fourth and final ancillary substance to be discussed is *water*, the simplest of all substances mentioned here. As we discussed in Chapter 19, it is so vital that it is second only to oxygen in keeping the body functioning the way nature intended. It should *never* be overlooked, never taken for granted, or ever assumed to be in adequate supply in the body. If you are engaged in vigorous training, even in the water, you will sweat as your body temperature rises along with the ambient temperature and humidity. Sweating is a physiologic must to keep the body from reaching dangerously high temperatures. *Waiting for the thirst alert is a physiologic mistake.*

Nutrient delivery, tissue repair, detoxification, and pain are all directly influenced by hydration, and injury and wound healing greatly increase the body's need for water. Adequate hydration positively influences circulation, which enhances nutrient delivery and waste removal during the time of healing and recovery. People suffering trauma can help speed their own recovery without much effort by forcing fluids. As adequate hydration is crucial to wound healing, patients should be encouraged to drink two to three quarts of water or thin liquids daily or eat foods that provide these.

From vitamins, proteins, and minerals to natural body substances and simple water, there are many options (in addition to appropriate medication and physical procedures) to help the trauma patient heal wounds faster. Yes, time heals, but it can always use some help.

CHAPTER 22

Ergogenics

"Ergogenic" means enhancing the ability to perform work. I like this word and what it stands for. Work is the key to success. No matter what the goal, if you are not prepared to do the work, why start? Of course, there is either the hard way or the smart way to embrace the work ethic. The smart way is to analyze the realistic goal, set the straightest course, and embrace all aspects that will guide you there. Anything that will enhance the athlete's efforts is worth a look-see. Ergogenics are usually substances that are not included in an athlete's normal food intake. I list what I feel are important supplements to nutrition, taken to power the needs of competitive swimmers. Every athlete or coach must make his or her own informed decisions about whether and how to supplement. The three main criteria that govern *my* selection for this short but important list are: (1) Does it function up to its claims? (2) Is it safe to use with no long-term deleterious effects? and (3) Is it legal to use in competition under the rules of the various governing bodies of the different swim organizations? This last proviso seems to take the lead position in today's headlines regarding many sports. The temptation is great to abandon ethics and live a lie. But an honest account always comes due, sooner or later, and you have to live with yourself for a long time.

The Science of Performance

Ergogenic supplementation can range from simply taking in enough fluid in order to hydrate the muscles properly to very sophisticated products that provide energy molecules for enhancing the ability to perform vigorous exercise. Questions of *what* to, *how much* to, and *when* to eat or drink have become the golden fleece of physiologic science and sports medicine. Simply relying on the body's thirst or hunger mechanisms is foolhardy. Rather than waiting to feel the need to eat or drink something, the knowledgeable athlete will now select several substances, some in liquid form, that will allow him to train and race at a higher level, maximizing the potential to perform. In other chapters we have discussed the specific action of some ergogenics in exercise and recovery. What follows here is a listing and thumbnail description of all the products I feel can enhance the body's ability to perform work or recover from it.

Ribose

This 5-carbon sugar is needed by the body to synthesize adenosine triphosphate (ATP), deoxyribonucleic acid (DNA), and ribonucleic acid (RNA); these last two substances are nucleic acids that make up the genetic code of life, governing how cells divide, multiply, function, and repair all types of tissue. Ribose is also needed to make riboflavin (vitamin B_2). Though glucose, a 6-carbon sugar, is the main substance that the body uses for energy, do not be fooled into thinking that simply removing a single carbon atom to get the 5-carbon ribose is an easy occurrence. It takes time, enzymes, and energy to produce this limiting factor in the ATP molecule. For intense training and competition, ribose can aid in something called the *salvage pathway*, in which by-products from energy metabolism (adenosine diphosphate and adenosine monophosphate, ADP and AMP) are rebuilt quickly to form ATP and shorten recovery time. If ATP is not regenerated quickly, some of its building blocks can be lost, to the detriment of overall energy production. Several studies have shown that the salvage pathway works much better in the presence of ribose and that the fast-twitch muscle fibers are affected to a greater extent than the slow-twitch fibers, which adapt the swimmer more to power or sprint swimming than pure distance.

Medical historians are pretty sure now that Pheiddipides, the first person to run a marathon distance when he was instructed to tell the Greeks that their army defeated the Spartans, who ran the 26+ miles to the city of Marathon, died of coronary exhaustion after delivering his message. The reason for this in an otherwise healthy 24-year-old was that he must have depleted all his ATP and ADP from his cardiac (heart) muscle. In the heart, once AMP is produced in great quantities, it can not be utilized to regenerate the needed ATP. The use of ribose prevents this depletion and is now being tried in large doses to treat heart attack victims to help get them back on their feet quickly with a heart able to handle the extra stresses of everyday life. A sickly heart, deprived of oxygen and the concomitant ATP from a compromised circulation due to clogged arteries, takes up to 72 hours to regenerate sufficient ATP to handle additional stresses of every day life.

Recommended ribose dosages are from 3 to 10 grams daily. It is quite sweet in its white, finely powdered form, so it can be mixed with anything, but it is best to take it on a near-empty stomach. It is also found in combination products with another ergogenic useful for muscle power and endurance, creatine.

Creatine

This powerful ergogenic has been much studied and found to be safe, effective, and legal for all swimming competitions. The NCAA has regulations saying that college-sponsored teams cannot push the product to its athletes. They did this to help level the field cost-wise, to prevent the more afflu-ent schools from having a financial advantage over the smaller schools. It is still legal to use creatine in NCAA competition, it just cannot be actively or overtly promoted by the schools. But knowledgeable sports staffs know that it works, so creatine is utilized by many competitors. The increased muscle power created with creatine during intense muscular con-traction has been verified in many sports that require immediate force and speed.

Exogenous creatine works by increasing its avail-able concentration in the muscle fibers by way of the creatine-phosphate system. This is the immediate backup to the readily-available ATP that the body is able to store a little of (about 10 seconds' worth throughout all the musculature). By ingesting extra creatine, the average athlete can have more than double the immediate and near-immediate supply of creatine and is able to produce more ATP as it is needed more quickly than one who does not take it.

Though conflicting studies on sprint swimming have produced some confusion as to its effectiveness, I am convinced that creatine makes a difference. The people I've tested have all shown benefit from it over and over. I am convinced that creatine plus ribose is a case of synergy, where one + one = three.

As discussed in Chapter 2, a safe dose of creatine is 5 grams per day, taken either one hour before exertion or right afterward to enhance recovery. Manufacturers sometimes suggest a "loading dose" of 20 grams per day for five to seven days to saturate the body quickly, but this much creatine this quickly

can contribute to its potential side effect of muscle cramping, and it carries a heavy dose of nitrogen from the two natural amino acids (arginine and glycine) that make it up. This nitrogen needs to be excreted safely and thoroughly from the body by the kidneys; otherwise toxic levels could rise to the point of causing liver failure and other physiological prob-lems. Before taking creatine for an extended period, any athlete should undergo complete blood testing to ensure good working order of the kidneys, liver, and other internal organs that regulate all the bio-chemical goings-on of a body in training.

Safe supplementation with creatine can more than double Nature's original supply and allow for more intense training, faster recovery between intense efforts, and, we hope, stronger racing. It even has the ability to neutralize lactic acid to some degree, allowing muscle tissue to fire longer before the inhibiting effect of this *immediate* waste prod-uct. A major caveat is that the swimmer *must* take in enough fluid to force hydration of the muscle fibers; otherwise, the fibers will rub against each other as they would normally do upon contraction, but they will not have enough bathing liquid in the immediate area to help lubricate them. Insufficient lubrication produces excessive heat and friction, which can lead to muscle cramping, possible tears, and reduced performance.

When creatine is taken in supplemental form, the body senses that enough or more than enough is present and stops making its own supply. This does not cause physiologic distress, since more than enough creatine is present to meet demands, but if the athlete quickly stops taking the (exogenous) sup-plemental creatine, there will be a lag time before the body resumes making its own supply. Sometimes this can last a week or more. A swimmer who stops supplementation and keeps training may feel weaker both in the water and in the weight room during this "down" time. This said, it should be obvious that if the athlete decides to take creatine, he needs to stay on it at least through his competitive season. The body does not like on/off creatine ingestion.

It should be noted that some coaches believe creatine should not be given to athletes younger than 18, on the theory that before physical maturity, too many changes are taking place in the body for the effects of such a supplement to be known. As I mentioned at the beginning of the chapter, athletes and coaches must decide such questions for themselves to suit their own levels of caution and their individual training philosophies. But I have had strong swimmers as young as 16 take creatine with their parents' permission and full understanding of its function in the body, with no deleterious side effects.

Mitochondrial Energy Boosters

New research has brought to light several components that specifically work to fuel, refuel, and help maintain the functionality of the mitochondria, the "powerhouse" areas of each working cell. Mitochondria have their own membranes and their own RNA and DNA (genetic material for replication) and have been produced by Nature for the single function of producing energy. The most important substance of force and movement, adenosine triphosphate (ATP), is the end product of the biochemical reactions occurring in mitochondria. Though absolutely needed for all movement to occur, producing ATP also causes the immediate production of free radicals right at the site of mitochondria, which can damage their function. This would seem to present as a biochemical mistake: having the site where energy must be produced negatively affected by the energy production. But Nature provides for checks and balances.

We naturally have moderate amounts of protective substances; but with vigorous extended exercise, these can become depleted rather quickly. If we choose to increase energy production, we need to provide correspondingly more protective substances.

Ingesting greater amounts of the substance acetyl L-carnitine (AL-C) as a nutrient increases transport of long-chain fatty acids (fats) into mitochondria and increases their energy production, but AL-C should not be taken alone because it increases oxidative stress on the mitochondria from free radicals. What needs to be added here is a powerful "universal" antioxidant which acts through all areas of the body (fat-soluble and water-soluble) to protect the mitochondria by sacrificing itself against free radicals. This substance is alpha lipoic acid. This can be utilized to recycle inactive (oxidized) vitamin C, vitamin E, co-enzyme Q10 or other molecules of alpha lipoic acid back into active antioxidants. It also has activity by assisting with the metabolism of glucose (the main form of sugar the body uses for fuel).

Research has also shown that the enzyme coenzyme Q10 (CoQ10) is needed by mitochondria for biochemical electron transfer in order to produce more energy (more ATP). CoQ10 is another powerful antioxidant which is utilized to protect mitochondria from free radicals. CoQ10 drops in concentration as the body normally ages, so an exogenous (outside) source of this is the smart way to go as we push through demanding training sessions. The combination of all three substances—alpha lipoic acid, acetyl L-carnitine, and CoQ10—seems to be the best combination of ingredients for mitochondrial energy-production and protection, the perfect balance biochemically and physiologically.

Further study has shown that all three seem to aid neurological function (memory, coordination, and muscle memory) and that they are cardioprotective (they protect the heart). There is now a product on the market containing the above ingredients plus other nutrients all together in capsule form: it is called Mitochondrial Energy Booster and is produced by the Nutraceutical Sciences Institute (NSI).

Prescription Medications

Many athletes need prescription medication to treat acute and chronic conditions. A surprisingly large number of swimmers have asthma: chronic, from which they suffer continuously and from many causes; or intermittent, which is exacerbated by specific elements like vigorous activity, poor pool chemistry, illness, cold air, allergies, and/or pollution; or undiagnosed. I have done extensive research concerning asthma in swimmers. Here, I will briefly discuss exercise-induced bronchospasm (EIB), the most common form of asthma and the type that manifests as the athlete pushes hard in workout or competition, and I'll discuss the "ergogenic" effects of the medications that an athlete may use to treat it.

EIB can affect swimming performance as much as 50%. It is found in chronic asthmatics, highly-allergic individuals, and in about 15% of the otherwise healthy population. One hallmark of EIB (if no medication is taken) is the fact that symptoms usually develop between 6 and 12 minutes into the exercise bout, especially after inadequate or inappropriate warm-up, and can take as long as 90 minutes after exercise stops to resolve. Of course, symptoms can occur more quickly and can last a lot longer, depending upon the sufferer's state of health and the ambient air around the pool and in the surrounding area. Chemicals from the pool area can be a great irritant to the respiratory system of an EIB sufferer, as can cold, dusty, smoky air, cigarettes, noxious exhaust fumes, and various perfumes.

Inhalation medication that reduces inflammation and opens up the constricted bronchioles is absolutely indicated, and there are several formulas now available to really make a difference, along with oral medication (Singulair™) that works to complement the inhalers by keeping certain chemicals in the body from forming that would otherwise bring about an attack. The inhalants should be taken at least one hour before exercise to give them enough time to work thoroughly.

Nonprescription Medications

Acid reflux, the condition whereby the sufferer experiences sometimes intense burning in the upper chest and into the back of the throat from stomach acid allowed to back up into the esophagus, is not an uncommon suffering for swimmers. The athlete is constantly putting pressure on the abdominal region while moving intensely through the water in an already prone position. If he ate improperly by consuming hard-to-digest foods, spicy or fatty foods, or foods that contain caffeine too soon before practice or competition or he has taken medications that can cause reflux like inhalation sprays for asthma or decongestants—anything that relaxes the esophageal sphincter and prevents it from working to keep stomach contents in the stomach—he can suffer this most annoying of conditions. It can be controlled by antacids as well as acid reducers, both of which can be purchased over the counter in pharmacies. Taking these products about 20 minutes before needed allows them to work yet dissipate from the mouth so no remnants are left to irritate the swimmer (especially if his mouth gets dry during practice or in the anxious moments just before the race).

Oral and nasal-spray decongestants help open up the upper respiratory system to enhance breathing and are usually part of a cold medication regimen.

The sprays act locally to shrink the mucous membranes and the blood supply of the nose and upper sinuses, which provides almost instantaneous but temporary relief. If taken too often, they can produce "rebound congestion" and make stuffiness worse. The oral decongestants do not cause rebound congestion, and their effects last longer. But they can also have a stimulant effect on the heart, aid the mind in present-time focusing, and they can help the muscles fire with more force. (The over-the-counter oral decongestant with the greatest effect in this area is pseudoephedrine, which must now be purchased at the pharmacy counter instead of simply taking it off the shelves.) This class of drugs (taken orally) was not allowed to be ingested before competitions up until 2006 in USA Swimming sanctioned events. But it is now on the permitted list even though it is structurally related chemically to amphetamines, which are known banned potent stimulants. And there are no listed restrictions on either the oral or nasal forms in national collegiate, YMCA, and high school competitions.

Each year more and more former prescription items can be bought over the counter. This allows athletes and coaches to choose pretty powerful stuff to take without the guidance of either a physician or pharmacist. Nonsteroidal anti-inflammatory drugs (NSAIDs) can help the body recover from trauma or overuse by keeping inflammation of the muscles, joints, connective tissue, and bones under control, providing mild to moderate analgesia, reducing swelling, and shortening down time for any injured athlete.

It is almost a given that NSAIDS are often recommended or dispensed by trainers, coaches, or teammates to help bring an athlete back from injury. The main caution here is to take the medication with food, never on an empty stomach, and for no more than five days at a time. If healing is seen and the athlete feels better, he may ease back into training with caution. Training can continue with the medication, but after that five-day period, the athlete must take at least a two-day "drug holiday" to protect several organs of the body (stomach, liver, kidneys, adrenals).

As an untoward side effect, NSAIDs, which are classified as prostaglandin inhibitors, reduce important blood flow to various organs (not good), along with reducing the inflammation (good). Without an appropriate nutrient base from the blood supply, several organs are put under extra stress, especially the kidneys. If they are deprived of appropriate blood supply, they begin to function less effectively. If these organs are continually exposed to this class of medication, eventually they lose their ability to function at full capacity. In time, they begin to fail and work less and less efficiently. In fact, the single most important cause of kidney failure in the United States today is excessive use of NSAIDs, which started around 30 years ago. So it is wise to take them with caution, and also to take them with antacids or over-the-counter acid reducers to protect the stomach.

Certain antacids are being used quite extensively in various sports to help neutralize lactic acid as intense muscular contractions take place. Some researchers claim that lactic acid is not a waste product of anaerobic metabolism; that it can be reoxidized in the liver to provide fuel for continued activity. If we stretch out the physiology, yes, this may be true, but for the immediate moment of intense movement that we are seeking to enhance, having lactic acid *in situ* (at the site of production) is having a waste product develop, because it greatly hinders muscle movement at that time and place. I claim it is a waste product of metabolism during the time it is being manufactured in the muscle. If it inhibits the quality of movement we desire, it cannot be called anything else than a waste product. Much work has been done with sodium bicarbonate, which has proved effective in delaying lactic buildup. But there is a price to pay: gas, cramping, and loose stools have been seen often enough to make many think twice about its use. Other lactic neutralizers have been tried and found to work, though not as well, including calcium carbonate and sodium citrate. Several studies have shown that 300 mg/kg of body weight of bicarbonate seems to work best to delay lactic acid if the exercise lasts from one to seven minutes. Less than one minute or more than seven and the lactic-acid buffering has little effect, but since most swimming events fall within this range, taking something like this can prove helpful, especially in someone who makes a lot of lactate…such as a sprinter!

Knowing how much bicarbonate to take and at what point before the competition is key. As an example, a working protocol that I use for a 190-pound swimmer is 30 double-strength chewable tablets taken 6 at a time, starting one hour before anticipated need and repeated every 15 minutes, with the final six chewed and rinsed down five minutes before the race.

Phytonutrients

Fruits and vegetables provide many physiological benefits. Some help the body to handle the rigors of intense exercise. Examples are: grape juice, which prevents the platelets in the blood from clotting, allowing blood to circulate better, and pineapples, which provide a healing enzyme (bromelain) that helps the body recover for the next exercise bout. I have included a quick listing of the benefits that the phytonutrients (plant-derived nutrients) in these fruits and vegetables bring to the table. I call this my Rainbow of Health. Try to get five or six servings of a mixed group of these offerings per day.

GAKIC®

This relatively new product, discovered and researched at the University of Florida, is being hyped to power muscles, increase endurance, and allow more work per training session. GAKIC is made up of two amino acids and an organic acid that work in concert to actually aid the muscles in a different way than ever before. The two amino acids *glycine* and *L-arginine* together form creatine and act together with muscle tissue to aid in its function and tissue repair. The organic acid *alpha-ketoiso-caproic acid* acts to neutralize and remove ammonia, a toxic waste product of anaerobic (power) muscle function. Taken up to an hour before exercise, GAKIC has been found to provide almost immediate benefit, unlike creatine, which needs several days to build to a concentration that will make a noticeable difference. Time will tell whether this product proves to be the next great discovery for energy expenditure. Stay tuned….

Caffeine

Besides the known mental stimulation of caffeine and its ability to help the user focus in on the moment, caffeine has the physiological effect of allowing the body to break down free fatty acids (FFAs) for energy, thus sparing glycogen for powering the muscles toward the end of a competition. Many studies in the literature show how caffeine expedites the use of FFAs for energy. Several studies have shown caffeine's effectiveness, and a pertinent investigation with swimmers has been done in Canada with college-level athletes. Six men and six women had to swim a 1,500-meter freestyle for time in a double-blind crossover study. Without knowing

The Rainbow of Health

Color	Action	Phytonutrient(s)	Source
Red	Protects against prostate cancer, heart and lung disease	Lycopene	Watermelon, tomatoes and pink grapefruit
Red/purple	Helps the heart and aids blood circulation by preventing platelets from sticking that could otherwise form clots	Anthocyanins, especially resveratrol	Red/blue grapes, red grape juice, blueberries, strawberries, beets, eggplant, red wine
Orange	Protects the skin from free radical damage and repairs DNA	Alpha- and beta-carotene	Carrots, mangoes, cantaloupe, and sweet potatoes
Orange/yellow	Prevents heart disease and helps heal damaged tissue	Beta-cryptothanxin; enzymes: papain and papase	Oranges, peaches, papaya, nectarines, and passion fruit
Yellow/green	Reduces risk of cataracts and age-related macular degeneration	Lutein and zeaxanthin	Spinach, corn, avocados, and honeydew melon
Pale yellow	Supplies a healing enzyme (bromelain) that destroys only damaged tissue and also aids digestion	Bromelain	Fresh pineapples
Green	Inhibits action of carcinogens	Sulforaphane, isocyanate, and indoles	Broccoli, cabbage, kale, and Brussels sprouts
White/green	Protects against tumors	Quercitin, kaempferol, and allicen	Garlic, onions, celery, and pears

whether they were being given the caffeine first or a placebo, each group had to perform two swims, three days apart, allowing for adequate rest and recovery, while the caffeine and placebo were switched. To everyone's surprise, not only did those taking caffeine swim faster than they did on the placebo (an average of 29 seconds faster), but they all *perceived* that the faster effort was easier.

Of course, caffeine should be used with caution. More than the recommended maximum dose of 400 mg taken at any one time can bring on skeletal muscle hyperactivity (twitching), excessive nervousness, and acid stomach leading to acid reflux. And at the highest levels of competition, the level of caf-feine in the urine is monitored, since it is an active stimulant. It is allowed to be present because it is consumed all over the world in many foods and drinks, but abuse is not tolerated.

Carbohydrate and Protein Combinations

Carbohydrates fuel the muscles and brain. With muscle-friendly high-quality protein (whey) added to the carbohydrate mix (4 parts carbohydrate, 1 part protein), the carbohydrates have been shown to be taken into the muscles faster and more thoroughly while the muscle fibers undergo refueling and healing more quickly due to the protein. Now this formula has been patented and made available in two useful products, Accelerade® (which it is advised to take about one hour before exercise for energy) and Endurox® (which is recommended immediately after exercise for recovery). The difference between the two is mainly the inclusion in the latter formula of antioxidants, which are in place to prevent as much tissue damage as possible—damage resulting from the sought-after metabolic oxidation we need to move through water. The label on the Endurox also instructs to take two scoops of the product as opposed to one scoop of the Accelerade which simply provides twice the energy and recovery substances the muscles crave. I suggest that the Endurox can be used both before and after exercise. I submit that the antioxidants would have greater benefit if taken before exercise to keep oxidative damage to a minimum, rather than trying to repair the damage afterward. I can testify (as can my swimmers) that these products do provide sufficient amounts of energy to make a noticeable difference in continuous training and repeat competition efforts. What's more, the American Dairy Association has now released test results in which they submit that good old low-fat chocolate milk has been proved to aid recovery after intense exercise as well as the above products. If analyzed, this should not come as too great a surprise. The contents of this type of product provide the quality carbohydrates and proteins that Mother Nature, with a little help from food scientists, had intended as the near-perfect food.

Steroids and Hormones

Unless you have been hiding in a cave, you've heard about anabolic steroids in sports. You may have even heard about human growth hormone. Simply put, to use these substances in sports is to put the body at risk in order to make it dramatically more powerful in a relatively short amount of time.

Anabolic (tissue-building) steroids act to make muscle fibers more receptive to physical training with any type of resistance (weights, latex tubing, dry-land exercises, power swimming). The fibers *that are in place* hypertrophy (get larger) and become more powerful for the moment of use. Muscle size and definition become outstanding in a matter of just weeks whereas with the natural path to power in the weight room, incremental benefits are seen over a period of months. Some athletes are genetically gifted to make muscle more easily than others; steroids can level the field, so to speak, by allowing everyone who takes them to increase muscle size and power. The muscles may develop an increase in endurance as well, but that is secondary.

Growth hormone, on the other hand, makes *more* muscle fibers develop, building a larger "army" of fibers from which to recruit energy and force. A distinguishing characteristic of growth hormone use is greatly increased endurance along with increased power. In swimming, with distances greater that 50 yards/meters, all athletes begin to slow down toward the end of their race. Those taking growth hormone would slow down much less, even to the point of being able to accelerate to the finish because of the greater number of muscle fibers producing force upon demand.

The most important thing to know about steroids and human growth hormone is this: *these substances are illegal* in all areas of swimming, as they are in any athletic endeavor. To use them is unconscionable, glaringly unsportsmanlike, and always unsanctioned by any governing body in competitive sports.

CHAPTER 23

Swimming for Mind and Spirit

Youth is not a time of life; it is a state of mind, a product of the imagination, a vigor of the emotions, a predominance of courage over fright, and an appetite for adventure.

Nobody grows old by living a number of years. People grow old when they desert their ideals. Years may wrinkle the skin, but to give up enthusiasm most definitely wrinkles the soul. Worry, self-doubt, fear, and anxiety: these are the culprits that bow the head and wither the heart.

But whether you're 16 or 60, there exists in the spirit of every person who loves life the thrill of a new challenge and an insatiable appetite for what is coming next. You are as young as your dreams or as old as your fears.

As I mentioned a few times, we are prisoners of our minds. We may not be the top of the food chain specimen-for-specimen (I wouldn't want to wrestle a polar bear for the day's survival food), but we are the top of the "think chain." Given this innate ability to reason, analyze, organize, and summarize, humans should always be at the top of their game emotionally. Unfortunately, life doesn't always allow for same. We need to work just as hard mentally as we do physically to clearly make a path to our goals, so that the mind and the body work together.

Exercise and Emotional Health

Just about everyone on the planet accepts that appropriate exercise can keep us "young" in terms of our physical well-being. What many people are now learning from magazines, newspapers, television, radio, and simple word of mouth is that the same devotion to exercise can also have a positive effect on our *emotional* well-being. Emotional factors such as reduction in anxiety and depression, enhanced self-esteem, a surprising ability to channel thoughts to appropriate resolutions, and normalized sleep patterns are all positively influenced by exercise. And emotional well-being has definitely proved to help maximize athletic performance. I wrote earlier that we are prisoners of our minds. Here's a corollary in rhyme: *Emotional well-being sets you free to be the best that you can be.*

There have been hundreds of studies of the effects exercise has on human psychological makeup and resiliency. Thousands of subjects have been tested under all kinds of circumstances over the years, and all this information has been collated and its effects on the human mind categorized in studies of the studies, called meta-analyses. All this research has asked: Which type of exercise (aerobic, anaerobic, on land, in the water) produces what type of response (neutral, positive, negative) and in what amount (great, moderate, slight, or none)? In particular, how do the benefits of swimming (and the training and cross-training for it) provide the healthy psychological balance that we all seek in our modern-day, multi-tasking, stress-filled society?

Most of us have experienced anxiety in varying degrees, from relatively benign doses when performing on tests or in competitions to more emotion-consuming situations of troubled relationships, worrying finances, or declining health. But when anxiety begins to interfere with normal functioning, then attention to treatment must be a consideration.

It seems that anxiety in the United States is on the rise. In our complex and closely interactive world, the effects of outside events often touch us at a personal level, contributing to feelings of generalized uneasiness leading into frank anxiety, to such an extent that about 10% of the U.S. population has to cope with emotional negativity intense enough to interfere with normal functioning.

Since I am a pharmacist, biochemist, and physiologist, one might think I would immediately turn to medication, to treat any imbalance in the body chemically. Not the case. Knowing the ramifications of consuming potent chemicals, I would first opt for an alternative approach where appropriate. And treating mild-to-moderate emotional distress is one area where at least an adequate trial effort with exercise should be made. If exercise does not elicit the desired results within a reasonable time (usually a few weeks), *then* it may be time to consider additional help from medication or professional consultation or other mind/body practices.

Exercise and Anxiety

Stress-related emotions such as anxiety, for instance, are common among healthy individuals but can unfortunately affect their approach to life and their social and professional interactions if these emotions cannot be dealt with appropriately. Anxiety is typified by behavior such as worry, self-doubt, and apprehension, often attributed to demands that tax or exceed the normal coping resources of the individual. This emotional strain is sometimes accompanied by physiological responses, such as elevated heart rate, high blood pressure, muscle tension, and increased blood cholesterol, which can usually be traced back to stress-induced excess adrenaline being released from the adrenal glands. (Adrenaline can raise heart rate, blood pressure, and muscle tension and it uses cholesterol as its basic building block in its formation.) The current interest in prevention and treatment of emotional distress has heightened our feeling that exercise is a safe, non-invasive alternative or adjunct to traditional treatments, such as psychotherapy or medication. It can even produce results more quickly, at reduced cost, and with greater all-around benefits, such as reduced blood pressure, increased muscle tone, and weight loss.

Between 1960 and 1991, six major studies examined the relationship between exercise and anxiety reduction. All six found that exercise was significantly related to a reduction in anxiety, with effects ranging from small to moderate depending upon the type, duration, and intensity of the exercise. We found that the most substantial effects on anxiety reduction were seen in aerobic exercise where air exchange was kept in the relative comfort zone of the participant. Swimming, running, and cycling were the forms of exercise most chosen. When oxygen demand rose markedly because of increased intensity or duration, people not adequately trained or adapted to this intensity actually experienced *increased* anxiety as discomfort set in. But as the body became more conditioned to and the participant became more familiar with the physiologic demands of increasing intensity, the emotional component became less of a problem and the sought-after benefits began to emerge.

It was found that the most effective period of time for the aerobic training sessions was at least 10 weeks—preferably more than 15 weeks—and that the subjects entering the study initially with lower levels of fitness or higher levels of anxiety, such as coronary and panic disorder patients, got the most

benefit. It was also found that anxiety returned to its original level within four to six hours after the exercise bout if whatever was causing the emotional problem was not resolved. Anaerobic exercises like handball and strength and flexibility training had less effect on reducing anxiety.

Exercise and Depression

In addition to anxiety, exercise works against depression. Mild-to-moderate depression is quite prevalent in today's society, and at least 5% of the population is burdened with more severe clinical depression.

Research on exercise and depression actually has a history dating back to 1905, when one study suggested a relationship between exercise and mood. Since then over 100 studies have reconfirmed that exercise results in a significant reduction in the symptoms of depression. In fact, depression responds *more* positively and *more* dramatically than anxiety to vigorous exercise.

These beneficial effects start off as moderate, not mild, in magnitude—more pronounced than the effects of exercise on anxiety—and grow from there, helping subjects classified from mildly depressed to mentally ill. The findings also indicate that the antidepressant effects of exercise begin as early as the first session and persist beyond the end of the exercise program. The effects are consistent across age, gender, exercise group size, and type of depression, and they are seen to produce the same benefits as psychotherapy, behavioral interventions, and social contact.

Take note that with anxiety, more intense exercise sometimes negated the benefit or even made the condition worse. The exerciser had to stay in her comfort zone. But with depression, increased intensity had a definite positive effect in lifting the depression.

There were significant benefits for younger exercisers as well. In both boys and girls aged 15 and under, aerobic activity of sufficient intensity and duration increased feelings of self-worth even more than learning new sport skills. Those who derived the greatest benefit were those who came to the training sessions more out of shape and those with disabilities. It is not hard to see how these youngsters would truly benefit from increased aerobic training and capacity.

These findings point the way to the most important possession I know, expressed in three words: *peace of mind*. As an example, one response — called a "compensatory adaptation" — the body produces in response to exercise is a longer, deeper, more restful sleep with a quicker onset. What greater testimony to emotional well-being than to have adequate restful sleep on a regular basis?

Of the various types of exercise offered in the above-mentioned studies, it stood to reason that the type of exercise had to be comfortable and doable for the exerciser. Obviously, a nonswimmer, becoming so stressed when pressed to move through water, would not get much benefit from activity in the pool. But for those who could swim or were made to feel comfortable in water, the aquatic exercise elicited special emotional responses of its own. One such response I label the "cocoon effect" — the feeling, almost an emotional bonding, of being surrounded by a safe, protective environment that provided some moments of escape from troubling issues. This worked better for depressed subjects than for anxious subjects, but the anxious swimmers got relief in the pool, too, as long as they were able to remain in their aerobic comfort zone. Of course, general adaptation to the stresses of swimming allows swimmers to *expand* their comfort zone faster and farther as the training bouts progress. But

the depressed swimmer has to be made aware of this and correctly guided along the path to greater ability and confidence in the water.

Swimming and Survival

I mentioned at the start of this book that the Nessel family had suffered more than one tragedy. There are two types of shock and grief that can injure the psyche and render the mind helpless: immediate shock in consequence of a tragedy that takes place quickly, leaving the survivors to cope, as in the sudden deaths of my two sons, with extra negative emphasis due to one dying in my presence. Then there is the emotional trauma that must be endured over time, as in my wife's illness, a serious and progressive disabling disease that science and medicine have been unable to stem. In both cases, I believe that swimming and training and coaching and just being in and around pools and those wanting to move through water more efficiently have probably kept the Ol' Coach emotionally able to carry on.

I am proud of my association with Cullen Jones, a brilliant rising star with tremendous sprint ability. Cullen came to me as a tall, skinny 14-year-old who would rather swim than play basketball, as his dad wanted. He reminded me of a mad stork, tall, skinny, and angular, so I nicknamed him that.

Cully took to the water, I am told, at an early age, but his family sought me out to help nurture whatever talent he might possess. He came to me with lots of desire and little else. Looking at it all from several years' worth of hindsight which is usually 20/20, I am honored to have been given the opportunity and challenge to help Jonesey along his way to becoming world class. His dad would come and stay for every practice, watching me as much as he was watching Cullen. We had many almost comical discussions about why I thought Cully should swim and he thought Cully should shoot baskets.

As Nature and bad luck would have it, Cullen's dad died painfully from disseminated lung cancer into the brain; his mom, one of the nicest ladies I have ever met, had to keep the family intact and on course while coping with cancer of her own. Being an only child, Jonesey leaned on me; I had lost both my sons; he lost his dad. I needed him as much as much as he needed me…it was a good fit, and I adopted him as a sort of surrogate son.

As his talent grew and his races became something to watch, I noticed an increasing amount of anxiety and uneasiness. It was understandable, considering what emotional baggage Cully brought to the blocks each time he had to perform against better and better competition. Beyond just coaching him, I constantly worked to get into his head, keep him focused; I had to sweep away all the negativity to the point where I could make him believe he could walk on water. He knew what I was doing, and he knew what he needed. He kept saying to me, "I'll be all right, Coach, once I get into the water." Picking up from Jonesey, I usually say the same thing: I'll be all right once I get into the water. So will you.

About the Author

Coach Ed Nessel moved to Central Florida (near the Kennedy Space Center) from New Jersey in 2004. While in the Garden State, he was an All-State champion breaststroker, coached various teams over his 38+ years on the pool deck, and produced several All-State, high school All-Americas, college All-Americas, and NCAA champions and three Olympians. Coach Nessel developed Cullen Jones from the age of 14 through his college career: he was the fastest swimmer in the world in 2006.

Ed moved south after retiring from his position as swim coach and racing camp presenter and coordinator at his alma mater, Rutgers University. He is academically trained as a pharmacist, biochemist, and physiologist and was selected to be an active member of both the National Masters Swimming Sports Medicine Committee and the Coach's Committee. Ed trains his athletes by applying the science of swimming as well as the physiology of aging.

Coach Nessel was selected as the United States Masters Swimming Coach of the Year in 1998 and has garnered many awards and national championships, both as a competitor and coach. His enthusiasm for the sport of swimming and for his athletes is known nationwide. It has been stated by many in the swimming community: "With Coach Nessel, it is not about him, it is about his swimmers." After reading this book, we hope that you will feel the same way.

Index